Public Speaking:
Prepare, Present, Participate

Cheri J. Simonds
Illinois State University

Stephen K. Hunt
Illinois State University

Brent K. Simonds
Illinois State University

Allyn & Bacon

Boston • Columbus • Indianapolis • New York • San Francisco • Upper Saddle River
Amsterdam • Cape Town • Dubai • London • Madrid • Milan • Munich • Paris • Montreal • Toronto
Delhi • Mexico City • Sao Paulo • Sydney • Hong Kong • Seoul • Singapore • Taipei • Tokyo

Editor-in-Chief:	Karon Bowers
Series Editorial Assistant:	Susan Brilling
Development Manager:	David Kear
Senior Development Editor:	Carol Alper
Associate Development Editor:	Angela Pickard
Marketing Manager:	Blair Tuckman
Production Editor:	Patrick Cash-Peterson
Manufacturing Buyer:	JoAnne Sweeney
Editorial Production and Composition Service:	Nesbitt Graphics, Inc.
Interior Design:	Nesbitt Graphics, Inc.
Photo Researcher:	Jessica Rui, Martha Shethar
Cover Designer:	Kristina Mose-Libon

Cataloging in Publication Data is on file at the Library of Congress

10 9 8   V092 15

Photo Credits

P. 3, REUTERS/Ray Stubblebine; p. 6, Dylan Simonds; p. 9 left, Dylan Simonds; p. 9 center, Alamy; p. 9 right, Hulton Archive Photos/Getty Images; p. 21, John McCoy/WireImage; p. 29 top, Allen Einstein/NBAE/Getty Images; p. 29 bottom, Dylan Simonds; p. 33, Barry Rosenthal/Getty Images; p. 36, AP Photo/Jennifer Szymaszek; p. 38, Photofest; p. 40, National Communication Association; p. 47, Alamy; p. 48, AP Photo/Harpo Productions Inc., George Burns; p. 54 top, John Atashian/CORBIS; p. 54 bottom, Newscom; p. 65, Masterfile Royalty-Free; p. 68, Michael D. Margol / PhotoEdit Inc.; p. 69, Digital Vision/Getty Images; p. 71, Image Source/Corbis; p. 72, AP Photo/Steve Helber; p. 83, Alamy; p. 86, Rachel Epstein/The Image Works; p. 90, Dylan Simonds; p. 93 left, Lucas Jackson/Reuters/Corbis; p. 93 right, Andrew Lepley/Redferns/Getty Images; p. 97, Image Source/Corbis; p. 106 top, AP Photo/Judi Bottoni; p. 106 bottom, Jim Spellman/WireImage/Getty Images; p. 111, AP Photo/Matt Sayles; p. 115, REUTERS/Jim Young; p. 120, Peter Kramer/Getty Images; p. 123, DreamWorks/Photofest; p. 129, Bob Daemmrich/PhotoEdit, Inc.; p. 135, Dorling Kindersley; p. 138, Dylan Simonds; p. 141, Dylan Simonds; p. 145, PAUL J. RICHARDS/AFP/Getty Images; p. 146, David S. Holloway/Getty Images; p. 148, Getty Images; p. 149, Brad Barket/Getty Images; p. 159, Lucas Jackson/Reuters/Corbis; Dylan Simonds; p. 163, Tom Carter/PhotoEdit, Inc.; p. 165, AP Photo/Charlie Neibergall; p. 168, Bettmann/CORBIS; p. 169, MGM Studios/Getty Images; p. 170, Universal/Gordon/The Kobal Collection; p. 175, VALERY HACHE/AFP/Getty Images; p. 195, Matt Stroshane/Getty Images; p. 202, Paramount/The Kobal Collection; p. 205, AP Photo; p. 207, PAUL J. RICHARDS/AFP/Getty Images; p. 211, Jason Kempin/FilmMagic/Getty Images; p. 212, Alan Powdrill/Getty Images; p. 214, AP Photo/Yuri Gripas; p. 217, NASA Headquarters; p. 222, REUTERS/Aaron Josefczyk; p. 231, AP Photo/Rich Pedroncelli; p. 237, Dorling Kindersley; p. 240, Bettmann/CORBIS; p. 245, The Advertising Archives; p. 251, AP Photo/Rich Pedroncelli; p. 254, Bettmann/Corbis; p. 256, Courtesy of Michael Shermer; p. 257, Tony Korody/Sygma/Corbis

Allyn & Bacon
is an imprint of

www.pearsonhighered.com

ISBN-10: 0-13-194558-0

ISBN-13: 978-0-13-194558-6

Contents

CHAPTER 13   Delivering the Presentation   194

UNIT III CONSTRUCTING PERSUASIVE MESSAGES—PARTICIPATE

Preface

What makes a good textbook? What makes an effective class? What should happen before, during, and after class? What should students learn in a public speaking course? And, how should they learn it?

As basic course directors for the last several years, we have been asking you these very questions. We have had informal conversations, attended conferences, taught seminars, and paid attention to current trends in higher education and society.

From all of these experiences, we have learned that a good textbook is one that motivates students to make critical connections between the text and their own experiences.

We have heard you say that you want a text that is brief and easy to read, but thorough in its coverage of key communication concepts. We have heard you say that the text needs to incorporate strategies that encourage students to read before coming to class and motivate them to participate in class discussions. We have heard you say that critical thinking, information literacy, and media literacy skills are absolutely essential outcomes of the public speaking course you teach. And, we have heard you say just how important civic engagement is in higher education—that students should come to understand how core communication competencies can and should be used to advance the common good.

We have had many conversations with students about what they want in a text and, not surprisingly, they say many of the same things that you do. Students want a brief text that is easy to read but that prepares them to become critical thinkers, savvy information users, and engaged citizens in their communities. Students want to be heard. Students want to participate.

Public Speaking: Prepare, Present, Participate is a text designed to address these questions—a text designed to meet your needs and the needs of your students. Specifically, we tie the theories and skills presented in the text to students' personal, professional, and civic lives. Ideally, students will come to realize that the communication skills they gain in this course will allow them to be successful students, employees, and citizens.

Approach of the Text

This text offers a delivery and implementation strategy that aligns with contemporary education goals and helps faculty insure better student and program performance. In doing so, we provide a concise presentation of the principles and skills of public speaking (using text, discussion prompts, and critical and media interactions in tandem), which will motivate students to read and engage with material prior to class. This pedagogy is embedded in the text so that as students read the concepts, they are provided with opportunities to critically reflect on and interact with the material. In other words, the text can be used as an impetus for classroom discussion—where learning takes place through student contributions of personal examples and insights.

For example, students can be assigned to read a brief chapter, engage in critical and media interactions, and answer questions about the material that will allow them to prepare to participate in class discussions. These strategies can change the way students spend time out of class, which will have implications for the way teachers and students spend time in class. Rather than lecturing over material that students should have read, teachers can engage students in higher order discussion of the content knowledge as well as more experiential activities. These strategies are predicated on students coming to class with a common content knowledge base from which the instructor can build to higher levels of learning. We also provide various instruments to formally assess student preparation for participation both in and out of class.

This book is written especially for undergraduate college students who are taking communication courses as part of their liberal arts or general education requirements. We have been developing, testing, and using these materials and instructional tools as part of our general education course at Illinois State University for the last twelve years. In addition, we have conducted and continue to conduct multiple assessments (including authentic portfolio assessment) of the efficacy of the course and program to promote student learning and have published the results of these studies in *Communication Education, The Basic Communication Course Annual, Communication Studies,* and *Communication Teacher.* Even though our charge has been challenging and our responsibilities have been great, we love what we do. So, we were extremely honored when our program received the 2008 Inaugural *Program of Excellence Award* by the Basic Course Division of the National Communication Association.

With the teaching tools provided by this text (which include videos that illustrate the pedagogical approach and models of expected performance), faculty will be able to manage the interactive classroom, assess interaction, and, as a result, better meet the goals of a general education program. Additionally, this text will provide faculty members with the necessary tools for evaluating and assessing student and course goals to report overall program quality to interested stakeholders.

In this book, we address several themes to help students become more effective communicators and public speakers. After taking this course and reading and thinking about this text, students should become more competent, confident, and ethical communicators, better critical thinkers, and more media and information literate. This book will provide students with opportunities to enhance their public speaking skills for academic and professional development. We believe that this will ultimately provide students with opportunities to become active citizens in their communities.

Organization of the Text

This text is organized into three units. In the first unit, students *prepare* to communicate by gaining a foundation of the communication concepts involved in becoming competent, confident, and ethical public speakers. In the second unit, students learn to construct clear messages so they can *present* a speech to an audience. And, in the third unit, students learn about the argumentation and critical thinking skills needed to *participate* as citizens in a democracy.

The first unit is composed of four chapters that lay the foundation for the communication principles necessary for students to present ideas in a competent, critical, ethical, and confident manner. Chapter 1 provides an introduction to communication goals, processes, and models. Additionally, the chapter introduces the woven themes of the text with emphasis on media and information literacy skills. Chapter 2 defines communication apprehension (CA) and presents the causes, effects, and strategies for dealing with CA. Chapter 3 provides an ethical framework by which students can become ethical consumers and producers of information. Chapter 4 discusses the principles of listening and its relationship to critical thinking.

The second unit contains nine chapters aimed at teaching students the principles and skills necessary for constructing clear messages. Although many of these principles are discussed in terms of the first major assignment—the informative speech—distinctions between contexts (special occasion, group, persuasion) are integrated throughout. This unit addresses the presentation of ideas as a goal-directed activity. Once learned, these principles can be adapted to a variety of rhetorical contexts. To begin, Chapter 5 discusses the selection and development of topics, purposes, and thesis statements. In this chapter, we introduce a series of example speeches (Tornadoes, Roman Coliseum, and Delta Blues) that are integrated throughout the unit. With each principle or skill presented, students will see how the information is incorporated using each of these examples. We also offer complete preparation and speaking outlines as well as videos of each of our speech examples. Chapter 6 introduces audience analysis by considering demographics, attitudes, and beliefs. These considerations are then carried throughout the text. Chapter 7 presents information literacy skills, including how to identify, locate, evaluate, and incorporate support material. Chapter 8 provides information on the organization of ideas, and Chapter 9 discusses principles of outlining for public speaking. Chapter 10 advises students on techniques used in beginning and ending presentations. Chapter 11 discusses appropriate language use in considering audience needs as well as message clarity. Chapter 12 describes the benefits and types of presentation aids and offers advice for creating, designing, and integrating them into a presentation. Students will also gain knowledge and skills necessary for evaluating media. Finally, in the last chapter of this unit, students will learn how to deliver their presentations extemporaneously, which enables the presentations to be adapted to other speaking situations.

The third unit includes three chapters on the context of persuasion and builds on the information from the second unit. Chapter 14 provides information on the types of persuasive statements as well as how to organize persuasive claims. Chapter 15 discusses the use of proof in the development of persuasive arguments. This chapter builds on the critical thinking skills presented earlier by discussing logical argument development in both the production and consumption of messages. Finally, this unit and text close with information on equipping students to become civically and politically engaged.

Features of the Text

Our instructional strategy is to make this book brief and clear, yet substantive—particularly suited to undergraduate collegiate experiences. The intent is to have a textbook that students are motivated to read. The readings are intended to provide a framework for higher order discussion and to promote critical thinking in the classroom. To accomplish this, we provide several features that prompt students to consider ways to contribute to class discussion.

Preparing to Participate 7.4
Evaluating Supporting Materials

 Knowledge
What should you consider when selecting and incorporating support material for your speech?

 Application
What are the implications for using support materials that may violate one of these considerations?

Preparing to Participate boxes are provided at the end of each major section in the chapter. The first question directs the students to the content knowledge of the readings. By answering these questions, students are addressing the chapter or reading objectives. If students prepare these answers before coming to class, the instructor can then move beyond the knowledge that these answers provide to higher levels of learning and to promote critical thinking. These questions are noted in the text with the owl icon.

The next set of questions asks students to apply and extend the content to their own experiences. These questions prompt students to consider how they might contribute to class discussions. These questions are noted in the text with the icon of an owl in flight. This is where the high order discussion begins. Note that student answers to the knowledge-level questions will all be the same, whereas student answers to the application-level questions will all be different as a result of their own personal connections and experiences. Thus, every discussion will be different depending on the make-up of the students. In other words, you can never have the same discussion twice.

Critical Interaction 11.3
Inclusive Language

Consider the following statements. Are they inclusive or exclusive? If you determine they are exclusive, how can they be rephrased to be inclusive?

1. Dr. Martin, a leading female psychologist, offers her insights into chronic depression.
2. The male nurse treated Adam in the Emergency Room.
3. All right, you guys, listen carefully.
4. I wonder if the mailman delivered the mail today.

Critical Interaction boxes provide students with opportunities to actively engage in various exercises throughout the text and to enhance critical thinking. To do so, these interactions allow students to critically reflect on course concepts and apply them to real life or public speaking contexts. As students progress throughout this course, they will sharpen their critical thinking skills by gaining new knowledge (e.g., knowledge of the different types of speeches and their functions) and comprehension (e.g., understanding how to draw conclusions on the basis of evidence presented) of communication concepts. Students will also apply (e.g., organizing ideas effectively in a speech) this knowledge and use their understanding of communication concepts to analyze (e.g., recognize fallacies of reasoning in a speech), synthesize (e.g., writing and delivering a speech), and evaluate (e.g., judging whether a speech was effective) communication. The *Critical Interaction* boxes can be assigned in advance or completed in class.

Media Interactions are provided for each chapter. A media interaction is an engagement opportunity that asks students to critically reflect on the messages they consume in the media and the way these messages apply to course concepts. These opportunities allow students to engage in critical thinking as well as enhance their media and information literacy skills. We provide discussion prompts for each of the interactions that allow students a low-risk opportunity to report the results of their interaction in the form of class participation.

Comic Strips with discussion prompts are also provided, when appropriate, to help students make additional connections between course concepts and public speaking applications.

Media
Interaction 3.1

Ethical Codes in Journalism

Log onto the Internet and listen to the *NewsHour* stories found at this URL: http://www.pbs.org/newshour/bb/media/july-dec98/media_ethics_7-1a.html

1. What factors do you think played a role in the unethical behavior of these journalists?
2. Do you think these factors might affect you when you present your research for your speeches?

Zits

Comic 4.1

1. How often have you heard someone but not listened?
2. What were the consequences?

Zits ©Zits Partnership, King Features Syndicate

End of Chapter Materials include *Key Terms* for student review purposes, and *Additional Engagement Opportunities*, which include *Civic Engagement Opportunities* for students to further enhance their critical thinking of course concepts, prepare additional contributions for class discussion, and become more civically engaged.

SUMMARY

The audience plays a crucial role in the success of your speech. By understanding and considering the characteristics of your audience as you produce your presentation, you are engaging in competent and ethical communication. As you begin to get to know your audience, you will also feel more confident in speaking before them. In this chapter, we provided you with both formal and informal methods of conducting an audience analysis. We have also talked about ways to adapt your message according to your analysis. It is one thing to know your audience, but it is quite another to be able to take that information and use it to accomplish your goals.

KEY TERMS

audience analysis (84)
frame of reference (85)
audience demographics (86)
speaking situation (88)
captive audience (88)
voluntary audience (88)

attitudes, values, and beliefs (89)
interviews (91)
open and closed questions (91)
questionnaire (92)
scaled or continuum questions (92)

ADDITIONAL ENGAGEMENT OPPORTUNITIES

Now that you have finished reading the chapter, it is also important to make connections between the course content and your own experiences. These activities will help you understand, apply, analyze, evaluate, or synthesize course concepts. You can use these activities to provide evidence of your preparation for participation in class as well as to plan additional contributions to class discussion. The Civic Engagement Opportunities (CEOs) are designed to help you become more engaged in campus and community life and apply course concepts to important social issues.

1. Listen to a song that inspires you. Who is the intended audience for this song? Are you part of this audience? Why or why not. In a short paper, reveal the song and the artist(s). Discuss whom you believe the intended audience is and how the artist(s) captured your attention. Be sure to include several lyrics to support your claims.

2. Visit the American Rhetoric website (www.americanrhetoric.com) and look at how presidents adapt to their audience in State of the Union or inaugural speeches. You could compare the Clinton-Bush-Obama speeches.

Resources in Print and Online

Name of Supplement	Available in Print	Available Online	Instructor or Student Supplement	Description
Instructor's Resource Manual (ISBN: 0131946021)	√	√	Instructor Supplement	Prepared by Allison Rattenborg, Cheri Simonds, and Stephen Hunt, Illinois State University, this comprehensive instructor resource is organized into 3 parts: Part 1: Chapter-by-Chapter Instructor Resources has all the standard offerings: Chapter Objectives, Teaching Notes, Chapter Outlines, Weblinks, Classroom Exercises/ Activities, and Additional Media and Print Resources *plus* Answer Key to Student Preparing to Participate boxes with Instructor Discussion Questions! Part 2: *Teacher Training* includes everything a new instructor needs to successfully teach the course. Lesson plan construction, quiz and test construction, choosing appropriate instructional strategies, criterion-based speech evaluation training, and much more! Every activity, assessment, and idea has been thoroughly classroom tested. Part 3: Test Bank contains approximately 400 classroom tested multiple-choice, true/ false, matching, and essay questions organized by chapter. Each question is referenced by page.
MyTest (ISBN: 0131945963)		√	Instructor Supplement	This flexible, online test-generating software includes all questions found in the Test Bank section of the printed Instructor's Resource Manual. Available at www.pearson-mytest.com (access code required).
PowerPoint™ Presentation Package (ISBN: 0131945971)		√	Instructor Supplement	Available for download at www.pearsonhighered.com/ irc (access code required), this text-specific package, prepared by Allison Rattenborg and Brent Simonds, Illinois State University, provides a number of dynamic, discussion-stimulating PowerPoint™ slides for each chapter of the book.
Instructional DVD (ISBN: 0131945947)	√		Instructor Supplement	A collection of brand new video clips for both instructors and students that cover a range of topics: Leading Instructional Discussions, Preparing Students to Participate, Presentation Aids, model speeches on tornadoes, the Coliseum, Delta Blues, and more! For adopters only. Some restrictions apply.
Pearson A&B Contemporary Classic Speeches DVD	√		Instructor Supplement	This exciting supplement includes over 120 minutes of video footage in an easy-to-use DVD format. Each speech is accompanied by a biographical and historical summary that helps students understand the context and motivation behind each speech. Speakers featured include Martin Luther King Jr., John F. Kennedy, Barbara Jordan, the Dalai Lama, and Christopher Reeve. For adopters only. Some restrictions apply.
Pearson A&B Public Speaking Video Library	√		Instructor Supplement	Pearson Allyn & Bacon's Public Speaking Video Library contains a range of different types of speeches delivered on a multitude of topics, allowing you to choose the speeches best suited for your students. Please contact your Pearson representative for details and a complete list of videos and their contents to choose which would be most useful in your class. Samples from most of our public speaking videos are available on www.mycoursetoolbox.com. For adopters only. Some restrictions apply.

Allyn & Bacon Digital Media Archive for Communication, Version 3.0, Third Edition (ISBN: 0205437095)	√		Instructor Supplement	The Digital Media Archive CD-ROM contains electronic images of charts, graphs, maps, tables, and figures, along with media elements such as video, audio clips, and related weblinks. These media assets are fully customizable to use with our pre-formatted PowerPoint™ outlines or to import into instructor's own lectures. (Windows and Mac).
Public Speaking Transparency Package, Version II (ISBN: 0205494692)	√	√	Instructor Supplement	100 full-color transparencies created with PowerPoint provide visual support for classroom lectures and discussions.
Preparing Visual Aids for Presentations, Fifth Edition (ISBN: 020561115X)	√		Student Supplement	Prepared by Dan Cavanaugh, this 32-page visual booklet provides a host of ideas for using today's multimedia tools to improve presentations, including suggestions for planning a presentation, guidelines for designing visual aids and storyboarding, and a walkthrough that shows how to prepare a visual display using PowerPoint. Available separately for purchase.
Pearson Allyn & Bacon Public Speaking Study Site (Open access)	√		Student Supplement	The Allyn & Bacon Public Speaking Study Site features practice tests, weblinks, and other study aids that are organized around major topics in your public speaking textbook. Available at www.abpublicspeaking.com
Public Speaking in the Multicultural Environment, Second Edition (ISBN: 0205265111)	√		Student Supplement	Prepared by Devorah A. Lieberman, Portland State University, this supplemental booklet helps students learn to analyze cultural diversity within their audiences and adapt their presentations accordingly.
Outlining Workbook (ISBN: 032108702X)	√		Student Supplement	Prepared by Reeze L. Hanson and Sharon Condon, Haskell Indian Nations University, this workbook includes activities, exercises, and answers to help students develop and master the critical skill of outlining.
Study Card for Public Speaking (ISBN: 0205441262)	√		Student Supplement	Colorful, affordable, and packed with useful information, Pearson Allyn & Bacon's Study Cards make studying easier, more efficient, and more enjoyable. Course information is distilled down to the basics, helping students quickly master the fundamentals, review a subject for understanding, or prepare for an exam. Because they're laminated for durability, these Study Cards can be kept for years to come and students can pull them out whenever they need a quick review.
Multicultural Activities Workbook (ISBN: 0205546528)	√		Student Supplement	By Marlene C. Cohen and Susan L. Richardson, of Prince George's Community College, Maryland, this workbook is filled with hands-on activities that help broaden the content of speech classes to reflect the diverse cultural backgrounds of the class and society. The book includes checklists, surveys, and writing assignments that all help students succeed in speech communication by offering experiences that address a variety of learning styles.
VideoLab CD-ROM (ISBN: 0205561616)	√		Student Supplement	This interactive study tool for students can be used independently or in class. It provides digital video of student speeches that can be viewed in conjunction with corresponding outlines, manuscripts, notecards, and instructor critiques. A series of drills to help students analyze content and delivery follows each speech.

Save time and improve results with

PEARSON
myspeechlab™

Designed to amplify a traditional course in numerous ways or to administer a course online, **MySpeechLab** combines pedagogy and assessment with an array of multimedia activities—videos, speech preparation tools, assessments, research support, multiple newsfeeds—to make learning more effective for all types of students. Now featuring more resources, including a video upload tool, this new release of **MySpeechLab** is visually richer and even more interactive than the previous version—a leap forward in design with more tools and features to enrich learning and aid students in classroom success.

Teaching and Learning Tools

E-Book: Identical in content and design to the printed text, the e-book provides students access to their text whenever and wherever they need it. In addition to contextually placed multimedia features in every chapter, the e-book allows students to take notes and highlight, just like a traditional book.

Videos and Video Quizzes: Interactive videos provide students with the opportunity to watch and evaluate sample speeches, both student and professional. Many videos are annotated with critical thinking questions or include short, assignable quizzes that report to the instructor's gradebook. Professional speeches include classic and contemporary speeches, as well as video segments from communication experts.

MyOutline: MyOutline offers step-by-step guidance for writing an effective outline, along with tips and explanations to help students better understand the elements of an outline and how all the pieces fit together. Outlines that students create can be downloaded to their computer, emailed as an attachment, or saved in the tool for future editing. Instructors can either select from several templates based on our texts, or they can create their own outline structure for students to use.

Topic Selector: This interactive tool helps students get started generating ideas and then narrowing down topics. Our Topic Selector is question based, rather than drill-down, in order to help students really learn the process of selecting their topic. Once they have determined their topic, students are directed to credible online sources for guidance with the research process.

Self-Assessments: Online self-assessments including the PRCA-24 and the PRPSA, as well as Pre- and Post-tests for each chapter, provide students with opportunities to assess and confirm their comfort level with speaking publicly, and their knowledge of the material in the course. The tests generate a customized study plan for further assessment and focus students on areas in which they need to improve. Instructors can use these tools to show learning over the duration of the course.

Speech Evaluation Tools: Instructors have access to a host of **Speech Evaluation Tools** to use in the classroom, including a Speech Evaluation Rubric that can be customized to individual needs. An additional assortment of evaluation forms and guides for students and instructors offer further options and ideas for assessing presentations.

ABC News RSS feed: MySpeechLab provides an online feed from ABC news, updated hourly, to help students choose and research their speech topics.

Cutting-Edge Technology

MediaShare: With this new video upload tool, students are able to upload their speeches for their instructor and classmates to watch (whether face-to-face or online) and provide online feedback and comments. Structured much like a social networking site, MediaShare can help promote a sense of community among students.

American Rhetoric.com partnership: Through an exclusive partnership with mericanRhetoric.com, MySpeechLab incorporates many great speeches of our time (without linking out to another site and without advertisements or commercials!). Many speeches are also accompanied by assessment questions that ask students to evaluate specific elements of those speeches.

Audio Chapter Summaries: Every chapter includes an audio chapter summary, formatted as an MP3 file, perfect for students reviewing material before a test or instructors reviewing material before class.

Online Administration

No matter what course management system you use—or if you do not use one at all, but still wish to easily capture your students' grade and track their performance—Pearson has a **MySpeechLab** option to suit your needs. Contact one of Pearson's Technology Specialists for more information and assistance.

A **MySpeechLab** access code is no additional cost when packaged with selected Pearson Communication texts. To get started, contact your local Pearson Publisher's Representative at **www.pearsonhighered.com/replocator.**

Authors' Background

Cheri J. Simonds is a Professor of Communication at Illinois State University and has taught basic communication courses including public speaking at the secondary and collegiate levels for 24 years. She has co-authored textbooks on classroom communication and intercultural communication and has published over 30 book chapters and articles in instructional communication and communication pedagogy. She has also co-produced (with Brent and Steve) several instructional videos.

Stephen K. Hunt is a Professor of Communication, Carnegie Foundation for the Advancement of Teaching Political Engagement Scholar, Co-Chair of the American Democracy Project, and Associate Director of the School of Communication at Illinois State University. He has taught basic communication courses at the collegiate level for the past 17 years. In addition, he has published more than 20 book chapters and refereed articles in instructional communication and communication pedagogy, persuasion, and the pedagogy of political engagement.

Brent K. Simonds is an Associate Professor at Illinois State University and has 12 years of university teaching experience in Presentation Media and Mass Communication. Before his academic career, Brent spent 14 years as a video producer/director, creating both broadcast programs and nationally distributed training/educational films. He continues to produce educational films and interactive media programs through various grant projects. He has received several national-level video production awards including the Telly Award for the instructional video included in this package, *Leading Instructional Discussions*.

Acknowledgments

This book is the culmination of many years of teaching public speaking. Many people have contributed to the development of these course materials. Thus, we would like to thank first all of our instructors, past and present, for their contributions to the successful delivery and implementation of our course. Your creative ideas and dedication to teaching have influenced our pedagogy—all of which are reflected in this book.

We would also like to thank our students who have challenged us to create a text that is brief, yet substantive and interactive. We are grateful for your enthusiasm and contributions to the learning environment with your preparation for and participation in our class discussions and activities.

In particular, we would like to thank our former students who have made specific contributions to the pedagogy of our course: Allison Rattenborg for her tireless dedication to and creation of our instructional materials; Todd Zessin, Carla Beck, and Bryan McCann for their outstanding performances on our sample Tornado, Coliseum, and Delta Blues speeches; and Greg Fairbanks for his excellent J.R.R. Tolkien activity.

We are also grateful to our staff at Allyn & Bacon for their efforts in this endeavor. They have supported us and challenged us to create the best product for our students. We are particularly indebted to Karon Bowers—editor-in-chief, David Kear and Sharon Geary—development managers, Carol

Alper—development editor, Patrick Cash-Peterson—production supervisor, Kathy Smith—copy editor, Susan Brilling, editorial assistant.

We are grateful to the many educators who read the manuscript and challenged us to make this a better book.

Donna Acerra, *Northampton Community College*

Nedra Adams-Soller, *College of Lake County*

Jonathan H. Amsbary, *University of Alabama, Birmingham*

Lana L. Baysinger, *Ozarks Tech Community College*

Jennifer Becker, *University of Oklahoma*

Francesca Bishop, *El Camino College*

Kay F. Blohm, *Baker College, Auburn Hills*

Penelope Britton, *Western Washington University*

Jodi Michele Bromley, *Old Dominion University*

Jack Byer, *Bucks County Community College*

Kimberly Conley, *Bellarmine University*

Elaine L. Davies, *Northern Illinois University*

Karen DeFrancesco, *Susquehanna University*

Joanne Detore-Nakamura, *Embry-Riddle Aeronautical University*

Terri Easley, *Johnson County Community College*

Gary W. Eckles, *Thomas Nelson Community College*

Kelsea Erbatu, *Spartanburg Technical College*

Amber K. Erickson, *University of Cincinnati*

Michael F. Fleming, *San Bernardino Valley College*

Amy Bowie Fountain, *Mississippi State University*

Joshua M. Galligan, *Virginia Commonwealth University*

Kevin Gillen, *Indiana University, South Bend*

Ava Good, *San Jacinto College*

Catherine Gragg, *San Jacinto College*

Phoebe Hall, *Fayetteville State University*

Carla Harrell, *Old Dominion University*

Tina M. Harris, *University of Georgia*

Emily Holler, *Kennesaw State University*

Diane Honour, *Lynn University*

Lawrence A. Hosman, *University of Southern Mississippi*

Sandra S. Johnson, *University of Maryland, Eastern Shore*

Brian Kline, *Gainesville College*

Ramona J. Klinger, *North Idaho College*

Karen Lada, *Delaware County Community College*

Maxine A. LeGall, *University of the District of Columbia*

Kurt Lindemann, *San Diego State University*

Leslie B. Maggard, *McLennan Community College*

Joseph P. Mazer, *Ohio University*

Charles R. McMahan, *Vincennes University*

Libby McGlone, *Columbus State Community College*

Christopher J. Miller, *College of DuPage*

Mary Moore, *Northwest Arkansas Community College*

Clay Redding, *Blinn College*

Heather Ricker-Gilbert, *Manchester Community College*

Douglas Rosenstrater, *Bucks County Community College*

Timothy Rumbough, *Bloomsburg University*

Gary Rybold, *Irvine Valley College*

James Schroeder, *Holmes Community College*

Steve Schwarze, *University of Montana*

Jeff Shires, *Purdue University, North Central*

Glenn Smith, *Mississippi State University*

June H. Smith, *Angelo State University*

Joseph M. Valenzano III, *University of Nevada, Las Vegas*

Nadene N. Vevea, *North Dakota State University*

Thomas W. Vickers, *Embry-Riddle Aeronautical University*

David Walker, *Middle Tennessee State University*

Susan Ward, *Thomas Nelson Community College*

Wyniese Way, *Blinn College*

CoraAnn Williams, *Lonestar College—Kingwood*

J. P. Williams, *Defiance College*

Alan Winson, *John Jay College – City College of New York*

Mark Woods, *Baker College, Auburn Hills*

Windolyn K. Yarberry, *Florida Community College at Jacksonville/Kent*

Tina Marie Zagara, *Georgia Perimeter College*

Finally, our families deserve a very special thanks. We are truly grateful to Sarah and Ethan and Dylan and Addison for their patience, love, and support during this process. Thank you for reminding us that writing is *what* we do, but you all are the reason *why* we do it.

1

Introduction to Communication

Anyone who forms a judgment on any point but cannot explain it clearly might as well never have thought on the subject.

—Pericles

CHAPTER OBJECTIVES

After reading this chapter, you should be able to:

- List and describe the three benefits of communication mentioned by the text.

- Understand the relationships among the six elements of the communication process.

- Explain the three models of communication.

- Explain the five goals the authors have for you as a communicator.

Kofi Annan

Communication is everywhere! You have been communicating from the time you were born. Even as a baby, your cries communicated whether you were hungry, in pain, or unhappy in some way. And since then, you have been communicating on a daily basis.

Consider for a moment the number of times a day you rely on communication. Before you leave your home in the morning for work or school, you express ideas, make plans, and manage relationships by speaking and listening. Using technologies such as a cell phone or e-mail, you plan your work and leisure time by sending and receiving messages. So, why study communication? You should be an expert by now, right? It seems as natural as breathing. We believe the quotation in the beginning of this chapter provides a justification for the formal study of communication. How often have you had a strong opinion or emotion about something and been unable to express your ideas or feelings adequately? This can be quite frustrating, and improving your communication skills can help you convey your thoughts more clearly. In this class, you will get an opportunity to practice your communication skills in the context of public speaking. As you learn to articulate and defend your ideas in your presentations, these skills will, in turn, improve your communication in other situations.

Benefits of Communication

Having poor communication skills can hinder us in many ways. It may cause difficulties in maintaining relationships, getting that dream job, or becoming an active member of society. On the other hand, understanding communication can provide many personal, professional, and social benefits.

Personal Benefits

Studying communication has many *personal benefits*. Effective communication can help you develop more meaningful relationships. Improving communication skills will help you to become more confident in expressing your ideas and justifying your point of view.

In this book, you will learn why one type of communication interaction works while another does not. You will be able to identify the problem when something goes wrong in the communication process and enact strategies to repair relationships when needed. Additionally, you will be able to communicate better with people who may be very different from you. You will understand how to become a better listener, which will motivate people to want to interact with you.

Throughout this text, we will provide you with opportunities to critically reflect on the information that you consume on a daily basis. For example, each chapter contains Critical Interaction boxes that build on your knowledge and comprehension of course concepts and encourage you to think more critically about the content. Thus, as you progress through this course, you will both sharpen your critical thinking skills as your knowledge and comprehension of the concepts increases and expand your ability to apply, analyze, synthesize, and evaluate communication events.[1]

Source Citation:
[1] Bloom, B. S., Englehart, M., Furst, E., Hill, W., & Krathwohl, D. (1956). *Taxonomy of educational objectives: Cognitive domain.* New York: David McKay.

In addition, we will provide various Media Interactions to improve your media literacy. For example, our first media interaction will direct you to a website that discusses how you can benefit from learning about communication. ⌐ The questions that follow the interaction will allow you to think about how this media source informs your communication decisions as well as your tasks in this class. In other words, this text will help you become a savvy consumer of information you receive from media sources. Think for a moment about the vast amount of mediated messages you consume every day through video games, television, radio, billboards, the Internet, and even T-shirts. Knowing how to analyze and evaluate mediated messages will allow you as a consumer of information to make better personal decisions.

The skills you learn in this class will help you with your other courses as well. Many college classes require a presentation of some sort. Often you will be asked to express and defend your ideas in conversation as well as to research and deliver a formal speech or report. This class will provide you with many opportunities for practicing these skills. The Preparing to Participate features in each chapter will help you come to class with the knowledge you need to contribute your own ideas to class discussions. In other words, this class will give you the confidence and skills to stand and deliver. You'll be ready if asked to give a wedding toast at your best friend's reception, or to provide a eulogy at a funeral. In fact, we have had students e-mail us and tell of their successes with such experiences. They expressed how this course helped them with the confidence they needed to deliver a strong presentation. They also indicated that the presentations were well received by their audiences.

Media Interaction 1.1

Communication Media Source

Log on to the Internet and visit the following website: http://www.mindtools.com/CommSkll/CommunicationIntro.htm

1. How can you benefit from learning communication?
2. How can this website help you in this class?
3. How can this website help you after this class?

Professional Benefits

There are also many *professional benefits* to studying communication. You will need communication skills to create a positive first impression during a job interview. In fact, according to the National Association of Colleges and Employers *Job Outlook 2008* survey, communication is the highest ranking skill that employers look for in new recruits.[2] According to the list, employers also seek recruits with interpersonal and teamwork skills. Employers value attributes such as honesty, integrity, the ability to analyze and synthesize information, flexibility, and adaptability—all of which can be improved by understanding the information you will be taught in this course and practicing the skills you learn. Regardless of your future career, you will likely find yourself in situations where you are required to deliver an oral presentation, and this course will certainly help you develop the verbal communication skills needed for such presentations. Beyond public speaking, the skills you learn in this course are transferable to the many communication contexts you will encounter in organizations—from face-to-face interactions to e-mail to communicating in teams. In other words, you will be a more competent communicator in all of these contexts because you will better understand how to tailor messages to specific audiences, build persuasive arguments, and organize and support your ideas.

Source Citation:
[2] *Job Outlook Survey 2008*. (2008). Retrieved March 28, 2008 from http://www.naceweb.org.

Source Citation:
[3] Milner, H. (2002). *Civic literacy: How informed citizens make democracy work.* Hanover: University Press of New England.

Media
Interaction 1.2
Communication Skills

Log on to the Internet and visit a career website such as monster.com or flipdog.com to locate a job listing for your "dream" job.

1. What communication skills are required for this job?
2. Can you think of a profession where communication does not take place?

Although most jobs also require company-specific skills such as the use of a particular technology, many employers provide on-site training for expertise particular to the organization. Effective communication skills will be crucial, however, in securing your opportunity to get that on-the-job training. ⌐ So, whatever your major or career choice, you will be expected to be an effective communicator to get and keep the job you want.

Social Benefits

There are also many *social benefits* to studying communication. You will learn how to influence people—to persuade them to your point of view. You will also become a critical consumer of the information you receive from a variety of sources including politicians, journalists, and advertisers. You will be able to distinguish a strong claim from a weak one and make decisions in both your own and your community's best interest. In this course you will learn how to access, use, and critically evaluate information from a variety of sources. Such skills form the foundation of what we refer to as *information and media literacy*. Information and media literacy are essential to engaged citizenship, as these skills enable individuals to sort through political messages, empower them to communicate their own messages to others, and enhance their decision making at the voting booth.[3]

Strong communication skills are required if you wish to be an effective and engaged participant in a democracy. You may become more influential in social situations by identifying problems and suggesting solutions to social injustices. In short, the skills you acquire in this course will help you to become a more effective producer and consumer of persuasive messages. For example, one of your authors recently attended a school board meeting where several high school students convinced the school board that it would not be a good idea to change the calendar to administer semester exams after the winter break. They presented several arguments, including the issue of retention of information after a vacation and the time necessary to travel or visit with their families. Five minutes after their impassioned and well-reasoned arguments, the school board voted to retain the calendar as it was, with exams taking place prior to the winter break.

Although this situation had immediate benefits for the students involved, communication can also be used in significant ways to benefit other members of society. For example, a doctoral student from the University of Missouri produced a documentary film about a death row inmate, Joe Amrine, who had been wrongly convicted of murdering a fellow inmate. After seeing the documentary and hearing the arguments it presented, the State Supreme Court of Missouri released the man from death row. Today, Amrine is a free man.

Unreasonable Doubt: The Joe Amrine Case. The effective communication skills of filmmaker, John McHale, had a life-changing effect on wrongly accused Joe Amrine.

Does that seem extreme or unrelated to your life? Consider this. There is a strong likelihood that you will serve on a jury in a criminal or civil trial during your lifetime. The attorneys in the courtroom will present evidence and arguments, and it will be up to you and your fellow jurors to weigh the information and reach a conclusion. This is serious business, and it is one of the responsibilities we have as citizens in a democracy. This course will help you hone the skills needed in this type of situation.

Preparing to Participate 1.1
The Benefits of Studying Communication

Knowledge
List and describe three benefits of studying communication.

Application
Think of a time when effective communication was beneficial in your personal or social life. Describe the communication encounter and the successful outcome.

The Communication Process

We know that communication happens all of the time and that we use it on a daily basis, but what is it? It is not something tangible that we can point to and say, "There it is." In fact, communication experts have offered multiple definitions and have debated the nature of communication for years. We know that it involves messages that are sent and received, but what if the meaning of the message gets lost along the way? Does your listener understand your message in the way you intended? Unfortunately, sometimes what we mean and what others think we mean are two different things.

Is communication always intentional? Or, can we send messages that we never intended? If your stomach growls in class and a classmate hears it and smiles at you, has communication taken place? Did you intend to communicate your hunger? Probably not, but an interaction between you and your classmate ensued.

Because many scholars still disagree on all of the factors that constitute communication, we do not provide a formal definition here. Rather, **the communication process** is composed of several elements we can identify that are necessary for any communication event. These include people (speaker and listener), the message, channel, interference, feedback, and context.

People

Communication involves interactions between **people**. It is important to understand that the speaker and the listener involved in the communication event each bring to the encounter their experiences, goals, values, attitudes, beliefs, age, and knowledge that affect everything they say and how they interpret the event. Furthermore, our culture and gender permeate our communication encounters. These life experiences make up our **frame of reference**. Later in this text, we'll talk more about how this frame of reference affects the entire communication encounter. For now, it is important to understand that your life experiences are extremely important to the outcome of your communication with others. In turn, other people's experiences will affect the way they communicate with you.

Because the people involved in the communication event have different frames of reference, they may construct and interpret messages very differently. For example, when a professor asked some first-year students at the beginning of the semester to share what sorts of things they thought were valued at the university, she was surprised when the students listed good looks, lots of money, and a nice car. What she expected to hear was intellectual curiosity, hard work, and punctuality. In the professor's social circles those are important values (although she has nothing against good looks, money, or nice cars!). Not surprisingly, because the professor didn't specify whose values the students were supposed to consider, they answered with those of their peer group.

In public speaking, the role of the people involved in the encounter is somewhat unique. In conversations, there may be turn-taking; however, in public speaking, the speaker has the floor. Because listeners may ask questions only when the presentation is concluded, the speaker must anticipate what questions might arise and plan for them in the presentation. In addition, the speaker needs to take into consideration the interests and attitudes (frame of reference) of the listeners. The listeners, in turn, have the responsibility to listen attentively to the message of the speech.

Messages

Communication also involves messages, which can be verbal or nonverbal. **Verbal messages** include the words we use in the encounter. This is what we say. As we construct our verbal messages, we make choices about the words we use. Obviously, we want our words to be appropriate, clear, descriptive,

Critical Interaction 1.1
Frame of Reference

Think about two different people with various backgrounds (e.g., different goals, values, attitudes, beliefs, knowledge, culture, or gender). Write a description of person A and person B. What might happen if these two people had a conversation about a current social issue such as an election, education, the environment, etc.? You get to pick the people and the topic. How does their frame of reference affect their interpretation of the communication event?

Using Symbolic Gestures. The meaning of nonverbal signs can change based on who is using the sign and in what context.

powerful, and accurate. The goal is to construct a message in such a way that the listener understands and correctly interprets our intended meaning. Given what we know about differing frames of reference, this can sometimes be challenging. In public speaking, there are strict time limits on the message. Thus, speakers must plan carefully the words and details of their presentations.

Communication is also nonverbal. This includes how we say words and use gestures. Tone of voice, face, eyes, and body language all serve to send messages that are either consistent or inconsistent with our words.[4] In addition, our actions or behaviors may communicate nonverbally. Just like verbal messages, **nonverbal messages** can differ based on the communicator's frame of reference. For example, we all use symbolic gestures. Ask a toddler how old he is, say hello to a hippie, or view a photo of Winston Churchill during World War II and you will see the same sign, but with three different meanings.

You can use nonverbal communication to help support your verbal communication by emphasizing your feelings associated with the message. You can also use nonverbal communication to indicate sarcasm in a message. It is important to note that you may not always be aware of how your nonverbal communication may support or betray the meaning of your message. Your listener, however, will be more likely to believe *how* you say something rather than *what* you say. For example, if your roommate yells at you to "Go ahead, turn on your television as loud as you want. I don't really need to study," do you dare push that button? In essence, what your roommate says is inconsistent with how she has said it. Knowing how verbal and nonverbal messages work together to create meaning will help you to become a more effective communicator and public speaker. For example, as a public speaker, if you cannot demonstrate an interest in your own topic through your nonverbal delivery, your audience is not likely to either. In this text, we will provide you with nonverbal delivery cues to help you give a formal presentation that is an honest reflection of your interest and enthusiasm for your topic.

Source Citation:
[4] Burgoon, J. K. (1980). Nonverbal communication research in the 1970s: An overview. In D. Nimmo (Ed.), *Communication yearbook 4* (pp. 179–197). New Brunswick, NJ: Transaction.

Channel

The medium through which we communicate is known as the **channel**, and the channel we choose can affect the message. We may speak to one another face-to-face or communicate through some medium such as a telephone (voice or text message), computer (e-mail, instant message, website), or video. By the time you read this book, there may be even more channels to consider.

It is important to understand the implications the channel has when you choose to communicate certain messages. For example, if you decide to quit your job, what is the most appropriate channel for doing so? Should you talk with your supervisor face-to-face or would an e-mail message be appropriate? Which one of these channels would increase your chances for a positive recommendation in the future? Or, consider the best channel for letting someone know that you don't want to date him/her anymore. Perhaps a text message or post-it-note is not the best communication choice!

Interference

Communication is not always easy, and it is sometimes affected by interference. **Interference** is anything that gets in the way of shared meaning between the speaker and the listener. Interference can be either external or internal.

External interference can be static or noise that distracts the speaker or listener from the message; it includes loud music, traffic, people laughing or talking, or a bad connection on your telephone or e-mail server. A room that is too drab, hot, or cold, can cause interference in communication.

Internal interference also affects a person's ability to listen or communicate. This type of interference can cause speakers and listeners to lack concentration and may include personal concerns, physical ailments, stress, or conflict. Have you ever found it difficult to listen to a lecture in one class because you were getting ready to take a test in your next class? Maybe you were up late studying and found it difficult to stay awake. Or, when you give a speech, perhaps your apprehension (internal interference) causes you to shake or stammer. These mannerisms, in turn, become external interference for your audience.

Feedback

Feedback is very important to the communication process and involves both the speaker and the listener simultaneously. As the speaker is sending the message, the listener is responding either verbally or nonverbally. As we send messages, we look to see whether our listeners understand or agree with us. Our listeners may ask questions for clarification, nod their heads in agreement, or express disagreement in their facial expressions. This feedback tells us what we should say or do next.

Feedback also tells us whether our listeners received the message we intended. An unexpected response from a listener (a raised eyebrow, a frown, a

Comic 1.1   *Hi and Lois*

1. How have our channels of communication changed over the years?

2. What implications do these channels have on the way we communicate with others?

Hi & Lois ©King Features Syndicate

confused look) can tell us that perhaps we should rephrase what we say. Recall that both the speaker's and the listener's frames of reference may affect the way each responds to a message. Additionally, in public speaking the audience may respond nonverbally during the presentation, but verbal feedback is delayed until after the presentation.

Context

Finally, communication happens in context. The time of day, location, or social situation all provide **context** to the communication encounter. For example, if you enroll in an 8:00 a.m. class, is this going to have an effect on your ability to concentrate on the instructor's message? Or, your classmates' ability to listen to your speech?

As students, you have different types of conversations in your dorm room than you do in class. Because of the classroom context, speeches become a little more formal than everyday conversation. Although time and place are important factors to consider, perhaps even more important is the social context of the communication event. What implications do the current economic, political, and social climates have for the topics you choose? What has happened in the news lately that might affect how people respond to your speech? Consider the social context of getting on a plane September 10, 2001 and then taking the same flight a week later. Everything you say and do happens in a climate that either makes your message appropriate or inappropriate, effective or ineffective, at any given time or place.

As you consider how all of these elements of communication work together, you are beginning to develop your own ideas about how you can use communication in your own life as well as in your speeches. We know that communication can involve all of these elements, but exactly how do they interact with one another to result in a successful encounter? The next section will help you understand the relationships among the elements of communication by providing pictures, or models, of what it looks like.

Preparing to Participate 1.2
Understanding the Communication Process

Knowledge
List and define the six elements of the communication process.

Application
What would happen if we eliminated feedback from the communication process during:

- A personal conversation?
- A job interview?
- A public speech?

Comic 1.2

1. How does the context change for Edison and his father in this situation?

2. How does their frame of reference change the message?

The Brilliant Mind of Edison Lee ©King Features Syndicate

Models of Communication

The following models of communication describe how each of these elements may or may not be present in every situation. Additionally, they describe how communication encounters unfold. The way we think about how these elements work together has evolved over the years. These models represent the changes in the way we view communication. It is important to remember that models are a way to lend visual form and therefore understanding to something that is abstract. These models are tools that allow us to think and talk about different communication encounters and contexts, but they do not suggest the way communication *should* happen. In other words, they are descriptive rather than prescriptive.

Action Model

Source Citation:
[5] Laswell, H. D. (1948). The structure and function of communication in society. In L. Bryson (Ed.), *The communication of ideas* (pp. 37–51). New York: Harper & Row.

Initially, communication scholars thought communication was primarily a linear process.[5] This is known as the **action model** of communication (see Figure 1.1). That is, a speaker sends a message to a listener who receives the message. This model views communication as something a speaker does to a listener. It also suggests that communication has a beginning and ending. Although we agree that communication is often much more complex than this, there are times when the action model best describes the communication event. For example, as you drive down the highway, you see the "Golden Arches." This symbol (placed there by someone who wants to communicate with you) represents something you are quite familiar with and tells you that

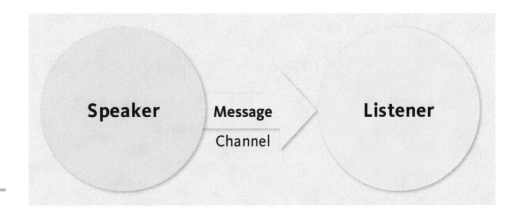

FIGURE 1.1

Action Model

a McDonald's restaurant is nearby. Do you take the exit or continue driving? The sender of that message may never know.

Another example of this kind of communication might occur if you phone a friend, only to get her answering machine or voice mail. You leave your message. Your friend may receive it, but may not. The power could go out, or another person may retrieve it first, and then erase it. An important part of the communication process is missing in this example. How will you know if your friend retrieved the message? Even if she did, how will you know if she understood it? How will you know if she reacted to the message the way you intended?

Interaction Model

The **interaction model** of communication takes into account the role of feedback in the communication process.[6] Feedback occurs when the listener responds to the speaker's message. In this model, however, the message goes back and forth between the speaker and the listener. In other words, they take turns sending and receiving messages (see Figure 1.2). There are times when this model describes the communication event, but the exchange is limited.

Source Citation:
[6] Schramm, W. (1955). *The process and effects of mass communication.* Urbana, IL: University of Illinois Press.

In this case, you and your friend are taking turns playing phone tag. Your friend calls you back, only to leave a message on your machine. You retrieve the message, and communication has taken place. Much like playing tennis, communication goes back and forth between sender and receiver. Although you and your friend are taking turns communicating, there is a delay in feedback.

Transaction Model

More recently, communication scholars have considered the **transaction model** of communication, which takes into account the simultaneous sending and receiving of messages that occur in context.[7] In this model, feedback is constantly being shared verbally and nonverbally between both people involved in the encounter. There is no one speaker or listener, but transactions that take place between people. This model also takes into account the context of the situation and the relationship between individuals (see Figure 1.3). This model best represents all of the elements of the communication

Source Citation:
[7] Barnland, D. (1970). A transactional model of communication. In K. K. Sereno & C. D. Mortensen (Eds.), *Foundations of communication theory* (pp. 98–101). New York: Harper & Row.

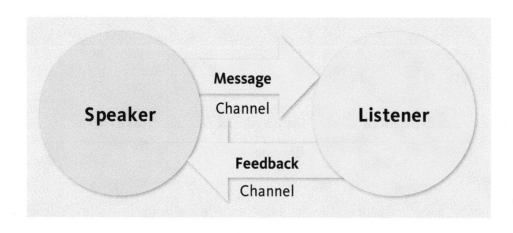

FIGURE 1.2

Interaction Model

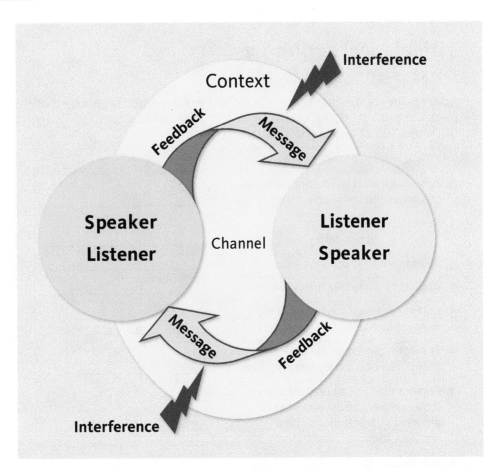

FIGURE 1.3
Transaction Model

process we described earlier (people, message, channel, interference, feedback, and context).

This time, when you call your friend, she answers the telephone. You want to invite her to dinner for her birthday, and she says she would love to, but doesn't seem too enthusiastic about it. You ask her if she is all right and she says she is not feeling well. You understand that your friend is under a lot of stress from school and work, so you suggest that tomorrow night might be better for both of you. She agrees and thanks you for your invitation. This model characterizes communication as a much more dynamic process.

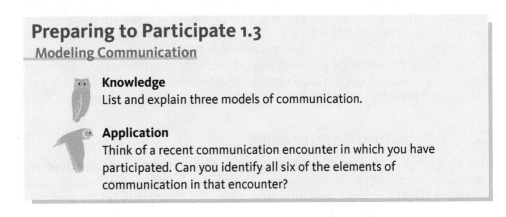

Preparing to Participate 1.3
Modeling Communication

Knowledge
List and explain three models of communication.

Application
Think of a recent communication encounter in which you have participated. Can you identify all six of the elements of communication in that encounter?

Critical Interaction 1.2
What Is Communication?

Read the following statements and indicate your initial reaction to each by checking whether you Strongly Agree (SA), Agree (A), Disagree (D), or Strongly Disagree (SD). Be prepared to defend your reactions.

	SA	A	D	SD
1. A message must be intentional to be considered communication.	____	____	____	____
2. Feedback is necessary for communication to take place.	____	____	____	____
3. You cannot NOT communicate.	____	____	____	____
4. Actions speak louder than words.	____	____	____	____
5. Communicating face-to-face is the most difficult channel.	____	____	____	____
6. The transactional model of communication is the most effective.	____	____	____	____
7. Communication can take place even if the speaker and listener have different interpretations of the message communicated.	____	____	____	____
8. A billboard sign communicates a message.	____	____	____	____

Themes for the Text

In this book, we will address several themes to help you become a more effective communicator and public speaker. These themes can be stated in terms of our goals for you. After taking this course and reading and thinking about this text, we hope that you become a more competent, confident, and ethical communicator, a better critical thinker, and a more media and information literate consumer. This course will provide you with opportunities to enhance your public speaking skills for academic and professional development. We believe that this will ultimately provide you with opportunities to become better citizens in a democracy. We will discuss each of these themes briefly here and ask that you think about how they apply to the rest of your readings and discussions.

Communication Competence

Our first goal is that you become a more **competent communicator**, which consists of four elements: knowledge, skill, motivation, and judgment.[8] After reading and thinking critically about this book, you will

Source Citation:
[8] Spitzberg, B. (2000). What is good communication? *Journal of the Association for Communication Administration, 29 (1)*, 103–119.

have knowledge of the factors that affect your communication personally, professionally, and socially. Because the goal of public speaking is to communicate effectively with an audience, you will have opportunities to practice the skills of producing and consuming messages to achieve your goals. Specifically, you will learn to choose and narrow topics; conduct research; and organize, outline, and present your speeches. Hopefully, you will become motivated to use communication effectively, and you will use your judgment on how to adapt and adjust your messages (or speeches) to your audience. Throughout this text we will apply concepts to multiple communication contexts that extend beyond giving a speech in classroom. It is our hope that by studying the fundamental elements of public speaking, you will develop an appreciation for how these concepts can be applied to the many contexts in which you will communicate for the rest of your life—from e-mail to face-to-face interactions to working with a group of colleagues. In other words, the competence you develop in this course will go well beyond public speaking.

Communication Confidence

Source Citation:
[9]Ayres, J. (1996). Speech preparation processes and speech apprehension. *Communication Education, 45*, 228–235.

Our second goal is that you become a more **confident communicator**. Because you will be afforded the opportunity to practice your skills in a variety of settings, you will begin to increase your communication confidence and decrease your apprehension in public, personal, and professional contexts.[9] In Chapter 2, we will discuss the causes of and strategies for managing apprehension in your communication with others. We will talk about how learning the process of public speaking will help you to feel more confident in giving presentations. By developing relationships with classmates and conducting audience analyses, you will feel more comfortable and confident about communicating in the classroom.

Ethical Communication

Source Citation:
[10]Johannesen, R. L. (2002). *Ethics in human communication* (5th ed.). Prospect Heights, IL: Waveland.

Our third goal is that you become a more **ethical communicator**. Ethical communication is characterized by honesty, clarity, accuracy, open-mindedness, and willingness to listen to others.[10] Ethical communicators are sensitive to the needs of the people they communicate with. These needs may be based on a speaker's or listener's past experiences, sex, culture, race, sexual orientation, and so forth. In Chapter 3, we will discuss ethical communication concerns when producing and consuming messages. As you prepare your speeches in this class, you will be continually faced with making ethical decisions on which sources to use as well as how to represent this information to your audience. You will be making these decisions at the same time you are considering the needs of your audience. As you listen to your classmates present their speeches, you will consider what they say, listen ethically, and make decisions about what is an appropriate response to their messages.

Critical Thinking

In addressing all of these previous goals, you will inevitably become a more *critical thinker*. You've probably heard this term before. What exactly does it mean? To us, **critical thinking** is characterized by the ability to defer judgment until you have enough information on which to act. Thinking critically means that you don't eagerly accept everything you are presented, yet you don't reject everything out-of-hand. It is a "wait and see" attitude. It involves a tolerance for ambiguity. It is a curiosity that drives you to seek high-quality information and recognize it when you find it. You will get opportunities to practice critical thinking in various contexts in this course. You'll consume and analyze mediated messages and you'll conduct research for your own speeches. Because of these opportunities, you'll enhance your media and information literacy.

Information literacy involves being able to find appropriate sources, analyze the material, evaluate the credibility of the sources, and to use and cite those sources ethically and legally.[11]

You will learn more about informational literacy in Chapter 7. In addition, we will provide you with opportunities to interact with several messages in the mass media and then ask you to critically consider what the producers of those messages are saying. (See the Media Interactions in each chapter.) That is, who are these people who are producing this content, and what are they trying to accomplish? What motivates the filmmaker, journalist, politician, blogger, or advertiser to communicate, what biases might they or the industry they work in have, and what constraints are placed on their ability to speak? This is referred to as **media literacy**, and we hope to show you how the communication principles and behaviors you will learn in this course can be used to critically evaluate all that you see and hear in the mass media. As you can see, media literacy focuses on a particular source of information available to you and requires the application of the same types of critical thinking skills that you will use throughout the speechmaking, delivery, and evaluation process.

Closer to home, you will also be provided many opportunities to reflect on and evaluate both your own and your classmates' communication behaviors. By realizing each of the goals we have set forth for you as themes in this book, you will be better prepared to enter into professional and civic life.

Source Citation:
[11] Eisenberg, M. B., Lowe, C. A., & Spitzer, K. L. (2004). *Information literacy: Essential skills for the information age* (2nd ed.). Westport, CT: Libraries Unlimited.

Citizens in a Democracy

By becoming a better communicator and public speaker, you will have the necessary tools to become a more informed **citizen in a democracy**. Competent and ethical communicators are central to advancing our democracy. These skills may give you the confidence you need to speak out for the greater good. Democracies function as a result of citizens using their critical thinking skills (including information and media literacy) to advance local, state, national, or international causes. Beyer and Liston point out that *common, community, and communication* all share the same linguistic root and that without these values it would be impossible to "establish a widely held social good."[12] In fact, Barack Obama often referred to our sense of common and mutual responsibility to public service in his presidential campaign speeches. To help you better understand the role communication plays in social issues, each chapter contains *Civic Engagement Opportunities (CEOs)* that provide ideas of how to apply communication concepts as a way of addressing significant social and political concerns in your community.

Source Citation:
[12] Beyer, L. E., & Liston, D. P. (1996). *Curriculum in conflict: Social visions, educational agendas, and progressive school reform.* New York: Teachers College Press. (p. 88)

Source Citation:
13 Hillygus, D. S. (2005). The missing link: Exploring the relationship between higher education and political engagement. *Political Behavior, 27,* 25–47.

As you become a more competent communicator, you also become better prepared to participate in our democracy. Think of it this way—our democratic system of government is an exercise of communication. In order to engage in political persuasion, an individual must have the verbal and argumentation skills to communicate a position. In fact, in one study of the effects of higher education, the author found that training in communication skills was the best predictor of a student's future political engagement.[13] This is where the social benefits of studying communication come into play. In Chapter 16, we will talk about how each of these themes comes together to give you opportunities you may never have considered.

Preparing to Participate 1.4
Putting It All Together

Knowledge
Describe the themes that will run throughout the course.

Application
What are your personal goals for this course? What strategies will you use to accomplish your goals?

SUMMARY

In this chapter, we have discussed the personal, professional, and social benefits of studying communication. We have also discussed how understanding the process of communication will enable you to become more *competent communicators* as well as public speakers.

Although there are many models and definitions of communication, scholars agree that the elements of communication (people, message, channel, interference, feedback, and context) will ultimately affect what is communicated or understood in any encounter. When our communication doesn't work for us, we can look back at these elements to determine what went wrong and where. This will make our future interactions more successful.

Finally, we have introduced some themes that will be threaded throughout the text. We encourage you to consider these as you read and prepare to participate in class discussions.

KEY TERMS

the communication process (7)

people (speaker and listener) (7)

frame of reference (8)

message (verbal and nonverbal) (8)

channel (9)

interference (external and internal) (10)

feedback (10)

context (11)

action model (12)

interaction model (13)

transaction model (13)

competent communicator (15)

confident communicator (16)

ethical communicator (16)

critical thinker (17)

information literacy (17)

media literacy (17)

citizen in a democracy (17)

ADDITIONAL ENGAGEMENT OPPORTUNITIES

Now that you have finished reading the chapter, it is important to make connections between the course content and your own experiences. These activities will help you understand, apply, analyze, evaluate, or synthesize course concepts. You can use these activities to provide evidence of your preparation for participation in class as well as to plan additional contributions to class discussion. The Civic Engagement Opportunities (CEOs) are designed to help you become more engaged in campus and community life and apply course concepts to important social issues.

1. Reflect on a conversation with a friend. Analyze the conversation, keeping the communication process model as your focus. What influenced the way each of you communicated? In other words, did certain aspects of your frame of reference bring clarity or confusion to the conversation? Were there any interferences? If so, were they external or internal? How did feedback affect your conversation? What provided context to your conversation? Did you feel the conversation was effective? If so, what allowed both of you to convey your messages effectively? If not, what hindered your communication, and how could you improve your communication next time?

2. Find a comic strip where communication is taking place. What is the gist of the strip? How does this connect to course content? Was it funny? What about the strip made it funny (or not funny)—the verbal or nonverbal aspects?

3. Your campus and community offer a wide variety of opportunities for involvement for students. Create a written plan of action for the semester. The plan should describe a coherent approach to getting involved in campus or community organizations, or attending out-of-class events this semester. The plan should meet the following requirements:

   • The plan should be related to developing a better understanding of communication (this shouldn't be difficult as every activity you'll participate in will involve communication).

   • The plan should provide a mechanism for reporting your attendance of at least 4 different types of campus/community events. For example, you could write short reports summarizing each of the events with ticket stubs enclosed, or you could write one longer report on all events. In other words, you need to be able to document that you attended and participated in the events

Communication Confidence

You have to have confidence in your ability, and then be tough enough to follow through.
                                              —Rosalynn Carter

CHAPTER OBJECTIVES

After reading this chapter, you should be able to:

- Distinguish between natural nervousness and communication apprehension.

- Understand the causes of communication apprehension.

- Describe the effects of communication apprehension.

- Explain and implement four ways to manage communication apprehension.

Halle Berry

Chances are, you are taking this course in communication because you are required to do so. As authors and instructors of this course, we realize that students are not flocking to our classes for the mere opportunity to give that first speech. Rather, you, like many others before you, are dreading the thought of it. But did you ever stop to ask why? Why is it that so many people indicate they are more afraid of public speaking than anything else?[1] The first answer to this question is that nervousness is a natural feeling when thinking about a public speaking performance.

Source Citation:
[1] Wallechinsky, D., Wallace, I. & Wallace, A. (1977). *The People's almanac presents the book of lists.* New York: Morrow.

Natural Nervousness

It is important for you to know that being nervous while speaking in public is a very normal thing. Your body is responding to your anticipated performance by producing extra adrenaline, which causes you to feel jittery. Sometimes the extra adrenaline you feel because of your nervousness will make your senses more acute and aware. We believe that a little **natural nervousness** provides speakers with the necessary energy to give successful presentations. Even the most skilled public speakers will admit to a few butterflies every now and then. The difference is that they know how to use the nervousness to their advantage. That said, there is a difference between natural nervousness and intense anxiety toward public speaking. Anxiety is more closely associated with communication apprehension and an extreme uneasiness about the prospect of giving a speech.

What happens to people who are anxious? And, more importantly, what can be done about it? It is important to know that your anxiety can be managed. In this chapter, we begin by addressing one of the overall goals for this course, which is to gain communication confidence. But first, you need to understand what communication apprehension is as well as the causes, effects, and ways to manage this anxiety.

Communication Apprehension Defined

Communication apprehension is one of the most widely studied phenomena in our discipline. James McCroskey, a communication professor from West Virginia University, and his colleagues have been studying people's fear of communication for over 40 years. Their early research in this area explored communication apprehension and public speaking anxiety.

At first, these scholars studied public speaking or oral communication apprehension specifically, but they have since explored the more general concept of communication apprehension in multiple contexts such as interpersonal interactions, groups, and meetings, as well as public speaking. **Communication apprehension** is defined as "an individual's fear or anxiety associated with real or anticipated communication with others."[2] In public speaking situations, this anxiety is heightened by concern about the outcome of the performance (being evaluated or graded) and the uncertainty of the situation (not knowing how the audience will react).

For their studies, McCroskey and his associates created measurements for individuals to assess their level of fear in each of these areas. The personal

Source Citation:
[2] McCroskey, J. C. (1977). Oral communication apprehension: A review of recent theory and research. *Human Communication Research, 4,* 78–96. (p. 78)

report of communication apprehension (PRCA-24) can be found on McCroskey's website ⌷ and will allow you to respond to statements regarding your feelings about communicating in small groups, large groups, pairs, and public settings. If, however, you are more concerned with your public speaking anxiety, you can access the personal report of **public speaking anxiety** (PRPSA) located on the same website. This report will measure your level of anxiety specifically associated with giving presentations. For example, you will be asked to respond (strongly agree to strongly disagree) to statements like "I feel relaxed while giving a speech," or "I feel anxious when the teacher announces the date of a speaking assignment." Thanks to the research of these scholars, communication apprehension can be understood and managed effectively.

The following sections summarize the research efforts of many scholars so that you may better be able to reduce your anxieties and increase your confidence in the tasks ahead of you in this class.[3]

Media
Interaction 2.1

Measuring Your Communication Apprehension

Complete one of the following measures found at http://www.jamescmccroskey.com/measures/ Personal Report of Communication Apprehension Measure (PRCA-24) or the Personal Report of Public Speaking Anxiety (PRPSA)

1. What was your score?
2. How did your score compare to those of other students?
3. Based on this information, what strategies, if any, will you use to improve your confidence level?

Source Citation:
[3] Daly, J. A., & McCroskey, J. C. (Eds.). (1984). *Avoiding communication: Shyness, reticence, and communication apprehension.* Thousand Oaks, CA: Sage.

See Also

McCroskey, J. C. (1982). Oral communication apprehension: A reconceptualization (pp. 505–527). In M. Burgoon (Ed.), *Communication Yearbook 6.* Beverly Hills, CA: Sage.

Richmond, V. P., & McCroskey, J. C. (1995). *Communication: Apprehension, avoidance, and effectiveness* (4th ed.). Scottsdale, AZ: Gorsuch Scarisbrick.

Behnke, R. R., & Sawyer, C. R. (1999). Milestones of anticipatory public speaking anxiety. *Communication Education, 48,* 165–172.

Preparing to Participate 2.1
Nervousness and Communication Apprehension

Knowledge
What is the difference between nervousness and communication apprehension?

Application
As you read in this chapter, public speaking is among people's top fears. Why are people afraid to speak in public?

Causes of Communication Apprehension

The real question is: are we born with communication apprehension or do we learn to become apprehensive? And if so, how?

Heredity

Some people experience anxiety because it is **hereditary**. They may be born with an enduring personality trait that causes them to be apprehensive. In other words, they may have a genetic predisposition for feeling anxious when communicating. Perhaps one of their parents or grandparents passed along this trait. This is known as **trait-like communication apprehension** and results in people feeling anxious in most situations. This form of apprehension can be very limiting in a person's relational and

Source Citation:
[4] Witt, P. L., & Behnke, R. R. (2006). Anticipatory speech anxiety as a function of public speaking assignment type. *Communication Education, 55*(2), 167–177.

professional success, but can be managed with proper training. The good news is that most people are not born with public speaking apprehension, but rather learn to become anxious.[4]

Learned Apprehension

Most forms of communication apprehension are related to the particular situation, audience, or context in which the communication occurs. In these cases, we are not born with the apprehension; rather, we learn to become apprehensive.

Situation-based apprehension occurs when we are anxious temporarily because of a particular event at a particular time. For example, you may be called to deliver the eulogy at a funeral for a dear friend and your grief intensifies your apprehension. Or, you may be anxious during a job interview because you really want or need the job. In this class, you may be uneasy because you are being evaluated on your speeches.

Audience-based apprehension, on the other hand, occurs when we are anxious because of the individuals with whom we will be communicating. You may be more anxious talking to adults than to children. Or, you may be uneasy in front of people you don't know. You may be anxious about speaking in front of teachers because of their authoritative role, or you may have a tendency to be more anxious about speaking in front of your peers and classmates.

Finally, **context-based apprehension** causes us to be anxious in certain settings such as one-on-one, groups, meetings, or public speaking. In these cases, we are socialized into thinking we are supposed to be apprehensive. In other words, we are not born with communication anxieties; rather, we are taught to be apprehensive. Perhaps you have known and admired someone (a teacher or friend) who was apprehensive about public speaking and you have learned to model that apprehensive behavior. Another explanation could be **childhood reinforcement**. Perhaps something in your past (a "show and tell" that went awry or a negative response from a teacher) has caused you to become apprehensive about future communication encounters. Any negative past experience can cause uncertainty and fear about future encounters related to that experience. For example, if you fear giving speeches because of an embarrassing childhood experience, this past negative experience will likely cause you uncertainty about future public speaking experiences and this uncertainty leads to fear.

If your main concern is that your classmates might not be interested in your topic or might find you unintelligent, then your anxiety comes from the audience. If your main concern is that you get a good grade on your speech, then your nerves stem from the situation.

Skills Deficit

Perhaps the source of the communication apprehension is neither because you were born with it nor because you learned it. Maybe you are fearful of public speaking because you simply do not know how to do it effectively. That is, you lack the skills and therefore the confidence to be a good public speaker. This is known as **skills deficit**. The good news is that by taking this course, you can learn how to eliminate this form of apprehension. In the process you may also overcome the other sources of apprehension.

As you will see in the rest of this text and through your experience in your class, public speaking requires certain sets of skills that by themselves are not difficult. Once you learn each step in the process of public speaking, you should become more comfortable with the prospect of your first speech.

Now that you understand why communication apprehension occurs, it is important to discuss what happens to people when they are anxious. Although this discussion may at first cause you some anxiety, it is only when we identify the symptoms of apprehension that we can begin to talk about remedies.

Preparing to Participate 2.2
Causes of Communication Apprehension

Knowledge
What are the three causes of communication apprehension? Explain each.

Application
Would you say that you are naturally nervous or extremely anxious? If you are anxious, to which of the three causes would you attribute your anxieties?

Effects of Communication Apprehension

Communication apprehension can manifest itself in many ways. Think about what happens to you when you feel anxious. When we ask our students what happens to them, this is the list they usually generate:

- Shortness of breath
- Sweaty palms
- Butterflies in the stomach
- Shaky hands or legs
- Forgetting what to say
- Breaking out in a rash or blotches
- Using filler words (*like, um,* or *you know*)

Sometimes when we ask students to ponder these things, they actually begin to feel some of these symptoms. Ask yourself, what you are feeling now. Can you add something to the list? It is important for you to be able to identify what happens so you can begin to develop strategies for dealing with your symptoms. For example, are your ailments internal or external, psychological or physical?

Internal Effects

The **internal effects** of communication apprehension stem from psychological issues that may have physical effects. If you suffer psychological discomfort while you anticipate a speaking situation, this internal state may actually lead to physical symptoms such as sweaty palms, shaky hands, and butterflies. It's easy to identify these physical effects, but the psychological effects may cause more than just physical symptoms. You may completely forget your presentation or even convince yourself that you are physically ill and cannot possibly show up for your presentation. It happens!

We call these *internal effects* because most of the time, the audience is unaware of our anxieties. In our experience, there have been many times when a student has sat down after a presentation and said, "I was so nervous," only to find the audience surprised by the statement.

External Effects

External effects of communication apprehension stem from behavioral issues such as avoidance or disfluency. First, the speaker may avoid communication altogether. If you were not required to take this course, would you? How long would you put it off—until your senior year? Were you previously enrolled in a communication course and withdrew prior to your first presentation? Or, do you avoid social situations because you are uncomfortable communicating with people you don't know very well?

Another external effect may come in the form of vocal disfluencies such as the repetition of filler words. Do you tend to use any of these? You might ask your friends to tally the number of times you say "um," "you know," and "like." How many times would they catch you using these filler words? To what extent do you think these vocal fillers would detract from your message or your credibility as a speaker?

Speaking from experience as instructors of this course, we have seen both the internal and the external effects of public speaking apprehension and the limitations they place on a person's ability to communicate effectively. Now that we know and have talked about what happens to us when we are anxious, let's talk about what can be done about it.

Preparing to Participate 2.3
Effects of Communication Apprehension

Knowledge
Describe the difference between internal and external effects of communication apprehension.

Application
Think of a time when you were apprehensive about a communication encounter. What happened to you physically and mentally?

Managing Communication Apprehension

There are several techniques you can use to manage your communication apprehension: systematic desensitization, cognitive restructuring, visualization, and skills training. We'll address each of these in this section. Please keep in mind, however, that the goal is to manage your apprehension, not eliminate it. Recall from our earlier discussion that nervousness is quite normal, and if managed appropriately, beneficial to a successful speech.

Systematic Desensitization

One way to manage apprehension of any type is by using a technique known as **systematic desensitization**. This is a formal term for learning how to relax by using a number of strategies. This technique is most useful when the symptoms are physical. For example, you could listen to some calming music. You may prefer the sounds of the ocean or the chirping of birds in nature to calm you, whereas a classmate might prefer the rhythms of hip hop. Use any music that encourages you to relax.

Another desensitization technique is muscle relaxation. This is where the identification of your symptoms is important. If you tend to get shortness of breath, then try deep breathing exercises before your presentation. Take three deep breaths just before your presentation. This will calm your nerves and can be disguised easily from your classmates. If your hands or legs get shaky, then try tensing and releasing the muscles in your hands and legs for 10 seconds—repeating the exercise three times prior to your speech. These techniques allow you to release the extra adrenaline you have associated with your nerves. Try walking up or down a flight of stairs or drinking a glass of water—whatever works for you.

Another way to use systematic desensitization is to gradually introduce yourself to the source of your fear over time. You may have seen television shows where people are exposed to their worst fears in order to overcome them. A person who is afraid of flying could use an airplane simulator before taking a first, short distance flight. Gradually, this person would become more comfortable with flying and might even be able to make that long-awaited trip overseas. In the case of public speaking, it would mean giving your speech initially to just a few people and then repeating the speech several times, gradually adding more members to the audience. Another strategy might involve increasing your participation levels in class throughout the semester so that when it comes time to give your presentation, you will have already practiced speaking in front of your audience.

Cognitive Restructuring

Another strategy for dealing with apprehension is known as **cognitive restructuring**, which can be directly linked to the psychological effects of

---

Blondie   Comic 2.1

1. Of the various strategies discussed for dealing with public speaking anxiety, which one is Dagwood suggesting? Which strategy has Mr. Dithers decided to use?

Blondie ©King Features Syndicate

Critical Interaction 2.1
Worst Case Scenario

Match the irrational fear on the right with its logical replacement on the left.

RATIONAL THOUGHT	IRRATIONAL FEARS
I will practice my speech and prepare careful notes.	My speech will be boring.
My audience will support me because I will support them.	I could trip in front of everybody.
I will ask my audience in advance if they are interested in my speech.	I could forget my speech.
I will be sure to eat a healthy meal before my speech.	I will get a bad grade.
I will rest up before my presentation.	I could get sick.
I will stand right back up.	The audience will laugh at me.
I will do thorough research, write my speech carefully, and practice my delivery.	I could pass out.

apprehension. This strategy involves getting people to identify their worst fears (irrational thoughts) and to restructure, or think differently, about them. The strategy is to replace the irrational thoughts with rational ones.

This is how it works. Ask yourself what the worst thing is that can happen when you give a speech. Do you think you might forget your speech or that the audience will laugh at you? Perhaps you fear getting sick or passing out. The key to this strategy is to brainstorm as many worst case scenarios as you can and then think logically about why they might be unreasonable or how you can prevent these things from happening in the first place. A student of ours once responded that he thought he would spontaneously combust, but that would be very unlikely—right? This example is a perfect illustration of where cognitive restructuring could be helpful in dealing with an irrational thought. Once you identify your worst fears (irrational thoughts), you can begin to logically replace them with rational ones.

For example, if you think that the audience will laugh at you, then consider the fact that the audience members will be in your position as a speaker in another class period and will most likely sympathize with you rather than laugh at you. Another thing to remember about the audience is that they are not judging you as a person. They are evaluating the quality and presentation of your information. If you have carefully planned your speech, this evaluation will be positive.

Or, if you think you will pass out or get sick, then tell yourself that if you get a good night's rest and eat a healthy meal, this will make you feel better.

If you are afraid your speech will be boring, remind yourself that you conducted an audience analysis and already know that members of your class are curious about your topic. Of course, this only works if you actually do what you propose.

Finally, reframe your thinking about public speaking by focusing on how rewarding or how much fun it can be to inform, persuade, or entertain an audience. This class will likely be unique in your higher educational experience in that you will be given the opportunity to speak to your peers about topics that are very important to you. In what other classes will you have a block of time set aside just for you to communicate your thoughts? In terms of persuasive topics, it can be empowering to realize that your words may actually change the attitudes, values, beliefs, or behaviors of your classmates. Maintaining such a positive attitude will go a long way toward helping you manage the anxiety associated with public speaking.

Visualization

Another management technique that is used often by athletes is known as **visualization**. If you suffer from the psychological effects of communication apprehension, perhaps visualization would be an appropriate technique for you.

Visualization. Just as Deanna Nolan of the Detroit Shock visualizes making a free throw, you should visualize delivering a successful presentation.

For example, if you visualize yourself giving a successful presentation, then you might boost your confidence before your presentation. Most likely you have seen athletes before a competition go through this process. They visualize themselves performing well and winning the competition. Basketball players visualize themselves making that free throw. Figure skaters run through a successful routine in their head, making and landing every jump. You can do the same with public speaking. As you learn the steps to public speaking, try visualizing yourself giving a great presentation that is received well by the audience and the instructor. In fact, you get an "A." Good for you!

Skills Training

The final strategy is one we will deal with for the rest of this text and this course—skills training. **Skills training** involves learning about the steps necessary to plan and present a public speech as well as gaining practice in doing so. Once you learn one skill, you move on to the next. No individual skill is very difficult, and once you put them all together and practice, you may even reduce the internal and external effects of communication apprehension.

Be Confident. Because Bryan has practiced his presentation, he is able to deliver it confidently.

This class will provide you with the skills you need to become competent communicators in everyday life as well as good public speakers. You will be provided instruction on how to plan, prepare, and present confident speeches. It is important to know that the more you prepare and practice, the less anxious you will become. Think about it—waiting until the last minute to develop your speech does not allow you the time to become comfortable with it.

Through audience analysis (see Chapter 6), you will get to know your audience and become more comfortable with them. Through class discussions, in this class and others, you will have opportunities to articulate and defend your ideas regularly. Consequently, you will be provided opportunities to practice your new skills. In doing so, it is our hope that you become a more confident communicator.

Many of our students have shared with us their experiences about their anxiety over the years. In the beginning of the semester (usually the second day of class), our students prepare and present an introductory speech. They share information about themselves to begin the process of getting to know one another. They often comment on how this first speech was the most "nerve wracking" because they did not know the audience or how to give a speech. By the time they reach the first graded speech, they feel much better. Our hope is that this course will reduce your apprehension, too.

Symptom	Management Strategy
Physical	
Butterflies	Systematic Desensitization/
Sweaty Palms	Skills Training
Shortness of Breath	
Shaky hands or knees	
Psychological	
Fearing the Worst	Cognitive Restructuring/Visualization/
Feel lack of confidence	Skills Training

FIGURE 2.1

Symptoms of Communication Apprehension and Strategies to Manage Them

Preparing to Participate 2.4
Managing Communication Apprehension

Knowledge
Describe the four ways to manage communication apprehension.

Application
Have you used any of these techniques in the past? If so, which ones, and how did the strategies work for you?

SUMMARY

In this chapter, we have discussed the differences between natural nervousness and communication apprehension or public speaking anxiety. We have identified the causes and effects of communication apprehension as well as provided strategies for managing your apprehension (for a summary, see Figure 2.1). Although this chapter may bring about feelings of anxiety at the thought of giving that first presentation, it is important for you to be able to identify exactly what happens to you when you are anxious.

For example, if your hands shake or you get weak in the knees, perhaps you could try tension/release exercises in your hands and legs. If you tend to talk too fast or get breathless and lightheaded, then try taking a few deep breaths before you begin your presentation. Although there are several causes and effects of communication apprehension, there are also several strategies to help you work through your worries. Taking this course is the first step toward developing the skills necessary to make you a more *competent communicator.*

KEY TERMS

natural nervousness (22)

communication apprehension (22)

public speaking anxiety (23)

heredity (23)

trait-like apprehension (23)

situation-based apprehension (24)

audience-based apprehension (24)

context-based apprehension (24)

childhood reinforcement (24)

skills deficit (24)

internal effects (25)

external effects (26)

systematic desensitization (27)

cognitive restructuring (27)

visualization (29)

skills training (29)

ADDITIONAL ENGAGEMENT OPPORTUNITIES

Now that you have finished reading the chapter, it is important to make connections between the course content and your own experiences. These activities will help you understand, apply, analyze, evaluate, or synthesize course concepts. You can use these activities to provide evidence of your preparation for participation in class as well as to plan additional contributions to class discussion. The Civic Engagement Opportunities (CEOs) are designed to help you become more engaged in campus and community life and apply course concepts to important social issues.

1. Take note of how many times you find yourself having negative internal dialogue regarding your conversations/communication throughout the day. For example, you might think, "Oh, I was short in that e-mail to Bob. I bet he thinks that I am mad at him." Now, try using the cognitive restructuring technique. You might think, "People realize that e-mail conversations can be short and more direct. I will call Bob to clarify my e-mail." After you practice the skill with your daily conversations/communications, try it regarding your public speaking experiences. How did this influence your thinking? How did it influence your outlook? How did it influence your performance?

2. Do a quick Internet search to find celebrities who have stage fright. What reasons do they provide for being apprehensive? How do they overcome their anxieties? Would any of their strategies be helpful to you?

3. 🗨 Find a politician who suffered from communication apprehension and determine what he or she did to overcome the fear.

3

Ethical Communication

It is not enough to show people how to live better: There is a mandate for any group with enormous powers of communication to show people how to be better.

—Marya Mannes

CHAPTER OBJECTIVES

After reading this chapter, you should be able to:

- Distinguish between ethics and ethical communication.
- Identify and apply ethical standards to decision making.
- Understand the principles involved in becoming ethical producers and consumers of information.
- Listen to and evaluate speeches.
- Create a classroom code of conduct.

R ecall from the first chapter that one of our overarching goals for you in this course is that you become a more ethical communicator. But why would that be so important to us? Who are we to tell you what is ethical? Well, as a communicator, you make choices about what to say and how to respond to what others say. And with these choices comes responsibility. This is where ethics comes in.

In the United States, the First Amendment protects our right to free speech, but does that mean that we can say anything we want anywhere we want to say it? In other words, it may be legal for you to say something, but it may not be ethical. This chapter will discuss the distinction between ethics and ethical communication, highlight various ethical standards, and present information on becoming ethical producers and consumers of information.

Ethics and Ethical Communication

Ethics are a set of standards that offer guidance about the choices we make and explain why we behave as we do. We often make choices based on what "we ought to do" as opposed to what "we want to do" in certain situations. To understand why we make these choices, it is necessary for us to learn about ethics. Ethics tell us what is right or wrong and good or bad, and provide standards and rules to guide our behavior. **Ethical communication** results when we apply ethical standards to the messages we produce and consume. The question becomes: What standards do we use to make decisions about our messages? As you will read in the next paragraphs, there are different ways of approaching ethical decisions. Choosing one standard over another may result in a different conclusion. Often, there are no universal answers to an ethical dilemma.

Preparing to Participate 3.1
Defining Ethical Communication

Knowledge
Describe the difference between ethics and ethical communication.

Application
Think of an example of something that may be legal, but not ethical. Is it possible for something to be ethical, but not legal?

Ethical Standards

When considering ethical guidelines that help us make responsible decisions, we often think in terms of what is legal or moral. But there are many other **ethical standards** that can be applied to decision making. Richard Johannesen, a leading ethics scholar, discusses the ethical responsibilities of communicators in contemporary society. He argues that we should "formulate meaningful ethical guidelines, not inflexible rules, for our communication behavior and for evaluating the communication of others."[1] In other words, we should consider our ethical practices as we both produce and consume messages. He describes various standards or guidelines to use in making ethical communication decisions. These standards may vary both by culture and by individuals within a culture.

Source Citation:
[1] Johannesen, R. L. (2002). *Ethics in human communication* (5th ed.). Prospect Heights, IL: Waveland.

A Political Perspective

The first standard, a **political perspective**, helps us to understand ethical practices based on a value system. The first step in using a political system as a standard for making decisions is to understand the values of that political system.

For example, many democracies in the Western world put a premium on the values of freedom of speech, the press, and religion.[2] We will go to great lengths to defend our own freedom, but what happens when our values conflict with those promoted by other political systems?

Source Citation:
[2] First Amendment of the United States Constitution.

For example, in the fall of 2005, a Danish newspaper published a series of political cartoons that featured images of the prophet Muhammad. Some people in the Arab world reacted violently with protests and bombings. A number of Muslims were deeply offended by the cartoons because they felt their sacred beliefs were being mocked; in addition, their religion prohibits visual representation of Muhammad.

Even within one particular political system and culture, people do not always agree on which view should prevail when competing values come into conflict. For example, filmmakers in the United States have often provoked religious controversy by exercising their rights of free speech. Mel Gibson's 2004 film *The Passion of the Christ* offended many people in the Jewish community; Kevin Smith's 1999 comedy *Dogma* caused some Catholics to picket and protest; and Martin Scorsese's 1988 film *The Last Temptation of Christ* infuriated many Christians because of its depiction of the life of Jesus. Of course, if free speech is valued in a society, audiences have the right—and responsibility—to make their voices known, especially if they disagree with the filmmaker, author, journalist, politician, or public speaker.

A Dialogical Perspective

Johannesen also discusses the **dialogical perspective** first articulated by sociologist Martin Buber.[3] This perspective says that interactions between people should promote the development of self, personality, and knowledge. That is, each participant in a communication event should make decisions based on his or her ability to improve mutual understanding and dialog between participants. Participants should have sound motivations for communicating and should listen to all sides of an issue before making an ultimate decision.

Source Citation:
[3] Buber, M. (1970). *I and thou.* (W. Kaufmann, Trans.). New York: Appleton-Century-Crofts.

Under this perspective, instructors might engage students in lively discussions about controversial issues. For example, the popular movies we mentioned earlier about Christ and Christianity have provoked much discussion in the United States. Documentary films such as Michael Moore's

Dialogical Perspective in Film. Michael Moore's documentary film *Fahrenheit 9/11* set box office records, but provoked much controversy.

Fahrenheit 9/11 don't leave too many audiences without strong political opinions. Religion and politics often touch us very deeply because they go to the heart of what we believe about ourselves as a people and how we go about creating our culture. At first, these discussions might be uncomfortable because of the controversy and conflict that may arise, but the resulting understanding of the issues becomes the ultimate goal. As in the case of the Muhammad cartoon, the dialogical perspective would conclude that media outlets should print the cartoon in order to communicate a point of view. French playwright and philosopher Voltaire perhaps summed up the intellectual tolerance necessary for a dialogical perspective best when he said, "I do not agree with a word that you say, but I'll defend to the death your right to say it."

A Human Perspective

Another standard that might be used to guide our decisions is a **human perspective**. This perspective says that we have a responsibility both to ourselves and to others to be open, gentle, compassionate, and critically reflective in our choices. For example, according to the values of the dialogical perspective above, the Danish newspaper had every right to publish cartoons critical of Islam. However, as a result, Danish citizens and other Westerners were put in danger and even died in the ensuing protests. The human perspective, on the other hand, requires us to consider the implications of our message making and to weigh the costs and benefits of exercising our right to free speech, and thus would argue against publishing the cartoons. So we see that the competing values of the dialogical and humanistic perspectives bring about different conclusions in making an ethical decision.

A Situational Perspective

Finally, Johannesen discusses the **situational perspective**, which takes into account the context of the communication event. This is where audience analysis comes in. Some contextual factors that would guide communication decision making are:

- the role of the communicator for the audience
- what is reasonable or appropriate for the audience
- how aware the audience is of the communicator's techniques
- what the audience's goals and values are
- what the audience's standards are for ethical communication[4]

Source Citation:
[4] Johannesen, R. L. (2002). *Ethics in human communication* (5th ed.). Prospect Heights, IL: Waveland.

For example, not all speech topics may be appropriate for the classroom. Take into consideration the situation of speech giving in the classroom. In this case, you may have a *captive* audience because of the requirements of the course. Is it fair to use this opportunity to advance a personal or political agenda? You may be thinking this is a "freedom of speech" issue—that you should be able to talk about whatever you want. But, with freedom of speech comes *the option for people not to listen to your message.* Does your audience have that option in the classroom? So, although you may talk about whatever you want in a public forum, the classroom context presents a little different situation. These are the questions you might ask yourself under the situational perspective.

No matter what career you choose when you graduate from school, there is sure to be a professional organization that requires or at least suggests ethical behavior on the part of its practitioners. For example, profes-

Critical Interaction 3.1
Ethical Dilemmas

Analyze the following dilemmas using each of the standards mentioned in this section (political, dialogical, humanist, and situational). Did your decision change depending on which perspective you used?

1. Your classmate, Jackson, wants to do an informative speech on how to tell successful lies and asks you, as a member of his audience, what you think about his topic.

2. You decide that you want to do your persuasive speech on stricter laws against drunk drivers. You are aware that one of your classmates has a family member who is an alcoholic and who is serving time for drunk driving. This classmate has confided in you and has expressed that he would be uncomfortable with some of your arguments.

Media
Interaction 3.1
Ethical Codes in Journalism

Log onto the Internet and listen to the *NewsHour* stories found at this URL: http://www.pbs.org/newshour/bb/media/july-dec98/media_ethics_7-1a.html

1. What factors do you think played a role in the unethical behavior of these journalists?
2. Do you think these factors might affect you when you present your research for your speeches?

sionals in medicine, law, accounting, and business are expected to follow strict ethical codes for the good of society and the organizations they work for.

It should come as no surprise to you that some people do not always live up to the ideals of their professions, and ironically seem to get ahead by "taking shortcuts." In 2009, Wall Street financier, Bernard Madoff pled guilty to operating an illegal investment scheme by cheating his clients out of huge sums of money. Madoff may have benefited in the short term by his actions, but in the end was held accountable for his illegal and unethical behaviors. In another example, Governor Rod Blagojevich of Illinois was accused by federal agents of attempting to sell Barack Obama's former senate seat. He was subsequently removed from office by Illinois lawmakers.

The *Society of Professional Journalists* is a group that hopes to raise the stature and ethical practice of journalism in this country by encouraging its members to "seek truth and report it." However, there have been situations involving young journalists who fabricated stories, such as Stephen Glass at *The New Republic*. These situations seem to undermine the intentions of professional groups advancing a code of ethics. This story was re-enacted in the 2003 film, *Shattered Glass*. 🖳 But that is exactly the point. Without an ideal toward which to aim or a standard to which you can compare your own behavior, it would be difficult to know how to act.

Professional Ethics. The film, *Shattered Glass*, recounts the true story of a young journalist who fabricated his stories.

Preparing to Participate 3.2
Four Ethical Standards

Knowledge
List and explain four standards that can be used to make ethical communication decisions.

Application
Think back to an ethical communication dilemma you have faced. How did you decide what was right or wrong in your situation? Did you consider any of the standards or perspectives discussed in the chapter? Did any of these standards help you make your decision? Would another standard or perspective have resulted in a different decision?

Ethical Credo

Because of the various perspectives that may be used in decision making, scholars from the National Communication Association (NCA) decided to create and adopt a **credo** or code of ethics to guide our communication behaviors (see Figure 3.1). Because you will be asked to produce messages and evaluate the messages of others in this class, it is important for you to

Calvin and Hobbes

1. What decision is Calvin trying to make in this situation?

2. What would be the consequences for the various decisions he is considering?

understand the ethical principles that communication scholars use to guide their behaviors. These guidelines should help you to understand further the relationship between ethics and ethical communication. This credo is based on the First Amendment, respect for others, access to information, democratic decision making, and responsibility for our behavior.

In the remaining sections of this chapter, we will talk about how you might use the previous ethical perspectives or the NCA credo as you engage in critical decision making when both producing and consuming messages.

Preparing to Participate 3.3
Understanding Ethical Credos

Knowledge
Describe the premise of the National Communication Association Credo for Ethical Communication.

Application
Which of the ethical standards mentioned earlier do these premises relate to?
Can you think of a speech topic that might violate the NCA credo?
Do you think that some speech topics should be banned from being presented in the classroom?

Source Citation:
[5] Morreale, S., & Andersen, K. (1999). Intense discussion at summer conference yields draft of NCA credo for communication ethics. *Spectra*. National Communication Association.

FIGURE 3.1

National Communication Association Credo For Ethical Communication

Source: Reprinted by permission of National Communication Association, www.natcom.org.

Questions of right and wrong arise whenever people communicate. Ethical communication is fundamental to responsible thinking, decision making, and the development of relationships and communities within and across contexts, cultures, channels, and media. Moreover, ethical communication enhances human worth and dignity by fostering truthfulness, fairness, responsibility, personal integrity, and respect for self and others. We believe that unethical communication threatens the quality of all communication and consequently the well-being of individuals and the society in which we live. Therefore we, the members of the National Communication Association, endorse and are committed to practicing the following principles of ethical communication:

- We advocate truthfulness, accuracy, honesty, and reason as essential to the integrity of communication.
- We endorse freedom of expression, diversity of perspective, and tolerance of dissent to achieve the informed and responsible decision making fundamental to a civil society.
- We strive to understand and respect other communicators before evaluating and responding to their messages.
- We promote access to communication resources and opportunities as necessary to fulfill human potential and contribute to the well-being of families, communities, and society.
- We promote communication climates of caring and mutual understanding that respect the unique needs and characteristics of individual communicators.
- We condemn communication that degrades individuals and humanity through distortion, intimidation, coercion, and violence, and through the expression of intolerance and hatred.
- We are committed to the courageous expression of personal convictions in pursuit of fairness and justice.
- We advocate sharing information, opinions, and feelings when facing significant choices while also respecting privacy and confidentiality.
- We accept responsibility for the short- and long-term consequences for our own communication and expect the same of others.[5]

Becoming Ethical Producers of Information

In this class, you will be expected to create and develop speeches either to inform or to persuade. With each step of the speech-making process, you will be making ethical decisions, starting with your selection of a topic.

Add to the Body of Knowledge

According to the dialogical or situational perspectives of ethical standards, you will want to choose a topic that you think will benefit your audience or add to the general body of knowledge.

According to the NCA credo and the human perspective, you want to choose a topic that advocates truthfulness, accuracy, and honesty. So, would a topic on how to get away with lying be an ethical one?

Be Credible and Reliable

As you research your topic, you will want to use information that is credible and reliable. You will want to use sound evidence and reasoning so you do not pass off information that could be misleading to your audience. As you develop your speech, you will want to be sensitive to the differences within your audience. In doing so, be sure to use language that is not abusive or offensive. As a speaker, it is your responsibility to be fully prepared for your presentation.

Avoid Plagiarism

Finally, you will want your presentation to be honest. That is, you will want to avoid plagiarism. ⬜ **Plagiarism** occurs when you present someone else's words or ideas as if they were your own. Plagiarism can be intentional or unintentional. If you intentionally plagiarize, you knowingly steal someone else's ideas or words and pass them off as your own. **Intentional plagiarism** can occur on a **global level** (taking entire passages or speeches) or on a **partial level** (using key words and phrases within your own speech). If you knowingly piece together several excerpts from various sources and pass them off as your own, this is still considered intentional plagiarism. The key to avoiding partial plagiarism is to attribute the information to each source. Intentional plagiarism is an offense that comes with serious consequences. At most institutions, you would probably fail the course, and could even be expelled from the college or university.

  Unintentional plagiarism occurs because of carelessness. Perhaps you neglected to take careful notes while researching or failed to cite your source

Media
Interaction 3.2

Avoiding Plagiarism

Log onto the Internet and read the information about plagiarism found at this URL: http://www.plagiarism.org/index.html

1. What tips does this site offer to help you avoid plagiarism?
2. How is plagiarism detected?
3. What information did you find about citing sources?

Critical Interaction 3.2
Plagiarism Check

1. Your roommate has waited until the last minute to prepare his speech on Greek architecture. You are both architecture majors and your speech is on Frank Lloyd Wright. Your roommate, who is also your friend, asks to see your research because he wants to change his topic. He then asks to see your completed outline. You agree to let him see the outline, but find out later that he used the entire outline for his own speech. What will you do?

2. You are a music major and you want to do an informative speech on Miles Davis, your favorite jazz musician. You have read many articles and books about him and have listened to all of his recordings. Because you are well informed about the topic, you don't see the need to conduct any further research. You use many facts about his life without attributing this information to a particular source. Have you committed plagiarism? If so, what kind?

appropriately. Perhaps you think that if you paraphrase someone's ideas, you do not have to give them credit. Or, you think that if you provide a reference page, you do not need to also provide an oral citation during your speech. In Chapter 7, we will address how to take careful notes and provide oral citations so that you do not unintentionally plagiarize.

Another, more subtle, form of plagiarism can occur when you and a friend decide to collaborate on a speech topic. Collaboration is good, right? We should all learn how to work together and get along. But if you work on a speech together, whose ideas belong to whom? Let's say that you and your roommate are both members of the gymnastics team and you want to use your experiences to write an informative speech, so you choose the same topic. At what point does the collaboration of your work become plagiarism? You may want to discuss this with your individual instructors, but at our university, we use the authorization and acknowledgement criteria. If both instructors are not informed of the collaboration and both speech writers are not acknowledged in the process, the speeches are plagiarized. If the presentations use the same organization at any point, or identical wording or phrasing, the speeches are plagiarized.

You should become aware of your own college and instructor expectations regarding academic honesty. In addition, you might also need to be aware of specific course policies, particularly with regard to presenting your ideas in the form of a speech.

Preparing to Participate 3.4
Becoming an Ethical Producer of Information

Knowledge
Define plagiarism.
Explain the difference between intentional and unintentional plagiarism.

Application
Plagiarism is a problem on college campuses. Do you know of anyone who has plagiarized a paper or speech? Why, do you suppose, did they choose to plagiarize? What were the short-term consequences of their action? What could be long-term consequences of their action?

Document Your Resources

At this point it should be clear that you have an ethical responsibility to properly document the source(s) of the information you incorporate into your speech. This is especially important to public speakers given that the audience likely will not have a paper copy of the speech; they will depend on the speaker to attribute credit to those responsible for the ideas being communicated.

Another important reason for fully citing your sources orally is to establish the credibility and reliability of your supporting material. Of course, your audience will likely not find you to be a credible speaker unless they perceive your claims are based on reliable sources of information. The procedures for locating and citing information will be discussed in much greater detail in Chapter 7.

Foxtrot

1. What kind of plagiarism did Peter commit?

2. How could he avoid this in the future?

Persuade Ethically

There are some particular ethical issues to consider when preparing a persuasive speech. Because the goal of persuasive speaking is to influence others, you have to be particularly ethical in the strategies you use and the choices you make. Under the political perspective, Johannesen applies ground rules for public or political communication.[6] In doing so, he synthesizes from various sources the following ethical criteria for persuasion.

Source Citation:
[6] Reprinted by permission of Waveland Press, Inc. from Richard L. Johannesen, *Ethics in Human Communication, 5/e.* (Long Grove, IL: Waveland Press, Inc., 2002). All rights reserved.

1. Do not use false, fabricated, misrepresented, distorted, or irrelevant evidence to support arguments or claims.
2. Do not intentionally use unsupported, misleading, or illogical reasoning.
3. Do not represent yourself as informed or as an "expert" on a subject when you are not.
4. Do not use irrelevant appeals to divert attention or scrutiny from the issue at hand.
5. Do not ask your audience to link your idea or proposal to emotion-laden values, motives, or goals to which it actually is not related.
6. Do not deceive your audience by concealing your real purpose.
7. Do not distort, hide, or misrepresent the number, scope, intensity, or undesirable features of consequences or effects.
8. Do not use "emotional appeals" that lack a supporting basis of evidence or reasoning.
9. Do not oversimplify complex . . . situations into two-valued, either-or, polar views or choices.
10. Do not pretend certainty where tentativeness and degrees of probability would be more accurate.
11. Do not advocate something in which you do not believe yourself.

Can you imagine what our political campaigns would look like if candidates were to follow these rules?

Becoming Ethical Consumers of Information

Throughout this course, you will be asked to listen to your instructor and classmates discuss course content and present speeches. As you consume these messages, you are asked to do so ethically. Well, what does that mean? We've already discussed what that means on a day-to-day basis in class discussions, but how do we *listen ethically* to our classmates' presentations? You may want to think about this in terms of "the golden rule." Listen to others as you would have them listen to you. If everyone in your class follows this rule, each speaker will feel much more comfortable and confident with the speaking environment. So, by teaching ethical communication, we also improve communication confidence. You should be confident in the fact that your classmates know and understand what it takes to be an ethical listener. We will discuss listening in more detail in Chapter 4, but for now, let's describe what an ethical listener does.

- An ethical listener shows respect by paying attention to the speaker.
- An ethical listener is open to new ideas.
- An ethical listener avoids pre-judging the speaker.
- An ethical listener provides nonverbal feedback to the speaker.
- An ethical listener is aware of his or her own biases.

Ethical Norms

As you begin to understand the various ethical standards and to decide which of them you will employ to guide your own communication behavior, you are developing your own **ethical norms**, or rules of behavior. As the members of your class expand upon their own norms and develop a **classroom code of conduct**, you will begin to consider the ethical responsibilities that all students have for classroom participation as well as for listening to presentations. Here are a few examples you might consider:

- Speakers and listeners will be on time to class.
- Speakers will be fully prepared to present.
- Speakers will be truthful and use credible sources.
- Listeners will never enter or leave the room while someone is speaking.
- Listeners will fully pay attention to all speakers.
- Listeners will be open minded and free of bias.

You can probably imagine that if everyone in the class agrees to and follows these norms, the climate of the classroom (particularly on speaking days) will become more positive and less threatening. As such, these norms serve to promote not only better ethical communicators but also more confident communicators.

SUMMARY

Questions of right or wrong are inevitable as you produce and consume information. In this chapter, we have discussed four possible standards you can use to make *ethical* decisions as you communicate with your classmates and present your speeches. These considerations can also be used in your day-to-day communication with others.

We have discussed how you make ethical decisions during each step of the speech-making process as well as while consuming the messages of your peers. By considering a classroom code of conduct, you and your classmates may reduce speaking anxieties by realizing that everyone expects ethical communication in the classroom. This, in turn, will make all of you more comfortable with one another as you present your speeches. Trust in your classmates will breed *confidence* in your communication.

KEY TERMS

ethics (34)
ethical communication (34)
ethical standards (34)
political perspective (35)
dialogical perspective (35)
human perspective (36)
situational perspective (37)
credo (38)

plagiarism (41)
intentional or unintentional
  plagiarism (41)
global level or partial level
  plagiarism (41)
ethical norm (44)
classroom code of conduct (44)

ADDITIONAL ENGAGEMENT OPPORTUNITIES

Now that you have finished reading the chapter, it is also important to make connections between the course content and your own experiences. These activities will help you understand, apply, analyze, evaluate, or synthesize course concepts. You can use these activities to provide evidence of your preparation for participation in class as well as to plan additional contributions to class discussion. The Civic Engagement Opportunities (CEOs) are designed to help you become more engaged in campus and community life and apply course concepts to important social issues.

1. Brainstorm several ethical dilemmas that you face as a student, as a friend, and as a citizen. Be ready to discuss your dilemmas with your classmates, as well as what standards you can use to manage the dilemmas. What are the possible outcomes? What are the consequences of your decisions?

2. A classroom code of conduct is a list of rules that will govern speakers and listeners in your class during discussions and speech presentations. The chapter provides a list of suggested rules that you and your classmates may wish to follow in your classroom. What others can you offer?

   • Speakers and listeners will be on time to class.

   • Speakers will be fully prepared to present.

   • Speakers will be truthful and use credible sources.

   • Listeners will never enter or leave the room while someone is speaking.

   • Listeners will fully pay attention to all speakers.

   • Listeners will be open-minded and free of bias.

3. 🗨 As noted in this chapter, the political perspective is a useful way of approaching ethical issues from a values orientation. Assuming that you value freedom of speech, do you agree with the claim made in this chapter that members of this society have a responsibility to exercise their free speech rights and make their voices heard when they confront injustice? Why or why not?

4 Listening

It is the province of knowledge to speak and it is the privilege of wisdom to listen.

—Oliver Wendell Holmes

CHAPTER OBJECTIVES

After reading this chapter, you should be able to:

- Describe two reasons why effective listening is an important skill.
- List and explain the six interrelated activities associated with the process of listening.
- Avoid four common barriers to listening.
- List and explain five types of listening.
- Become a better critical listener and critical thinker.
- List several tips to improve your listening skills.

Take a moment, close your eyes, and attend to the sounds around you. What did you hear . . . the wind rustling leaves, birds chirping, the whirring of a computer? These sounds are around us all the time, but because we are not listening, we typically are not aware of their presence. It is one thing to hear a sound, but quite another to listen to it. Although hearing is the first step in the listening process, it is a necessary, but not sufficient condition for listening to occur. To become more motivated to listen, it is necessary to establish why it is important to listen.

Importance of Listening

Source Citations:
[1] Bohlken, B. (1999). Substantiating the fact that listening is proportionately most used language skill. *The Listening Post, 70,* 5.

See Also

Janusik, L. A. & Wolvin, A. D. (2006). *24 hours in a day. A listening update to the time studies.* Paper presented at the meeting of the International Listening Association, Salem, OR.

[2] Conaway, M. S. (1982). Listening: Learning tool and retention agent. In A. S. Algier & K. W. Algier (Eds.), *Improving reading and study skills* (pp. 51–63). San Francisco: Jossey-Bass.

We spend most of our waking time communicating in some way—writing, reading, talking, or listening. Of that time, we spend more time listening than all the other forms of communication combined.[1] Interestingly, although listening is the communication activity we engage in the most, it is the skill we are taught the least. Many communication textbooks offer just one chapter on listening, and few departments offer listening courses, even though listening is the skill with which we are expected to perform at very competent levels. For example, as students, how much class time do you spend listening as opposed to talking? For purposes of this class, you'll spend time listening not only to your instructor but also to many of your classmates as they present their speeches.

Listening is also an important survival skill. Research indicates that effective listening skills are essential to academic success.[2] Because listening allows us to make decisions as to what is important, it is necessary for effective note taking. This, in turn, can improve study habits and increase retention of material. In addition, communication scholars and employers cite listening as

Making Connections.
Television interviewers such as Oprah Winfrey demonstrate effective listening skills in order to be successful.

the top skill necessary for success in the business community.[3] We acquire knowledge, develop language, learn professions, enhance relationships, and communicate respect through listening. Judi Brownell, a professor at Cornell University, describes two very important functions of listening. First, listening helps you to accomplish tasks through understanding, recall, feedback, decision making, and problem solving. All of these skills are required for effective speech making. Additionally, listening promotes relationships by attending to emotions, understanding needs, improving self-disclosure, enhancing authentic trust, and valuing diversity and respect for others.[4] For example, Oprah Winfrey makes personal connections with her guests through her attentive listening behaviors. In return, they trust her and feel comfortable disclosing information about their personal lives. Have you ever had a conversation with someone who really listened to you? Someone who asked questions about *you* rather than always talking about herself or himself? How did this make you feel about that person? By nature, we are attracted to people who listen to us and we avoid people who don't.

Source Citations:
[3] AICPA. (2005). *Highlighted responses from the Association for Accounting marketing survey. Creating the future agenda for the profession–managing partner perspective.* Retrieved July 28, 2006, from http://www.aicpa.org/pubs/tpcpa/feb2001/hilight.htm

[4] Brownell, J. (2006). *Listening: Attitudes, principles, and skills.* Boston, MA: Allyn & Bacon.

Preparing to Participate 4.1
The Importance of Listening

Knowledge
Discuss two reasons why listening is important.

Application
What are the consequences for not listening?

- To a family member or friend
- To an instructor
- To a classmate giving a speech

Process of Listening

Listening is a much more complicated process than simply hearing. Brownell describes listening according to what she calls the **HURIER model,** which represents six interrelated activities associated with listening: hearing, understanding, remembering, interpreting, evaluating, and responding.[5]

Source Citation:
[5] Brownell, J. (2006). *Listening: Attitudes, principles, and skills.* Boston, MA: Allyn & Bacon.

Zits

Zits ©Zits Partnership, King Features Syndicate

Comic 4.1

1. How often have you heard someone but not listened?

2. What were the consequences?

Hearing

Since *hearing* involves the physiological process of accurately receiving sounds, we must focus our attention and concentrate to begin the process of listening. For example, earlier, when we asked you to close your eyes and attend to the sounds around you, you were able to hear things you might not have otherwise noticed because you stopped to call attention to the sounds you were hearing.

Understanding

We may hear sounds, but we may not always comprehend them. Listening for *understanding* improves with practice. It involves a thought process within us and requires reflection. We begin to think of the sounds around us and what they mean. For example, suppose you are driving and you hear a siren. You immediately check your speedometer and see that you were not speeding. Then you realize it is a fire engine in an emergency situation and you think to pull over.

Remembering

Source Citation:
6 Brownell, J. (2006). *Listening: Attitudes, principles, and skills.* Boston, MA: Allyn & Bacon.

According to Brownell, "remembering is essential if you intend to apply what you have heard in future situations."[6] How often have you been introduced to someone and forgotten his or her name only moments later? Perhaps this is because you are not attending to the name, but rather forming in your mind first impressions of the person. *Remembering* requires a conscious effort on the part of the listener. For example, if you repeat someone's name just after being introduced, you are more likely to remember it.

Interpreting

Media
Interaction 4.1

Interpreting a Message

Access the following songs on the Internet.

1. Access Nine Inch Nails versions of "Hurt" at http://www.youtube.com/watch?v=iFx2Tm QfM-o
2. What are your first impressions of this song? What feelings does it evoke?
3. Now, access Johnny Cash's version of "Hurt" at http://www.youtube.com/watch?v=Sm VAWKfJ4Go
4. How is this interpretation of the song different from the first? What feelings are evoked in this version?
5. How do the videos create a context to the story?

Interpreting messages involves the ability to see a situation from another person's perspective. Would someone else (perhaps someone from another culture) interpret the message differently than you? For example, when a Native American child hears in her history classes that *"In 1492, Columbus sailed the ocean blue,"* thus discovering the new world, she might be a little confused and think, *"Wait a minute . . . our ancestors were here before Columbus and didn't need to be discovered!"* In addition, interpreting requires that you pay attention to the meaning and the context of the message. For example, would a speaker's message change if the situation were different (recall the pre and post 9/11 example of air travel in Chapter 1)? Or, perhaps the message remains the same, but the context causes you to interpret the meaning of the message differently. For example, near the end of his life, Johnny Cash recorded and made a video of the song "Hurt" by Trent Reznor of *Nine Inch Nails*. Reznor's original version is interpreted as a young man's struggle with drug addiction. Cash's version, however, becomes a much broader, sweeping saga of the pain and regret of an elderly musical icon near death.

Evaluating

We *evaluate* messages through our past experiences, attitudes, and values. Based on these predispositions, we analyze the messages we receive. Are they consistent with your beliefs? If not, how are they different, and will you accept or reject the messages? In our example above, the Native American child is confused when the teacher talks about Columbus discovering America because it is not consistent with what she knows about her own heritage. Thus, whereas most European-American children may take this part of their history lesson for granted, it causes the Native American child to wonder. Consider another example. Suppose that you're sitting in a classroom listening to a speaker advocate against gun control legislation. The speaker argues that gun ownership is safe, deters crime, and is constitutionally protected. Further, imagine that your cousin was killed, accidentally, by a gun he was playing with just a few years ago. How might this experience affect your evaluation of the speaker's message?

Responding

Once we have listened to a message, we must decide how we will *respond*. What will we do with the information? Will we use it to construct new information? Or, will we reject it because it is not consistent with what we already know? Given our previous discussion, what do you think the Native American child will do with the notion of Columbus discovering America? Similarly, how might the audience member whose cousin was killed by a gun respond to the topic of gun control? Would that person react differently to the arguments about gun safety, deterrence, and constitutionality than someone who had not had that experience?

Preparing to Participate 4.2
The Listening Process

Knowledge
What activities are associated with the process of listening? *Hint:* HURIER

Application
How many times have you heard, "You are hearing, but you are not listening to me." What is the difference?

Barriers to Listening

Listening is a complex process, and there are many things that can get in the way of our ability to listen effectively. Recall that in the first chapter, we discussed communication interferences that can get in the way of shared meaning

Source Citation:
[7] Golen, S. (1990). A factor analysis of barriers to effective listening. *Journal of Business Communication, 27, 25–36.*

between a speaker and a listener. Below, we will elaborate on how and why this occurs. We'll look at four major categories of listening barriers, which include physical, mental, factual, and semantic distractions.[7]

Physical Distractions

Physical distractions are external sources of interference. These include any distractions from our environment that keep us from focusing on the speaker and the messages. Examples include time of day, temperature in the room, and noises both inside and outside of the room.

Mental Distractions

Mental distractions are the first of three internal sources of interference. Mental distractions occur when your mind wanders from the subject at hand. You are supposed to be listening to the teacher, but instead you are concerned about your exam in the next class. You are supposed to be listening to a friend, but instead you are wondering what on earth she was thinking when she got that haircut. Or, perhaps you are listening to a speaker and are prejudging him based on appearance or the fact that you don't like his topic. Mental distractions occur when our own mind gets in the way of our ability to concentrate and listen.

Factual Distractions

Factual distractions, another internal source of interference, occur when we concentrate so hard on a speaker's message that we miss the main point. This may not be entirely your fault. The speaker may be providing too many details so that you become overwhelmed and can't concentrate on the message. Let's say there is a speaker on your campus who is talking of the perils of war. The speech is full of statistical information, names of people you don't know, and specific dates and locations of various battles. You may become so overwhelmed with the details of his message that you overlook the underlying purpose and importance of it.

Semantic Distractions

Semantic distractions are also internal sources of interference and occur when we have an emotional response to particular words or concepts the speaker is presenting. It may be that the word is offensive to us or causes us to remember a traumatic event in our past. For example, as a child, suppose you were severely bitten by a dog. One of your classmates is doing a presentation on the need to prosecute people who participate in the underground activity of dog fighting. The speaker is vividly describing a scenario where dogs fight to the death. This use of imagery causes you to remember your own incident and you are unable to concentrate on the rest of the speech. The emotional reaction does not always have to be negative, however. The speaker could say something that causes us to recall positive experiences as well. In this way, the words a speaker uses can cause you to stop listening. You now have a mental distraction caused by words or phrases.

Preparing to Participate 4.3
Listening Barriers

Knowledge
Describe the four major barriers to listening.

Application
Name a situation or context in which you find it difficult to listen. Explain the situation, discuss barriers that impede your listening, and brainstorm strategies you can use in that situation or context that will help improve your communication.

Critical Interaction 4.1
Overcoming Listening Barriers

Consider the concrete steps you can take to overcome listening barriers:

Physical Distractions

Consider your listeners before you begin to speak. Survey the environment to see what changes you can make that will remedy any physical distractions. You might open a window, close the door, adjust the thermostat, or rearrange the furniture.

Sometimes you will have to adjust your behaviors to overcome a distraction you cannot remove. Consider whether you can move away from a lectern and closer to your audience, speak more loudly, or use an amplification system.

Mental Distractions

Whenever you take part in a listening activity, focus your concentration on the speaker. If you find your mind wandering away from the listening task, gently tell yourself to attend to the here and now. If your mental interruption is important, make a note to yourself to attend to it after your current listening task is finished.

Factual Distractions

Pay close attention to the speaker's introduction, where he or she previews the main themes. Look and listen for the speaker's gestures, transitions, and signposts throughout the speech that often signal important passages.

Semantic Distractions

Monitor your own reactions to the speaker. Just being aware can help you stay focused on the message instead of the emotions.

Types of Listening

We have established that listening is a complicated process and that many things can affect our ability to listen. It takes time and energy. But, why do we listen? There are many reasons or purposes for listening. Andrew Wolvin & Carolyn Coakley discuss these reasons in terms of various types of listening: discriminative, comprehensive, appreciative, empathic, and critical.[8]

Source Citation:
[8] Wolvin, A., & Coakley, C. (1996). *Listening* (5th ed.). Dubuque, IA: W. C. Brown.

Appreciative Listening. Johnny Cash and Trent Reznor deliver different interpretations of the song, "Hurt." Based on our own experiences and preferences, we as listeners may appreciate them differently.

Discriminative Listening

Discriminative listening is the most basic type of listening and occurs when we distinguish between verbal and nonverbal messages. You may hear a friend tell you he is fine, but his actions tell you otherwise. He seems troubled and distracted. Because you are able to discriminate between the nonverbal and the verbal messages, you inquire further to see how he really is.

Comprehensive Listening

Comprehensive listening occurs when we are attempting to understand a message for a particular reason—to gain knowledge or complete a task. We still must be able to discriminate between verbal and nonverbal messages, but with comprehension, you need to not only understand the message but also retain the information for future use. Examples include listening to directions or concentrating on a lecture to prepare for an exam.

Appreciative Listening

Appreciative listening is an individual process because it involves personal enjoyment. What some people enjoy, others may not. If you could just spend time listening to something for sheer enjoyment, what would it be? Listening to music is the perfect example of appreciative listening, but to whom would you listen? Would it be Johnny Cash or Trent Reznor? Are there some bands that give you more enjoyment than others? Sometimes you listen to music to understand a message, sometimes you listen to learn how to hit a note or play a key, sometimes you listen to decide if you will buy the CD, and sometimes you just listen. This last purpose is listening for appreciation, and even then your choices can change because of your mood. Sometimes you may want to dance, sometimes mosh, and sometimes just be quiet and reflective.

Empathetic Listening

Empathy is the ability to feel for the other person—to put ourselves in their shoes. Thus, **empathetic listening** occurs when we want to support or help another person—perhaps a friend or family member. Our sole purpose is to listen and not talk. Perhaps your friend needs to vent about a problem and all she wants from you is an empathetic ear. In this way, she is able to talk through her problem while you listen. It is important for you to signal nonverbally your listening and support. Have you ever tried to discuss a problem with someone who did not indicate that he was listening? Perhaps his eyes kept darting toward the television or a book he was reading. This can be very frustrating and lead to interpersonal conflict or withdrawal.

Critical Listening

The final and most complicated form of listening that we'll talk about is **critical listening**. Whereas the previous forms of listening ask you to take in some form of information, critical listening asks you to do something with it. Critical listening involves making judgments about the messages you receive. Is the information the speaker provides useful, meaningful, clear, valid, or reliable? Is it consistent with what you already know? If not, should you reevaluate your position? Is there a reason to doubt the information? Has the speaker considered all possible perspectives? In this way, you, the listener, evaluate and reflect on how you will use the information. You use critical listening as you consume messages from speakers. When you listen to your classmates present their speeches, you will engage in critical listening to evaluate the effectiveness and usefulness of their information. You also engage in critical listening as you are presented with messages in the media. Do you really need to buy that product? Will it do everything the advertisers claim? Which political candidate is most in line with your views? Whom should you vote for?

We will discuss strategies for listening critically and evaluating your classmates' speeches in more detail later in this chapter, but first it is important to distinguish between critical listening and critical thinking.

Preparing to Participate 4.4
Listening Types

Knowledge
Explain the five types of listening.

Application
When do you engage in each listening type? Do you participate in one type more than another? What strategies can you use to enhance your empathetic listening; your critical listening?

Critical Listening and Critical Thinking

Critical listening and critical thinking are integrally connected. We cannot listen critically without having the ability to think critically. However, we use critical thinking in contexts other than just listening. Whereas critical listening involves making judgments about messages we are being presented, critical thinking is much broader. In other words, we listen critically while consuming messages, and we think critically while both consuming and producing them.

When writing and researching your own speeches, you will engage in critical thinking as you evaluate evidence from your sources, decide how the information will be useful to your speech and your audience, organize your ideas, and develop your arguments. So, what is critical thinking? **Critical thinking** is the ability to make reasonable decisions about what to believe or do based on careful evaluation of available evidence and arguments.

1. What topic or question is being explored in this message/speech?
2. What is the author's/speaker's main point?
3. Does the author/speaker provide reasons to support the main point?
4. What evidence does the author/speaker provide in support of the main point?
5. Are the reasons and evidence given by the author/speaker believable, logical, or relevant?
6. If we were to accept the author's/speaker's reasons and evidence, would that be enough to warrant our acceptance of the author's main point?
7. What objections to the author's/speaker's position are likely to be made by someone who does not agree?
8. Would the author's/speaker's position be more reasonable if the main point were changed in some way? If so, how and why?

FIGURE 4.1

Questions for Critical Thinkers

At a very basic level, critical thinking is skeptical thinking. It occurs when you stop and say, "Hey, wait a minute, that doesn't make sense!" In other words, critical thinking happens when you don't *accept* or *reject* things automatically; rather, you question the information with an inquiring mind. In short, critical thinkers ask a lot of questions (see Figure 4.1). In doing so, critical thinkers have the ability to separate fact from fiction.

Critical thinkers are able to evaluate the quality of evidence and reasoning used to draw conclusions. Critical thinkers are able to identify relationships among ideas. All of these skills result in an outcome: the ability to make quality decisions or to produce quality messages. In other words, critical thinking is required to make a great public speech. Figure 4.2 provides an overview of the many ways in which critical thinking is required for effective public speaking. As we move through the levels of thought (from knowledge to evaluation) required to produce a speech, we advance our ability to think critically. This figure demonstrates how critical thinking is used in every phase of the speech preparation process. As we move through this text and this course, we will provide you with the tools you need to become an effective critical thinker and public speaker.

Preparing to Participate 4.5
Critical Listening and Critical Thinking

Knowledge
Explain the relationship between critical listening and critical thinking.

Application
Think of a situation where someone you know did not use critical thinking. What happened? What questions should he/she have considered before acting?
Can you identify an instance of when you use critical thinking without listening?

Knowledge Level Objectives

Effective public speakers are able to:

- distinguish among various types of speeches and their function.
- recall specific facts for use in speech development.
- identify the major criteria used by professionals in assessing a speech.
- identify criteria for testing the validity and reliability of evidence.
- identify methods for analyzing the audience.

Comprehension Level Objectives

Effective public speakers are able to:

- illustrate arguments using evidence in a manner the audience can easily understand.
- draw conclusions on the basis of evidence presented.

Application Level Objectives

Effective public speakers are able to:

- effectively organize and outline ideas in a speech.
- choose evidence appropriate for a given audience, topic, and situation.

Analysis Level Objectives

Effective public speakers are able to:

- recognize flawed assumptions in a speech.
- identify the main points of a speech.
- distinguish fallacies in arguments.
- compare the validity of opposing arguments.

Synthesis Level Objectives

Effective public speakers are able to:

- write a well organized speech.
- deliver a speech.
- plan and produce an outline of a speech.
- plan and execute a strategy for researching a topic.
- plan and execute a strategy for audience analysis.

Evaluation Level Objectives

Effective public speakers are able to:

- evaluate the effectiveness of a speech (using criteria for effective communication and argumentation).

FIGURE 4.2
Critical Thinking and Public Speaking

Critical Interaction 4.2 contains the Critical Thinking Self-Assessment (CTSA) instrument that can be used to help you become more aware of your critical thinking skills. This questionnaire is designed to help you examine your own skills by asking you to describe how you interact with things you read and hear. Doing this accurately can help you know what skills you need to work on and which ones you have already developed.

This instrument will also help you identify strengths and weaknesses in your own critical thinking. In addition, given the importance of critical thinking to communication, we will return to this topic throughout this course and this text. For now, let's revisit the process of listening and see how we can become better at it.

Critical Interaction 4.2
Critical Thinking Self-Assessment (CTSA)

Directions: Think about times when you have seen, read, or listened to professionally produced articles, stories, videos, books, speeches, or sermons that were designed to persuade you to believe something. Consider only those times when you paid attention. Please answer the following questions as honestly as you can. Please circle the appropriate response using the scale below (1 = never, 2 = rarely, 3 = sometimes, 4 = frequently, 5 = always).

	NEVER	RARELY	SOMETIMES	FREQUENTLY	ALWAYS
1. When I read or hear items like those described above, I am able to get the point.	1	2	3	4	5
2. I am able to follow a fairly complex line of argument, so that I can tell which things are offered in support of certain other things, and how it's all supposed to fit together.	1	2	3	4	5
3. After reading or hearing someone's line of argument on an issue, I can give an accurate, detailed summary of how the line of argument went.	1	2	3	4	5
4. I feel confident about deciding whether it is reasonable to believe a piece of evidence or a reason used in support of a conclusion.	1	2	3	4	5
5. I can tell when there are logical holes in the reasoning that is supposed to connect a conclusion and the reasons being used to support that conclusion.	1	2	3	4	5
6. I know how to tell the difference between a credible source and a garbage source of information or ideas.	1	2	3	4	5
7. I look for the hidden assumptions that are often present in an argument.	1	2	3	4	5
8. When I read reliable statistics that show two factors rise and fall together, I recognize that it doesn't necessarily mean one caused the other.	1	2	3	4	5
9. When I evaluate someone else's line of thinking, I consider the arguments rather than just deciding whether I agree with the conclusions.	1	2	3	4	5
10. I know how to go about deciding how strong an argument really is.	1	2	3	4	5

11. I am able to come up with acceptable reasons or evidence to support my conclusions when I write or give organized oral presentations.	1	2	3	4	5
12. When I write an essay or give a talk, I try to respond carefully to possible significant objections to my positions.	1	2	3	4	5
13. I am able to construct an organized, logical argument that stays on topic.	1	2	3	4	5
14. When I present an argument for a position, other people can follow what I'm saying.	1	2	3	4	5
15. When there are good arguments for contrary views on a subject, I know how to evaluate them and come up with the best conclusion.	1	2	3	4	5
16. I am willing to take the time and make the effort to think through an argument carefully before deciding what I think about it.	1	2	3	4	5
17. I enjoy thinking through an issue and coming up with strong arguments about it.	1	2	3	4	5

In order to obtain a score, simply sum all 17 items. Your CTSA score is _____. Look back over your answers. Do you see any patterns of weaknesses or strengths? You can compare your score on the CTSA to the scores of other students using the percentile chart below (the average beginning of semester CTSA score in a previous sample of students was 64.11).

Percentiles	Score
25	60.00
50	63.00
75	69.00

Source: From "Revising General Education," by Joseph P. Mazer, Stephen K. Hunt, and Jeffrey H. Kuznekoff, *The Journal of General Education*, Vol. 56, Nos. 3 & 4, 2007. Reprinted by permission of Penn State University Press.

Improving Your Listening

It is not until we understand the process of listening that we can become more effective listeners. It is important to note that improving listening skills will require time and effort as well as motivation. Here are several behaviors that can improve listening.[9]

1. **Remove, if possible, the physical barriers to listening.** You might simply relocate to another room or move the furniture in the room, turn the thermostat up or down, or close the door. Manipulate your environment to fit your needs. In the case of your classrooms, what can you do to remove any physical barriers to facilitate listening during speeches? Can you rearrange the desks or move a table at the front of the room to be closer to your audience?

Source Citation:
[9] Cooper, P. J., & Simonds, C. J. (2007). *Communication for the classroom teacher* (8th ed.). Boston, MA: Allyn & Bacon (pp. 70–71).

2. **Focus on the speaker's main idea.** You can always request specific facts and figures later. Your initial purpose as a listener should be to figure out the speaker's main idea. Again, you'll want to avoid prejudging the speaker or the topic so that you can listen for the main idea. In the next chapter, we'll discuss the thesis statement as the central idea of a speech. You can listen for the thesis statement to get the main idea for each speaker in your classroom.

3. **Listen for the intent, as well as the content, of the messages.** As you listen to speakers on campus or as your classmates present their speeches, ask yourself the following questions: Why is this person saying this? Does the speaker have anything to gain or lose in providing the message? Is this message an attempt to inform or persuade me? Does the intent of the message affect the content of the message?

4. **Give the other person a full hearing.** Too often, as listeners we spend our listening time creating our messages and responses rather than concentrating on the content and intent of the other's message. Recall from the last chapter that we talked about what ethical listeners do. They show respect, are tolerant of new ideas, avoid pre-judging, and are aware of their own biases. Here is the perfect opportunity to engage in these behaviors. As you listen to your classmates' speeches, do not begin your evaluation until you have listened to the entire message.

5. **Remember the saying that meanings are *in people*, not *in words*.** Try to overcome your emotional reactions to words. At this point, it might be crucial to consider that the speaker who is talking about dog fighting from our previous example is not aware of your past personal experiences. Focus on what you can agree with in the message and use this as common ground as you move into more controversial issues.

6. **Concentrate on the other person as a communicator and as a human being.** All of us have ideas, and we have feelings about those ideas. Listen with all your senses, not just with your ears. The well-known admonition to "stop, look, and listen" is an excellent one to follow. Focus on questions such as: What is her verbal meaning? Her nonverbal meaning? What's the feeling behind the message? Is this message consistent with those she has expressed in previous speeches?

The behaviors previously outlined should assist you in improving your listening skills by enabling you to become more actively involved in the process.

Preparing to Participate 4.6
Improving Listening

Knowledge
List the six behaviors that can improve listening.

Application
There are specific behaviors you can engage in to improve your listening. Try experimenting with these in one of your daily conversations. What happened? Did the person treat you differently?

Because this chapter is on listening, we will provide some suggestions on how to evaluate messages using critical listening here. This is an important life skill that will serve you well not only in this class as you listen to your peers' speeches but also in your future professional life as you offer feedback and advice to your colleagues. You may want to revisit this section after you learn more about producing speeches and as you begin consuming your classmates' presentations.

Evaluating Messages Using Critical Listening

One way to learn how to become a better speaker is to evaluate other speakers. As you learn the steps in the speech-making process, you will begin to identify effective and ineffective aspects of your own as well as your classmates' presentations. In this section, we will discuss some strategies for evaluating (not grading) the speeches of others. You will want to be sure that you ask questions about the content (what they say), the structure (how they organize it), and the delivery (how they say it). You will ask and answer these questions to arrive at some conclusion. Did the speaker accomplish his/her purpose? Was the message meaningful/useful to the audience? And, what can the speaker do next time to improve?

Once you answer these questions (by using your critical listening skills), you will need to provide feedback to the speaker. The purpose of feedback is for you to provide the speaker with a plan for improvement. The speaker will want to know what to repeat (things he/she did well) or change (things he/she could improve) next time.

So, what kinds of comments can you provide to help the speaker? In our research we have found that there is a relationship between the types of feedback provided and student improvement over time.[10] In our initial analysis of a large number of instructor evaluations, we found that generally instructors used four types of comments: positive nondescriptive, positive descriptive, negative, and constructive. Each of these is explained below.

Positive nondescriptive comments say that the speaker did a good job, but do not describe or detail how the task was accomplished. Examples:

Good eye contact

Nice references

Excellent visual aids

Plus marks (+)

Positive descriptive comments say that the speaker did a good job and specifically describe or detail what was liked about how the speaker accomplished his or her task. Examples:

Good job of engaging your audience through the use of facial expression and direct eye contact.

Nice job of incorporating full source citations into the flow of your presentation.

Your visual aids are very professionally produced and incorporated smoothly into the presentation.

Thus, positive descriptive comments provide a better plan for repeating successful behaviors than positive comments alone.

Source Citation:
[10] See Hunt, S. K., Simonds, C. J., & Hinchliffe, L. (2001). Using student portfolios as authentic assessment. *Journal of Excellence in College Teaching, 11*(1), 57–77

Reynolds, D., Hunt, S. K., Simonds, C. J., & Cutbirth, C. W. (2004). Written speech feedback in the basic communication course: Are instructors too polite to students? *Basic Communication Course Annual, 16,* 36–71

Stitt, J. K., Simonds, C. J., & Hunt, S. K. (2003). Evaluation fidelity: An examination of criterion-based assessment and rater training in the speech communication classroom. *Communication Studies, 54,* 341–353

Simonds, C. J., Meyer, K. R., Hunt, S. K., & Simonds, B. K. (2009). Speech evaluation assessment: An analysis of written speech feedback on instructor evaluation forms in the basic communication course. *Basic Communication Course Annual, 21,* 65–90.

Negative comments criticize the speech without providing suggestions for improvement. Examples:

Poor eye contact

Weak sources

Visual aids need work

Minus marks (-)

Constructive comments acknowledge the need for improvement in the speech and provide specific direction or detail on how to improve. Examples:

You need more direct eye contact. Try using fewer note cards and gaze more directly at more of your audience.

Try to provide more complete information for each source. I would suggest putting complete information on your note cards.

Your visual aids need to be larger and bolder. Practice incorporating them into the flow of your speech.

Thus, constructive comments should be used if the speaker is expected to improve next time. In short, if your feedback is to be effective (that is, help the speaker improve), you should concentrate your comments on the positive descriptive and constructive aspects of the speaker's content, structure, and delivery.

Preparing to Participate 4.7
Using Critical Listening to Evaluate Speeches

Knowledge
List and describe the four types of feedback for evaluating speeches.

Application
Which type is most likely to help them improve next time? Why?

SUMMARY

Listening is an important life skill that will help you in your daily tasks as well as in your relationships. Understanding the process of listening will enable you to become better listeners. In this chapter, we discussed why it is important to listen (motivation) and ways to improve listening as well as evaluating the messages of others (judgment). Because motivation and judgment are two skills involved in *communication competence,* becoming a better listener makes you a more competent communicator. Good listeners are also ethical listeners—they are open-minded and tolerant of new ideas. Giving a full hearing of someone's ideas is considered *ethical communication.* Listening is also related to *critical thinking* in that as you listen, you make judgments about what to do with the information you are being presented. As such, by improving your listening skills, you are also accomplishing many of the course goals we have for you. You are more competent, ethical, and critical when you practice good listening skills.

KEY TERMS

listening (49)

HURIER Model (49)

physical distraction (52)

mental distraction (52)

factual distraction (52)

semantic distraction (52)

discriminative listening (54)

comprehensive listening (54)

appreciative listening (54)

empathy (54)

empathetic listening (54)

critical listening (55)

critical thinking (55)

positive nondescriptive
   comment (61)

positive descriptive comment (61)

negative comment (62)

constructive comment (62)

ADDITIONAL ENGAGEMENT OPPORTUNITIES

Now that you have finished reading the chapter, it is also important to make connections between the course content and your own experiences. These activities will help you understand, apply, analyze, evaluate, or synthesize course concepts. You can use these activities to provide evidence of your preparation for participation in class as well as to plan additional contributions to class discussion. The Civic Engagement Opportunities (CEOs) are designed to help you become more engaged in campus and community life and apply course concepts to important social issues.

1. Keep a *listening* journal entry for one day. Take notice of your conversations with others, others' conversations that you observe, and students' behavior during class, interpersonal encounters, group encounters. Notice people's listening behaviors—verbally and nonverbally. At the end of the day, make a list of effective and ineffective listening behaviors. Declare a *listening winner*, the person you feel displayed the best listening behaviors overall! What made him/her the best listener?

2. Give an example of situation in which your emotions led you in the wrong direction. Then, give an example of how your emotions led you in the right direction. In terms of critical thinking, how do you explain the difference?

3. 🗨 For this CEO, first visit the International Listening Association's website at http://www.listen.org/. Do you agree with the ILA's contention that listening is the language of peace? Why or why not? What role does listening play in civic and political engagement? In what ways might ineffective listening preclude meaningful civic and political engagement?

5

Choosing Topics

*Develop an interest in life as you see it; the people,
things, literature, music—the world is so rich, simply
throbbing with rich treasures, beautiful souls and
interesting people. Forget yourself.*

—Henry Miller

CHAPTER OBJECTIVES

After reading this chapter, you should be able to:

- Select and narrow a topic.
- Identify a general and specific purpose.
- Write a clear and concise thesis statement.

Y ou would think that choosing a topic would be one of the most exciting moments in the speech-making process, but many students feel angst at the thought of it. In our experiences, students have difficulty choosing topics because they feel that so much of their success is riding on this choice. When we ask students what they hope to improve on most during the course of the semester, topic selection is at the top of many lists. So, how do you go about choosing a regret-free topic?

Selecting a Topic

When selecting a topic for any presentation, whether in this class or for future speaking opportunities, you need to consider three things: *yourself, your audience,* and *your occasion.* First, to maintain a level of excitement with your presentation, you need to choose something you feel passionate about. Perhaps you have some kind of personal connection to or interest in a topic because of your life experiences. To begin, consider your hobbies, job experiences, and talents. What is your major? What organizations do you belong to? You may want to choose a topic because a friend or family member has been affected by the issue in some way. This, in turn, gives you a personal connection to the topic. These connections help to establish your personal credibility on the topic, which will motivate the audience to listen.

You also need to consider your *audience* throughout the speech-making process, particularly when choosing a topic. Who are they? What are their interests and attitudes toward the topic? How might you relate the topic to their experiences? Most student insecurities about choosing a topic have to do with thinking the audience will not be interested in what they have to say. A few simple questions to indicate audience interests will go far in reducing these fears. Once you generate a list of possible ideas, ask members of your class what they know or think about your suggestions.

Finally, you need to consider your *purpose* and *occasion* for speaking. How much time do you have to research or present the information? For example, what can you accomplish with two weeks time to prepare? How much time will you have to present and what are the requirements of the assignment? What time of day will you be speaking? What is the social climate? Is there anything going on in the world or in your community at the time you present that will lend itself to one topic over another? For example, if you are assigned to present a speech some time in October, you might consider a topic on the history or significance of Halloween.

Generating Ideas

When generating ideas, you should consider topics that are of *significance* to you and your audience. **Significant topics** allow you to contribute information that your audience would not have known had you not given the presentation. You should try to think of a variety of topics that are worthy of your (and your audience's) time and energy.

For example, your audience may consist of students on a limited budget, but that doesn't mean they need to hear a speech on how to prepare Ramen Noodles. Chances are, they already know how. With that in mind, **brainstorming** is a good way to generate possible topic ideas.[1] Give yourself

Source Citation:
[1] Weiten, W. (1986). *Psychology applied to modern life* (2nd ed.). Belmont, CA: Wadsworth.

Potential Informative Topic Categories						
Places	Hobbies	Games	Natural Phenomena	Objects	Pets	Unusual (little known)
Australia	Pottery	Halo 3	Hurricanes	Guitar	Schnoodle	Noodling (hand fishing)
Iraq	Growing Herbs	Scene It	Volcanoes	Cello	Ferret	Doodle Breeding
Mt. Rushmore	Ultimate Frisbee	X-Games	Tornadoes	Clickers	Hermit Crab	Raising Emus

Potential Informative or Persuasive Topic Categories				
People	Organizations	TV Programs	Books	Events
Ghandi	N.O.W.	*The Amazing Race*	Harry Potter	Virginia Tech Massacre
MLK Jr.	Habitat for Humanity	*Lost*	*The Da Vinci Code*	Woodstock
Mother Theresa	Disney	*Survivor*	*The Kite Runner*	Presidential Election

Potential Persuasive Topic Categories			
Current Events	Social Issues	Local Issues	Beliefs
Election Reform	Homelessness	Parking	Liberalism
Terrorism	Same Sex Marriage	Smoking Ban	Conservatism
War in Iraq	Climate Change	Student Dress Code	Atheism
Wind Power	Affirmative Action	Free Speech Zones	Environmentalism

FIGURE 5.1

Personal Inventory with Brainstormed Topics

a reasonable time limit (5–15 minutes) to generate as many ideas as possible. You may want to organize your thoughts according to a **personal inventory** of things that interest you in some way. You can write categories across the top of a sheet of paper and fill in topics associated with each category. (See Figure 5.1 for an example of a personal inventory with brainstormed topics.) Because this is a brainstorming activity, some ideas that you generate may be more appropriate for speech topics than others. At this point, you can seek the advice of your classmates and your instructor to narrow the list of ideas.

For example, a personal inventory might be categorized according to people you know, places you've been, organizations you belong to, or hobbies you enjoy. The categories are endless and based on your interests. Other categories to consider for your personal inventory could include current events, social issues, local issues, beliefs, books, TV programs, games, natural phenomena, possessions, pets, little known or unusual information (our favorite), etc. These are just a few suggestions. Of course, the types of categories will be different based on your personal experiences and interests.

Timely Ideas. News web sites are a great place to find timely ideas for your speech topic.

The strategy is to try to come up with many ideas under multiple categories to create a variety of choices for speech topics. Once you generate as a wide range of ideas as possible, you may want to consult other members of your class to narrow the list until you have a topic that is of interest or importance to both you and your audience.

If you are having trouble coming up with some of your own ideas, try using the mass media to generate some ideas. Turn on the TV and watch a local or national news program. Pick up a magazine or newspaper. Log onto cnn.com or foxnews.com. Pay attention to the main stories or headlines. Generate a list of ideas from what is being talked about in the media.

One common practice of local media outlets is to take a story of national or international importance and find a local angle. Perhaps you could do the same. Choose a story in the media and find a fresh angle that affects your particular audience. For example, is there a national story about the state of the economy and job forecasts? What might that mean for people who are getting ready to choose a major or embark on a career?

You might also consider using a subject-based search engine to explore for topics. Some of the more popular Internet search engines include Google, Dogpile, and Yahoo! Many search engines, like About.com, provide a categorical breakdown of major topic areas. The deeper you go into the directory structure, the more detailed information you can retrieve about a topic.

Narrowing the Topic

Once you decide on a topic, you may need to narrow it according to your purpose and occasion. You will most likely have time limits placed on you that will require you to make specific choices about what information to include. Many topics can be divided into multiple subtopics.

You may want to start thinking about how to narrow your topic by conducting preliminary research on the more general topic. How many hits do you get when you type in the topic on a search engine? This will give you some clue as to how general your topic is. For example, a recent Google search for the term "blues music" yielded over 2.2 million hits. A search for "Delta blues music" yielded around 900 hits, whereas "pre-war Mississippi Delta blues" came up with a mere 14 hits.

The preliminary research you conduct will also give you some clues as to how the topic has been addressed by people who write and speak about it. Each topic can be divided differently based on the nature of the subject matter. Generally, any topic can be divided according to *time* (past, present, future), *place* (by space or location), or *subtopic* (of which there are many more ways to subdivide).

For example, a topic on the Pentagon can be discussed in terms of time (pre 9/11, post 9/11) or space (the five sides to the building), or subtopic (the divisions of the Pentagon). Let's brainstorm some additional ways that topics can be subdivided: categories, types, lists, steps, branches, functions, goals, dimensions, causes, effects, and so forth. Perhaps you can come up with some other ways to divide the topic you choose.

Remember, you can look at the research to see how other people have organized their thoughts with regard to your topic. Each time you think of a way to divide your topic to narrow it, you can take one of your divisions and narrow it even further until you come up with a focus to your topic that is manageable given your time limits. This is known as **concept mapping.** Figure 5.2 demonstrates this process by narrowing the topic of communication apprehension as it is discussed in Chapter 2 of this text. Let's say that you want to give a speech on communication apprehension, but cannot cover all of the information within the amount of time you have. How will you narrow the topic? You could discuss communication apprehension in terms of the people who research it (McCroskey and others), the causes (heredity, learned apprehension, skills deficit), the effects (internal, external), or the management strategies (systematic desensitization, cognitive restructuring, visualization, skills training). Each of the divisions noted in the parentheses are further ways of narrowing the topic of communication apprehension if needed.

Concept Maps

Choose one of the following links for developing concept maps:
http://telstar.ote.cmu.edu/environ/m2/s5/index.shtml
http://www.internet4classrooms.com/excel_concept_map.htm
http://www.udel.edu/chem/white/teaching/ConceptMap.html

1. Choose a topic based on your personal inventory.
2. Follow the directions in one of these links to create your own map.
3. Compare your map to those of other students who used a different link.
4. How are the maps alike? How are they different?

Subdividing Topics. If your speech was about the Pentagon, you would have several choices about how to divide the topic into smaller categories.

Preparing to Participate 5.1
Selecting a Topic

Knowledge
Name the three things to consider when selecting a topic for any presentation.
Describe two ways to generate ideas for a topic.

Application
Generate your own personal inventory.
Think about which topics would be interesting to your audience.
Which of these topics might be interesting to your instructor?
Be prepared to ask them in class.

General Purpose

General-purpose statements contain the overall intent of the message. Usually, most speeches fall under one of four categories: to inform, to persuade, to entertain, or to commemorate (to celebrate an event or person).

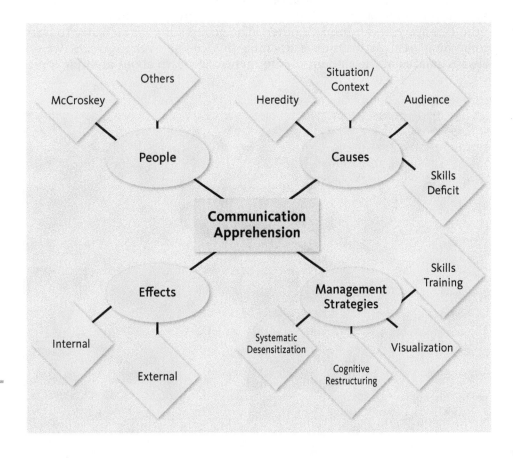

FIGURE 5.2
Concept Map of Communication Apprehension

For purposes of your first speech class, you will most likely be concentrating on speeches that inform or persuade. What you learn about giving these kinds of presentations will help you if you find yourself in the position to give presentations to entertain or commemorate in the future.

The communication you are learning about in this book is aimed at creating goal-directed messages, so understanding the relationships among general purposes, specific purposes, and thesis statements is imperative. Speakers hope that their audiences will change with regard to knowledge, behavior, or attitude. Thus, a presenter speaks with purpose and intent. For example, a presenter who tries to persuade listeners to change their eating habits based on the latest nutritional research hopes that the audience will indeed heed the message. Contrast that speaking situation with a ceremonial speech such as a wedding toast. In that situation, the presentation itself is the end—the audience should enjoy it on its own merits.

Speeches to Inform

When giving an **informative speech**, you, the speaker, serve in the role of *teacher*. It is your responsibility to present information that contributes something of significance to the body of knowledge of your audience. In other words, teach them about some *object, person, event, process,* or *concept* that they would not know otherwise.

Categories of topics that are especially well suited to informative speaking include people, places, organizations, hobbies, books, TV programs, games, natural phenomena, possessions, pets, or little known or unusual information. Perhaps you can think of others. The goal is for your audience to learn something new. As instructors teaching this course over the years, we are always amazed at the amount of information we learn about multiple topics

Ceremonial Speech. Wedding toasts are presentation opportunities that often rely on stories, jokes, and heartfelt sentiments that audiences enjoy.

Speech Topics. A speech about Lance Armstrong could either be informative or persuasive based on the direction you choose to take with the presentation.

in a given class. You should note that your instructor is also a member of your audience, and you should choose a topic you think he or she may not have heard before. This is why instructors particularly like novel and unusual topics.

Speeches to Persuade

When giving a **persuasive speech**, the speaker serves as an *advocate*. You choose a topic that is controversial in some way and attempt to influence your audience's attitudes, beliefs, or actions with regard to the issue. Some of the categories of topics we discussed earlier, such as current events, social issues, local issues, or beliefs, are particularly suited to persuasive speaking.

To come up with ideas for persuasive speech topics, it is a good idea to pay attention to what is happening around you. As suggested earlier, you can pick up a newspaper, watch a morning television program with news and feature stories, watch a nighttime news magazine program, or visit news websites (e.g., cnn.com or foxnews.com). What are the issues of the day? What is happening in the world today that would be worthy of taking a position on?

Some of the categories listed in your personal inventory may be suited to both informative and persuasive speaking, depending on the direction you take with the topic. Try choosing people, organizations, or TV programs that are controversial and attempt to influence the audience in some way about those topics. For example, suppose you are very interested in the career of Lance Armstrong. You know that you will be giving both an informative and a persuasive speech in your class. So, in which of these speeches will you choose to talk about Armstrong? You could inform an audience about Lance Armstrong, the seven-time Tour de France winner, or you could attempt to convince your audience that his wins are due to his hard work and determination as opposed to performance-enhancing drugs, which he has been accused of taking.

Preparing to Participate 5.2
General and Specific Purposes

Knowledge
What is the difference between an informative speech and a persuasive speech?

Application
What are the implications of making persuasive arguments in an informative speech?
Discuss the difference in the speaker's role when giving an informative speech versus a persuasive speech.

Speeches to Entertain

Entertainment speeches are designed to make an important point in a creative or humorous way. In general, it's a good idea to begin the process of creating a speech to entertain by thinking of the serious message you want to communicate and then finding ways to make your points in a humorous way. Keep in mind that your speech should have an identifiable thesis statement, main points, and supporting material. However, these elements will be presented in a much more subtle manner than in a formal informative or persuasive speech.

If you are thinking about ways to interject humor throughout your presentation, pay particular attention to the culture, values, attitudes, and beliefs of your audience. After all, these elements often determine whether your audience will deem your use of humor effective or offensive.

Speeches to Commemorate

Commemorative speeches are typically presented as part of celebrations of anniversaries, national holidays, or important dates and are accompanied by tributes to the person or persons involved. For example, a speech given to commemorate the anniversary of the massacre at Virginia Tech University might overview the events that happened on that day and pay tribute to those who lost their lives.

As with all other speeches, when planning a commemorative speech, it is imperative that you carefully analyze your audience as well as the situation in which the speech is to occur. Commemorative speeches are usually formal presentations, so your language use should be expressive, elegant, and eloquent.

When commemorating a person or event, you assume the role of an informative speaker by highlighting facts about the person or event being commemorated. In addition, you assume the role of an advocate by attempting to motivate and inspire the audience to build on the past to construct a better future.

As you develop your commemorative speech, work on isolating the particular actions and values of the person or event you are honoring and consider how those might be applied to your audience. Your speech is more likely to be effective if you can get your audience to vividly re-experience the emotions and feelings they have about the person or event you are discussing. Doing so should allow you to persuasively build a case for applying or transferring the values or actions to new contexts.

In summary, keep your general purpose in mind as you develop your topic. You should avoid messages that attempt to influence if your purpose is to inform. For example, you may give a presentation on a unique dog breed, but if you tell your audience they should adopt one of these pets, you have crossed the line of persuasion. Recall from Chapter 3 on ethical communication that you should remain true to your goals if you are to practice ethical speaking. The first way to do this is to keep your general purpose in mind.

Specific Purpose

Chances are, your general purpose in this course will be determined by the particular speech you are assigned. For example, everyone in your class will either be presenting an informative or a persuasive speech at the same time. Although your general purpose may be assigned by your instructor, your specific purpose is determined by the topic you choose.

Moving from the General to the Specific Purpose

The **specific-purpose statement** should focus on one aspect of the topic. Thus, once you know your general purpose and have chosen your topic, the specific purpose results from the process of narrowing your topic. What, specifically, will you be informing or persuading your audience about? The specific-purpose statement indicates the direction or focus you will take with your topic. In other words, it goes from general to specific. Choosing a specific purpose will allow you to make informed decisions about what to include, or not include, in planning your presentation within your given time frame. As you conduct research for your speech, you'll find some information that relates to your topic, but may not relate to your specific purpose. In other words, once you decide on a specific purpose, this decision will help you to focus your research and will serve as a guideline for all of your subsequent speech-making decisions. In our communication apprehension example, the specific purpose might be (for a 5–7 minute presentation):

> To inform the audience of the strategies for managing communication apprehension.

Notice how the specific purpose becomes a narrowed version (strategies for managing) of the more general topic (communication apprehension). In some instances, your general topic may become the specific purpose if your occasion allows you to discuss the topic in its entirety. For example, if your instructor had one hour to discuss communication apprehension, his or her specific purpose would be:

> To inform my students about communication apprehension.

Guidelines for the Specific-Purpose Statement

There are several items to consider when constructing your specific-purpose statement. Your statement should indicate (in as few words as possible) your general purpose, the focus of your topic, and your audience. Thus, the statement specifies not only what the speaker wants to talk about but also what the audience needs to know or think as a result of the speech. Because specific-purpose statements are written in terms of the audience, speakers are constantly reminded that the speech is intended with a particular goal and audience in mind. This becomes more important as we consider the process of audience analysis in the next chapter.

Because the specific-purpose statement should be written as clearly as possible, we offer the following suggestions and examples. Throughout the rest of this unit on constructing clear messages, we will use our current communication apprehension topic as well as three additional informative speech topics as running examples to clarify the process of public speaking. These three speeches will focus on tornadoes, the Roman Coliseum, and the Delta blues. (Complete outlines for each of these speeches are provided in the appendix.)

Write the specific-purpose statement to include the general purpose, the focus of topic, and the audience.

Ineffective:	Tornadoes.
More Effective:	To inform my audience about the phenomenon of tornadoes.

Avoid being too broad or general.

Ineffective:	To inform my audience about Rome.
More Effective:	To inform my audience about the Roman Coliseum.

Write the specific-purpose statement using as few words possible.

Ineffective:	To inform my audience that Blues Music is an amazing and soulful sound.
More Effective:	To inform my audience about the Delta Blues.

Write the specific purpose as a statement, not a question.

Ineffective:	What are tornadoes?
More Effective:	To inform my audience about tornadoes.

Write the specific-purpose statement as one distinct idea.

Ineffective:	To inform my audience about the historical significance of the Delta Blues and the musicians who epitomized the movement.
More Effective:	To inform my audience about the historical significance of the Delta Blues.
More Effective:	To inform my audience about the original musicians of the Delta Blues.

Be sure that your specific-purpose statement meets the requirements of your assignment and that the work can be accomplished in the time allotted. Finally, your specific purpose should be *relevant* (not too trivial) and *comprehensible* (not too technical) to your audience.

Critical Interaction 5.1
Specific Purpose—Effective or Ineffective?

For each of the following specific-purpose statements, decide whether it is effective or ineffective. If it is ineffective, be prepared to identify which guideline the statement violates.

	EFFECTIVE	INEFFECTIVE
1. *To inform my audience about war.*		
2. *To persuade my audience that homelessness is a significant issue that needs to be dealt with right here in our own community.*		
3. *What is Noodling?*		
4. *To persuade my audience that global warming is a threat to our future.*		

Thesis Statements

Your **thesis statement** is a clear and concise sentence that provides an overview of your entire presentation. Because it encapsulates your whole speech, it is the most important sentence of your presentation. Throughout your speech, you will reinforce the ideas presented in your thesis statement.

Moving from the Specific Purpose to the Thesis Statement

Once you decide on a focus for your speech, you can follow the narrowing process one step further to determine the main points of your presentation. These can be reflected in your thesis statement. Thus, the thesis statement provides even more information than the general and specific-purpose statements. Let's use our communication apprehension and Roman Coliseum speeches as examples to see the flow from a general-purpose to a specific-purpose statement and then to a thesis statement.

General Purpose:	To inform
Specific Purpose:	To inform my audience about strategies for managing communication apprehension.
Thesis Statement:	Communication apprehension can be managed using systematic desensitization, visualization, cognitive restructuring, and skills training.

Notice how the speaker streamlined the thesis statement by simply stating the main points of the speech without including the specific purpose (i.e., to inform, which is implied). In fact, the examples provided throughout the rest of the text will follow this pattern. As always, make sure to check with your instructor for her or his preferences for the wording of general-purpose, specific-purpose, and thesis statements.

General Purpose:	To inform.
Specific Purpose:	To inform my audience about the Roman Coliseum.

Thesis Statement:	To understand the historical impact the Roman Coliseum has had on civilization, it is important to learn of the architectural wonders of the Coliseum, the terror of the Roman Games, and the present plans for its restoration.

Notice how these thesis statements provide a great deal of information without using too many words. From these statements, we know several things:

1. the general purpose
2. the specific purpose
3. the topic and direction
4. the main points
5. the organizational pattern (which we'll discuss in more detail in a later chapter)

By listing the main points in the thesis statement, the speaker enables the audience to determine the organizational pattern of the presentation. For the purposes of this chapter, we'll preview organizational patterns by saying that in informative speaking, you will use one of three patterns: *time, space,* or *subtopic.* Recall that we used these categories earlier to talk about ways to divide a topic. Given this information, which organizational pattern does our Roman Coliseum thesis statement use?

One of the most difficult things about making a thesis statement clear and succinct is in how you label your main claims. Once you decide what two to five points you want to address with your topic (*in a 5–7 minute presentation, this is all you will have time for*), you need to use labels to identify them for your audience.

Generally, you will want to label each of your main points using one to three words. Why? Speeches rely on *oral style* to communicate ideas. Your audience only gets to hear your speech one time. Most likely, your audience will not have the benefit of reviewing a written copy of your presentation. Thus, the audience needs a clear and concise thesis statement that provides an overview of the presentation (labeling the claims) so they can follow along and listen attentively. If you label your claims clearly, chances are the audience will remember them. Here's an example using the tornado speech.

Ineffective:

1. What are the causes?
2. Types
3. Weird things that happen

Thesis using ineffective labels:

In discussing tornadoes, one should know what are the causes, types, and weird things that happen.

More Effective:

1. Causes
2. Classifications
3. Oddities

Thesis using effective labels:

There are several causes, classifications, and oddities associated with tornadoes.

Try to make your labels *parallel* in structure. That is, if one label is a two-word phrase, see if you can make all of them two-word phrases. If one label is a noun, then try to make all of them nouns. If one label has a one-word descriptor, then all of them should have one-word descriptors. The better your labels are and the more parallel the structure, the easier it will be for your audience to follow your presentation. Now, in the communication apprehension example, what could we do to make the labels of the main points more parallel?

1. systematic desensitization
2. cognitive restructuring
3. visualization
4. skills training

All but one of them are two-word descriptions. What if we took *visualization* and called it *positive visualization*? Now, all of our main points have two-word descriptions for labels.

1. systematic desensitization
2. cognitive restructuring
3. positive visualization
4. skills training

Guidelines for Writing a Thesis Statement

Remember our guidelines for writing the specific-purpose statement? These are the same suggestions we have for writing the thesis statement.

- Write the thesis statement to include general purpose, focus of topic, audience, and claims. Remember to clearly label your claims so the audience can follow your organization.
- Avoid being too broad or general. It is better to go in depth with a few claims than to not cover several of them sufficiently.
- Write the thesis statement with as few words possible. Remember, you have a lot of information to provide in this one statement. Avoid figurative language like metaphors and adjectives.
- Write the thesis statement as a complete statement, not a question. Remember your purpose is to provide the information, not ask for it.

One more note about thesis statements. This one statement should encapsulate your entire presentation. As instructors, we tell our students it is the backbone of your presentation. It is important to note that while we provide instructions for how to write a thesis statement in this chapter, you will need further information about constructing speeches before you are ready to complete this step. You cannot complete the thesis statement until you have analyzed your audience, located support, and organized your ideas. The next three chapters will provide more information about how to accomplish these steps. In the end, you cannot have a successful presentation without a strong thesis statement, so this will take time to develop. On the other hand, a good thesis statement is the beginning of a strong presentation. Take time with this statement. Make sure it provides the necessary information your audience is looking for in a thesis. The rest is just follow-through.

Critical Interaction 5.2
Thesis Statements—Effective or Ineffective?

For each of the following thesis statements, decide whether it is effective or ineffective. If it is ineffective, be prepared to identify which guideline the statement violates. How can the ineffective statements be improved?

	EFFECTIVE	INEFFECTIVE
1. Mount Rushmore is an amazing and historical landmark that includes the faces of four very important people.		
2. Cancun is a fun vacation spot.		
3. Autism is a developmental disorder that, if detected early, can be treated.		
4. Three conspiracy theories target Fidel Castro, the mob, and the CIA in the assassination of JFK.		

Preparing to Participate 5.4
Thesis Statements

Knowledge
Define what a thesis statement is and list the five components that should be included in a thesis statement.

Application
Why is it important to have a clear thesis statement? What are the implications to the audience of not providing a clear thesis statement?

SUMMARY

In this chapter, we have discussed several strategies for choosing and narrowing a topic. We have also talked about moving from general-purpose to specific-purpose statements, as well as creating thesis statements. These decisions are the first and perhaps the most important steps in the speech-making process. The guidelines provided in this chapter will help you make sound decisions in the early stages of your speech preparation. This will allow you to become *confident* in both your topic and your ability to present a successful speech. Becoming a better public speaker will help you become a more *competent communicator.*

KEY TERMS

significant topics (66)

brainstorming (66)

personal inventory (67)

concept mapping (69)

general-purpose
    statement (70)

informative speech (71)

persuasive speech (72)

entertainment speech (73)

commemorative
    speech (73)

specific-purpose
    statement (74)

thesis statement (76)

ADDITIONAL ENGAGEMENT OPPORTUNITIES

Now that you have finished reading the chapter, it is also important to make connections between the course content and your own experiences. These activities will help you understand, apply, analyze, evaluate, or synthesize course concepts. You can use these activities to provide evidence of your preparation for participation in class as well as to plan additional contributions to class discussion. The Civic Engagement Opportunities (CEOs) are designed to help you become more engaged in campus and community life and apply course concepts to important social issues.

1. Find a magazine, newspaper, or Internet article on a topic that interests you. After reading the article, determine if the speaker's goal was to inform or persuade you. If you were asked to write a specific-purpose and thesis statement for the article, what would it be?

2. If you were to sum up your life in a nutshell, what would you say? Create a concept map of your life. Write a thesis statement with yourself as the topic. Be sure to include your purpose and main points.

3. One relatively easy way to become more civically engaged in campus and community life is to research topics that are important in your area currently (such topics can also make for especially

relevant classroom speeches). For this CEO, conduct the necessary research to answer the following questions:

- What are the specific "hot" policy issues on your campus (e.g., tuition increases, parking regulations, free speech zones, etc.)?
- What are the key social issues facing members of your community (e.g., homelessness, discrimination, fair wages, relationships between community members and students at your institution, etc.)?

Analyzing Your Audience

*Make sure you have finished speaking before your
audience has finished listening.*

—Dorothy Sarnoff

CHAPTER OBJECTIVES

After reading this chapter, you should be able to:

- Understand the role of the audience in public speaking.

- Determine audience attitudes and beliefs.

- Gather information about an audience formally
  and informally.

- Adapt a message based on audience analysis.

Source Citation:
1 Behnke, R. R., O'Hair, D., & Hardman, A. (1990). Audience analysis systems in advertising and marketing. In D. O'Hair & G. L. Kreps (Eds.), *Applied communication theory and research* (pp. 203–221). Hillsdale, NJ: Lawrence Erlbaum Associates.

W hen you watch TV or pick up a magazine, you can be assured that the people who prepared those media messages took your interests, attitudes, and beliefs into consideration. Marketers spend an enormous amount of money trying to determine who their audience is for a given program or advertisement.[1] As you flip channels during commercials, you can tell something about who the audience is expected to be just by the products being advertised. Try it some time. If you are watching football, who are the commercials geared to? What about if you are watching cartoons or daytime programming? Answers can be found in the products being advertised.

Media
Interaction 6.1

Coding Commercials

Watch a 30-minute television program. Take note of the products being advertised and determine who is the target audience for each commercial. After coding the commercials, take a few minutes to analyze the target audience for the products and their relevant placement during the program.

1. Who is the target audience for the TV program? What types of products were advertised during this block? Is the audience consistent with the products that were pitched to them?
2. Do you think that the targeted audience would be persuaded to purchase any of these products?

Considering Your Audience

Why is it important to consider your audience as you develop or produce your message? If your goal is to inform or persuade, the audience is the target of your overall purpose and ultimately determines the success of your speech. If your goal is to inform, then your success is determined by the extent to which your audience clearly understands your message. If your goal is to persuade, then your success is determined by the extent to which your audience has been influenced by your message. This, in turn, determines whether you reach your goal. Consider what might happen if you were to give a speech to your classmates about the college application process. Although your topic may be perfectly suitable for a room full of high school seniors, the information may be too late for your current audience. Thus, how can you accomplish a goal that is not realistic or relevant for you audience?

In addition to accomplishing your goals, you will also want to be sure you are respectful of your audience. In Chapter 11, we will discuss using appropriate language to be inclusive of all members of your audience and to avoid offending anyone. For now, it is important to note that by conducting an audience analysis, you demonstrate respect for your audience. By considering their interests as you develop your speech, you will make appropriate choices that include your audience in your presentation.

Audience analysis is the process by which we gather and analyze information about our listeners and adapt our message to their knowledge, interests, attitudes, and beliefs. Audience analysis can be considered a crucial step toward accomplishing many of the course goals explained in the first chapter. First, by understanding and considering the characteristics of your audience as you produce your presentation, you are engaging in competent communication. Analyzing your audience allows you to predict their reactions to your message. Being able to adapt your message based on the information you gather will make you more credible to your audience.

Second, by taking your audience's interests and needs into account, you are engaging in ethical communication. Your analysis will enable you to maintain sound goals as you construct your message—to enrich their knowledge through an informative presentation or to get them to consider a controversial issue from various perspectives.

Third, in gathering information about your audience, you may become more comfortable and confident as you present your message. Specifically, the better you know your audience, the less anxiety you will experience when you actually give the speech.[2]

Recall from Chapter 5 how we talked about choosing topics that are worth your and your audience's time and energy to present and to listen to, respectively. Well, as you present, your audience will be asking themselves, *what's in it for me?* In short, audiences always put their needs ahead of yours.[3] Thus, speakers need to find ways to motivate the audience to listen. To do this, speakers have to conduct an analysis of who the audience members are.[4]

Source Citations:
[2] Richmond, V. P., & McCroskey, J. C. (1997). *Communication: Apprehension, avoidance, and effectiveness* (5th ed.). Boston, MA: Allyn & Bacon.

[3] Hoff, R. (1992). *I can see you naked*. Kansas City, MO: Andrews and McMeel.

[4] Backer, D., & Borkum-Backer, P. (1993). *Powerful presentation skills*. Chicago: Irwin.

Preparing to Participate 6.1
Considering Your Audience

Knowledge
Discuss why it is important to consider your audience while you are developing and producing your speech.

Application
What would be the consequences of not considering your audience? Can you think of an example of when someone said something without considering whom he or she said it to? What happened?

Identifying and Understanding Your Audience

So, if your success is determined by your audience's reaction to your message, then what do you need to know about them to achieve your goals? To identify and understand your audience, you will need to answer the following questions: Who are they? Why are they here? What do they know? What are their interests? What are their attitudes? In the following sections, we will discuss how you can obtain this information from your audience.

Analyzing Audience Characteristics

Recall from Chapter 1 that we discussed the elements of the communication process and how the people involved in interactions interpret events differently depending on their **frame of reference**. A person's frame of reference is composed of personal *experiences, goals, values, attitudes, knowledge, beliefs, age, gender, culture,* and so forth.

Some of these characteristics involve general information about your audience, whereas other characteristics are more specific to the speaking situation or topic. Gathering general information allows you to answer the question, "Who are they?" In other words, what is the general make-up of your audience? This is known as *audience demographics*.

Audience Diversity. Even though your classmates are probably near your age and may be from a similar geographic area, other factors should be considered when analyzing your audience.

Source Citation:
[5] Berko, R., Wolvin, A., & Ray, R. (1997). *Business communication in a changing world.* New York: St. Martin's Press.

Audience demographics include a number of general characteristics including:

- age
- sex
- gender
- sexual orientation
- cultural background
- income
- occupation
- education
- religion
- group membership
- political affiliation
- place of residence

Knowing this general information about your audience will help you choose and develop topics with your audience in mind.[5] For example, politicians rely heavily on certain demographics. Some of them court the younger vote; some of them court the female or minority vote. In the 2008 presidential election, Barack Obama was successful in engaging the youth population to vote for "change in Washington." He communicated his mes-

---

This is an anonymous demographic survey of your Public Speaking Classroom Audience. Please do not put your name on this survey.

What is your age?_____

Are you: Male   Female

Are you: Caucasian   Latino/Latina   African-American

                Asian/Pacific Islander   Native American

                Other: _____

What is your religious affiliation, if any (feel free to write "none" if you do not strongly identify with any religion)?

_____

What groups do you belong to? (Examples include Fraternity/Sorority, Band, Theatre, Clubs, etc.)

_____

_____

_____

Are you a: Democrat   Republican   Independent

                Not Politically Motivated   I Don't Know

Where are you from? _____

Are you from: Large metro area   Suburb   Rural Town

FIGURE 6.1

Sample Questions for Demographic Audience Analysis

sage to his target audience on social networks such as MySpace and Facebook. He even announced his running mate via text message. Some demographic information may be more or less relevant, given your topic. For example, if your purpose is to inform and your topic is on birth order, then you could ask the audience members to provide their ages relative to those of their siblings. You could then use this information to classify the members of your audience into first, middle, or last born and address them more specifically in the speech. On the other hand, you probably do not need to know their political affiliation.

Some information is particularly relevant when your purpose is to persuade. Let's say that you are attempting to persuade your audience that your state should legalize gay marriage. Knowing your audience members' cultural, religious, and political backgrounds will help you determine how to approach the topic. We have provided you a *demographic audience analysis survey* (Figure 6.1), which you can adapt based on your topic.

Because demographic information is general in nature, you should be careful not to make overgeneralizations (stereotypes) about your audience based on this information. For example, your classmates are all college students, but you cannot assume that all of your classmates enjoy partying. Likewise, you cannot assume that all males enjoy sports and all females enjoy shopping. To avoid making assumptions about your audience based on demographic information, you should gather specific information relevant to the speaking situation.

Preparing to Participate 6.2
Audience Demographics

Knowledge
Define *audience demographics*. Give examples of demographic traits.

Application
Consider your classroom audience. Which audience demographic traits will be important to consider with your topic?
Consider the various classes you are taking. How are the audiences in those classes different from this one?

Analyzing the Situation

Analyzing the **speaking situation** will provide you even more specific information about how to adapt your topic to your audience. This analysis will attempt to answer the questions: Why are they here? What do they know? What are their interests? What are their attitudes? The speaking situation is composed of the size and type of audience; the setting; and the audience's interests, knowledge, and attitudes toward the topic.

Size What is the *size* of the *audience* that you will be speaking to? Generally, the larger the audience, the more formal the presentation should be. For your purposes in the classroom, your audience will be medium size (20–30 students), which will enable you to connect with them on a more personal level than a large audience. As your confidence and competence increases, opportunities for addressing larger audiences are likely to arise. Think of the successful and influential people you know. Chances are, they often communicate with large audiences.

Setting   What is the *setting* of the *audience* for your speech? For the speeches you prepare for this course, you will be making your presentation in your classroom, but for speeches in other locations, it is important that you get a feel for your surroundings before you speak. Is the heating/air-conditioning going to be a factor? Are there external noises you may have to contend with? How large or small is the room? Will there be obstacles in your way (pillars, desks, electronic cords)?

The answers to these questions become even more important when the setting is unfamiliar. The setting may also affect the mood of the audience. Speaking in a church, mosque, or synagogue has a very different set of norms than giving a toast at a wedding or pitching an idea for a charity event during a fraternity or sorority meeting. The setting also gives you clues about audience type.

Type   A **captive audience** is required to attend a presentation and may not have an inherent reason for listening to a speech. A **voluntary audience**, on the other hand, attends a presentation with a particular interest in doing so. Why is your audience here? Are they *captive* or *voluntary*? Did they come to hear you speak because they were particularly interested in you or your topic? Or, are they required to be there to hear your speech because they are your classmates? Chances are, the latter is true.

What implications does a captive audience have for the way you approach your topic? Recall from Chapter 3 the ethical considerations for a captive audience. If your audience is required to attend your presentation, how does this affect what you will say (and not say)? In other words, will the audience accept what you say with joy and gladness in their hearts or will you need to pay special attention to winning them over? As you research and follow stories related to your topic, are there ways that you can make connections between the material you find and your audience's lived or future experiences? With a captive audience, you may have to generate interest in your topic to make these connections. With a voluntary audience, the interest may already be there.

Interests   What are your *audience's interests*? You might want to gather some information about your audience's hobbies, recreational activities, or job interests. What TV programs do they enjoy (or not), and what magazines do they subscribe to? This information can give you a sense of their interests. What subjects will they enjoy hearing about? You can use this information to relate your topic to your audience throughout your presentation.

If you know that many of your audience members enjoy watching crime shows on television, then they may be particularly interested in a speech on forensic science or crime investigations. What if spring break is around the corner? Should you describe the all-inclusive resorts they could visit in Mexico, or should you make them aware of an alternative spring break where they can provide a public service while still having fun?

Knowledge What is the level of *audience knowledge* about your topic? Knowing this information will help you determine how much and what kind of information to cover in your presentation. Remember, you are trying to enrich their knowledge and experience. You should avoid presenting information that is too general (audience already knows), too specific (audience doesn't need to know), or too complex (audience cannot understand).

Perhaps you are a music composition major and wish to inform the audience about the process of composing a symphony. Other music majors may appreciate and be able to understand a speech about scales, modes, harmony, and instrumentation, but a general audience may only be able to relate to music that has a good beat and is easy to dance to!

Attitudes **Attitudes** describe how your audience feels about your topic. Attitudes are rooted in value and belief systems. **Beliefs** are statements that your audience holds to be true, whereas **values** are the extent to which audience members attach importance or worth to those beliefs. Beliefs can change over time if new evidence is presented, whereas values are more enduring. Nonetheless, our values and beliefs are influenced by our families, our culture, our religion, our political affiliation, and our personal experiences.

Suppose you are planning to give a speech on legalizing gay marriage. From your audience analysis, you find that you have an audience member who has been taught that gay people choose their lifestyle and that their choice is wrong. Thus, your audience member has a negative value of what it means to be gay. Consequently, her attitude about a ban on gay marriage would probably be positive. Because you know this, you know that you need to find credible evidence that suggests that being gay is genetically determined rather than a lifestyle choice.

Understanding your audience's attitudes, beliefs, and values also helps you with topic selection. For example, you should avoid choosing a persuasive speech topic if everyone already agrees with you. Likewise, your chances of persuasion are slim if most of the audience is diametrically opposed to your position.

Thus far, we have talked about the kinds of information you need to know about your audience so that you can connect your speech to their experiences. In the next section, we will elaborate on how to collect that information.

Preparing to Participate 6.3
The Speaking Situation

Knowledge
List six factors to consider when analyzing the speaking situation. Then, note information to consider for each factor.

Application
Consider your classroom audience. Assess your speaking situation using the six factors to consider when analyzing your audience. How does speaking in a public forum differ from speaking in a classroom?

Critical Interaction 6.1
Audience Analysis

What are the demographic traits of the two audiences described below? How would you adjust your approach to preparing speeches on the two topics for each audience?

Audience 1

The members of this audience are senior citizens who meet daily for their noon meal at a state-funded center. These people live and worked in a rural area and did not retire with large pensions. Their retirements are funded entirely by Social Security.

Audience 2

The members of this audience are college-educated business leaders in a metropolitan area who collectively employ thousands of workers. A major concern of theirs is to attract and retain the brightest and most productive workers.

Topic 1

The local municipal government is considering raising property taxes to fund a new school, public park, and museum. Both business and private property tax rates will be affected.

Topic 2

A candidate for state representative is running a campaign that espouses core values of lower taxes, stronger police protection, and self-reliance.

Gathering Information

There are many ways to gather the necessary information you need about your audience. Some are informal, and others are more formal.

Getting to Know Your Audience. By interacting with your classmates, you gain insight into their interests and beliefs.

Informal Methods

As you proceed through this course, you will most likely have several opportunities to get to know your classmates. Typically, in the first week of a public speaking course, you will have the opportunity to give an introductory speech about yourself. These presentations not only help to relieve you of the stress of your first speaking assignment but also are your first step in the audience analysis process. As you listen to your classmates give their introductory speeches, you are learning information about their disposition toward your future speech topics.

Another way that you will get to know your audience is through class discussions. As you read this text and prepare for in-class contributions, you will not only get practice speaking in front of an audience but also begin to get a feel for your classmates' knowledge and experience with course concepts as they make their contributions. They may share personal examples or insights that you can relate to as you develop your speech. It is most impressive to an audience when you can take your classmates' comments from a class discussion and incorporate them into your speech.

Another strategy would involve spending time with your classmates both before and after class to get a sense of their interests, knowledge, and attitudes—particularly toward your topic. The better you get to know your classmates, the more comfortable you will be when you have to give your first major presentation. The more you know your audience, the more you can connect with them as well.

Formal Methods

Although there are numerous methods of collecting information, we will focus on the two methods most suitable to audience analysis. The first method is **interviewing**. This occurs when audience members are asked about their knowledge, interests, and attitudes toward a topic.[6] For example, marketers and advertisers often use a special type of interviewing technique known as *focus groups*. Focus groups are assembled from the target audience to share their thoughts on topics, products, political candidates, etc.

Source Citation:
[6] Berko, R., Wolvin, A., & Ray, R. (1997). *Business communication in a changing world.* New York: St. Martin's Press.

In your situation, individual interviews can be conducted before or after class and would be a good reason for you to start spending time with classmates outside of class. Interviews allow you to gather a great deal of information from a few people. The disadvantage of this method is that you may not have the time or the opportunity to interview all of your classmates, and you should be aware that a few individuals cannot speak for the whole group. However, talking to several individuals in the class can give you a general sense of where you should direct your topic.

There are different types of questions that can be asked in an interview. Questions can be open or closed. An **open question** allows the interviewee to respond in-depth. For example, you may ask:

What do you already know about (fill in your topic)?

What would you be interested in learning more about (fill in your topic)?

A **closed question**, on the other hand, gives the interviewee a choice between options such as yes or no. For example:

Have you ever had experience with (fill in your topic)? ___ Yes ___ No.

Do you know what (fill in term associated with your topic) is? ___ Yes ___ No.

In an interview, as the name implies, you gather and record information through the conversations you have with your classmates.

To gather additional information from more members of your audience, you could develop a **questionnaire** in which the audience would provide written answers to your questions. In Figure 6.1 on page 86, we provide you with an example of a questionnaire to gather demographic information. Using the information from the general demographic analysis, you could develop a few specific questions to determine your audience's knowledge, interests, and attitudes about your topic. When developing a questionnaire,

Scaled Questions
1. I know a great deal about the Delta blues.

Strongly Disagree	Disagree	Undecided	Agree	Strongly agree
1	2	3	4	5

2. I would like to know more about the Delta blues.

Strongly Disagree	Disagree	Undecided	Agree	Strongly agree
1	2	3	4	5

3. I would like to know more about how current artists have been influenced by the blues.

Strongly Disagree	Disagree	Undecided	Agree	Strongly agree
1	2	3	4	5

Open-Ended Questions
1. What do you know about the history of the Delta blues (please be specific)?
2. What specifically would you be interested in learning more about regarding the Delta blues?

FIGURE 6.2
Scaled Questions

there are several kinds of questions you could ask. The first kind of question is asked along a **scale** or **continuum**. For example:

On a scale of 1 to 5 (5 being strongly agree; 1 being strongly disagree), how do you feel about (fill in your topic)?

The scales, or range of responses, can be modified to fit your topic. These kinds of questions allow you to gauge attitudes on a continuum as opposed to a limited "yes" or "no" response. Once your audience completes your questionnaire, you can add up the responses (based on your scale) and divide by the number of items to determine your audience's general disposition toward your topic. Figure 6.2 provides you with some examples of *scaled questions*. You can also use both open and closed questions as you did in the interview, but have your audience respond to the questions in writing.

Once you have gathered the information from your audience, you will have a better idea of their general disposition toward your topic. You can then use this information to determine what research you will need to address any concerns they may have.

Preparing to Participate 6.4
Gathering Information

Knowledge
List and describe the informal and formal methods of gathering information about the audience.

Application
Considering your speech topic, what questions (both formal and informal) can you ask your audience?
How will you use this information as you research your topic and develop your speech? What will you say to connect your speech to your audience?

Adapting Your Message

As we have discussed, you should use audience analysis throughout the entire process of producing your message. ▭ In the previous chapter, we discussed how you consider your audience when selecting a topic, but you will also bear them in mind as you decide how to organize your speech, which supporting material to use, what presentation aids to use, and how to deliver your presentation.

The best speakers will competently consider what they know about an audience and use the information to develop effective informative or persuasive speeches. For example, if you know that several of your audience members love to listen to the Dave Matthews Band, then you could compare his style of music to a lesser known artist, Michael Hedges. In this way, you use information that is familiar to your audience to draw comparisons to something that is less familiar. The best speaker does this throughout the presentation and as often as possible.

If your purpose is to persuade your audience that the federal government should fund stem cell research and you know that some of your audience may disagree with the medical procedures for religious reasons, then you can use this information to highlight alternative methods of research. The best speaker does this through sound reasoning and evidence, and proceeds as carefully as possible without offending the values of the audience.

In our earlier speech examples (tornadoes, Roman Coliseum, and Delta blues) the speakers keep their audience (composed of

Media
Interaction 6.2
Analyzing Political Rhetoric

Log onto the Internet and access a speech by Barack Obama at the following URL: http://www.americanrhetoric.com/speeches/convention2004/barackobama2004dnc.htm

1. How did Obama use his personal background to identify with the audience?
2. How did he appeal to his party?
3. How did he appeal to Americans?
4. Which demographic variables (from the text) did he mention/illustrate through examples or stories in his speech? (example: "age"—children, elderly, etc.)

Now log onto the Internet and access a speech by Zell Miller at the following URL: http://www.americanrhetoric.com/speeches/convention2004/zellmiller2004rnc.htm

1. How did Miller use his personal background to identify with the audience?
2. How did he appeal to his party?
3. How did he appeal to Americans?
4. Which demographic variables (from the text) did he mention/illustrate through examples or stories in his speech? (example: "age"—children, elderly, etc.)

Adapting Your Message. It is a good idea to start with information your audience knows (in this case Dave Matthews), and then lead them into information about which they are less familiar (e.g., Michael Hedges).

Illinois college students) in mind throughout the presentation. Figure 6.3 provides an example of how one speaker utilized an audience analysis checklist to construct a speech about the Delta blues. 🖵

It is important to note that your job of analyzing the audience does not end when you finish developing the speech. In fact, competent communicators carefully analyze their audience and adapt their messages before, during, and after the speech.

As you deliver the speech, monitor your audience members' eye contact, facial expressions, and movement. All of these nonverbal behaviors will give you clues as to whether members of your audience are bored or excited, interested or uninterested, and so on. In addition, unresponsive facial expressions may signal that members of your audience do not comprehend your message.

These types of responses from the audience demand that you adapt as you present. Depending on the precise feedback you receive, you may find it necessary to alter your speech rate, use additional examples, pause for dramatic effect, or use appropriate humor. The key is to be flexible as the presentation unfolds so that you can respond appropriately to your audience.

You should also carefully reflect on your experiences after the speech so you can determine what you might do differently next time. Ask yourself these questions: Did you effectively analyze your audience before the speech? Did you adapt to your audience during the speech? Your goals in answering these questions should be to determine what strategies worked well and, of course, to identify areas for improvement.

Topic
Delta Blues

Who are they?
First-year students enrolled in my public speaking course. According to my audience survey, the majority of students are from the Chicago area.

Why are they here?
This is a required course for all first-year students.

What do they know?
According to my audience survey, most have some general knowledge of the blues tradition especially as it relates to Chicago blues (but most were unable to name more than one specific musician).

What are their interests?
All of the respondents to my survey indicated an interest in music. Several stated that they were interested in knowing more about how blues musicians influenced current artists.

What will you say in the speech?
I know that many of you are from the Chicago area. . . . I've discovered that the world famous "Chicago Blues" sound owes its origins to the Mississippi Delta Blues . . .. [These men] directly influenced some of the greatest blues musicians from the heyday of Chicago blues like Howling Wolf and Muddy Waters, who in turn influenced a whole generation of rock and rollers. . . .

FIGURE 6.3
Audience Analysis
for Blues Speech

We have another suggestion for you based on several years of teaching this course—don't overlook the feedback you receive from your instructor and peers! You should capitalize on this feedback by using it to prepare for the next speech.

SUMMARY

The audience plays a crucial role in the success of your speech. By understanding and considering the characteristics of your audience as you produce your presentation, you are engaging in *competent* and *ethical communication*. As you begin to get to know your audience, you will also feel more *confident* in speaking before them. In this chapter, we provided you with both formal and informal methods of conducting an audience analysis. We have also talked about ways to adapt your message according to your analysis. It is one thing to know your audience, but it is quite another to be able to take that information and use it to accomplish your goals.

KEY TERMS

audience analysis (84)

frame of reference (85)

audience demographics (86)

speaking situation (87)

captive audience (88)

voluntary audience (88)

attitudes, values, and beliefs (89)

interviews (91)

open and closed questions (91)

questionnaire (91)

scaled or continuum questions (92)

ADDITIONAL ENGAGEMENT OPPORTUNITIES

Now that you have finished reading the chapter, it is also important to make connections between the course content and your own experiences. These activities will help you understand, apply, analyze, evaluate, or synthesize course concepts. You can use these activities to provide evidence of your preparation for participation in class as well as to plan additional contributions to class discussion. The Civic Engagement Opportunities (CEOs) are designed to help you become more engaged in campus and community life and apply course concepts to important social issues.

1. Listen to a song that inspires you. Who is the intended audience for this song? Are you part of this audience? Why or why not. In a short paper, reveal the song and the artist(s). Discuss whom you believe the intended audience is and how the artist(s) captured your attention. Be sure to include several lyrics to support your claims.

2. 🗩 Visit the American Rhetoric website (www.americanrhetoric. com) and look at how presidents adapt to their audience in State of the Union or inaugural speeches. You could compare the Clinton-Bush-Obama speeches.

7

Integrating Support Material

The interesting thing is always to see if you can find a fact that will change your mind about something, to test and see if you can.

—Diane Sawyer

CHAPTER OBJECTIVES

After reading this chapter, you should be able to:

- Define and understand information literacy.
- Develop a research strategy.
- Incorporate supporting material into your speeches.
- Evaluate supporting materials.

Hopefully, you have chosen a topic that you are comfortable with—one that is relevant to both you and your audience. Now, what strategies will you use to find information on this topic? We hope your answer is not to settle on the first few hits you get on Google.

The ability to develop a research strategy for locating and evaluating information critically is a prerequisite to becoming an effective speaker, student, worker, and member of a democratic society.[1] As you will see throughout this chapter, supporting material can take many forms, including quotations, statistics, and examples. The use of credible supporting material will bolster your credibility as a speaker on the topic and help ensure that the audience takes your ideas seriously. When your aim is to change the audience's way of thinking or to take action, as is the case for persuasive presentations, the use of credible supporting material will significantly enhance the persuasiveness of your message. In this chapter, we discuss several types of supporting material as well as strategies for selecting, evaluating, and incorporating those materials into your speech.

Information Literacy

Before you begin to develop an effective research strategy, it is important that you understand what it means to be information literate. **Information literacy** involves being able to find appropriate sources, analyze the material, evaluate the credibility of the sources, and to use and cite those sources ethically and legally.[2]

To place this in the context of public speaking, you need to develop the abilities to:

- determine what information you need
- access information effectively and efficiently
- evaluate information critically
- use and incorporate information ethically and legally
- transfer these information literacy skills to new research tasks in the future[3]

Source Citation:
[1] DeMars, C. E., Cameron, L., & Erwin, T. D. (2003). Information literacy as foundational: Determining competence. *Journal of General Education, 52,* 253–265.

Source Citations:
[2] Eisenberg, M. B., Lowe, C. A., & Spitzer, K. L. (2004). *Information literacy: Essential skills for the information age* (2nd ed.). Westport, CT: Libraries Unlimited.

[3] For a more detailed set of information literacy competencies, see American Association of College and Research Libraries. (2000). *Information literacy competency standards for higher education.* Chicago: American Library Association.

Preparing to Participate 7.1
Information Literacy

Knowledge
Define information literacy.

Application
How can becoming information literate help you, as a speaker and a consumer of information, make decisions?

Developing a Research Strategy

In our experience, beginning public speakers often struggle with developing a strategy for locating supporting materials. Too often, students simply go to a library database or an Internet search engine, type in a few key words, and settle for the first four or five search results. This approach is problematic because it rarely results in locating the best available information on a topic.[4] Developing a research strategy will help you identify what supporting materials you need to access for your speeches. The key steps in developing a successful research strategy are outlined in Figure 7.1.

Source Citation:
[4] Jacobson, T. E., & Mark, B. L. (2000). Separating wheat from chaff: Helping first-year students become information savvy. *Journal of General Education, 49,* 256–278.

Create Research Questions

In Chapter 5 you learned the basic steps for selecting and narrowing a topic. Once you have selected a topic, the next step in developing a research strategy is to create research questions. Think about your topic. What do you want to know? What might your audience like to know? These become your

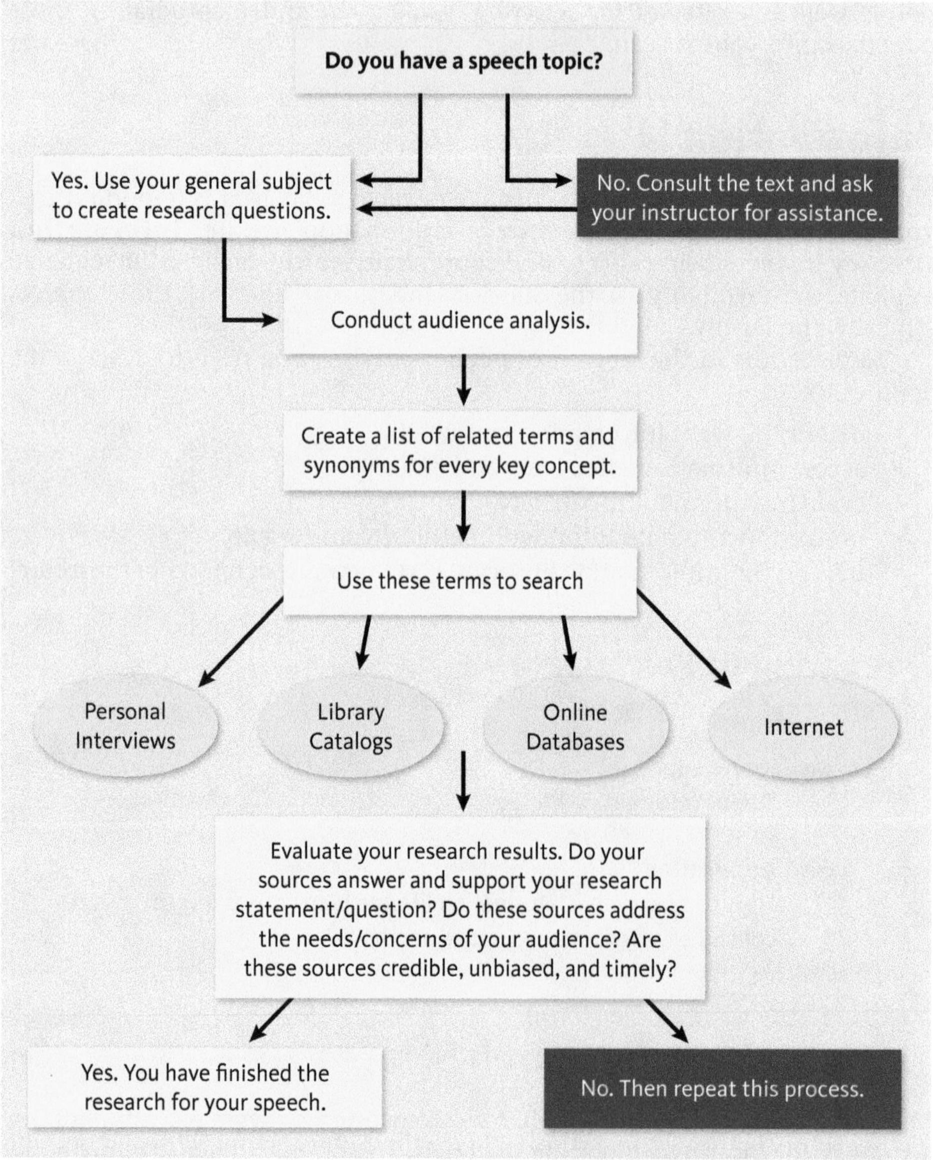

Do you have a speech topic?

Yes. Use your general subject to create research questions.

No. Consult the text and ask your instructor for assistance.

Conduct audience analysis.

Create a list of related terms and synonyms for every key concept.

Use these terms to search

Personal Interviews

Library Catalogs

Online Databases

Internet

Evaluate your research results. Do your sources answer and support your research statement/question? Do these sources address the needs/concerns of your audience? Are these sources credible, unbiased, and timely?

Yes. You have finished the research for your speech.

No. Then repeat this process.

FIGURE 7.1
The Research Process

Critical Interaction 7.1
Developing a Research Strategy

Consider the following questions about your speech topic as you develop your research strategy.

1. For your specific topic, what are your research questions? What, specifically, do you want to talk about? What do you think the audience will be interested in hearing about?

2. Brainstorm various terms that can be used to describe your topic.

3. What sources are most appropriate to use, given your topic? Do they answer your research questions? Do they address the needs/concerns of your audience? Are these sources credible, timely, or free of bias?

research questions. For example, if your speech topic explored reality television, you might pose the following research questions:

- What effect does reality television have on screenwriter employment?
- Can reality television be used to educate the public?
- What are the ethical issues associated with humiliation in reality television?

Using research questions in this way will guide you through the rest of the research process, thereby allowing you to explore a wide range of issues related to your topic that are of interest to you and your audience. Rather than simply taking the first few search results from a search engine, you will proceed in a much more focused fashion as you seek the best available information on your topic.

As you go through the process of developing research questions, it is important that you keep your audience in mind. Ask yourself the following questions:

- What topics are they most likely to appreciate?
- What information do they already have on this topic?
- What information would they like to have?
- What sources of information will my audience find credible?

Use the audience analysis strategies discussed in Chapter 6 to tailor the speech to your specific audience.

Generate a List of Synonyms

Before you begin searching available databases for supporting materials, you may find it helpful to generate a list of synonyms for each of your key concepts. A sample list is provided in Figure 7.2. Generating such a list will help you create search terms and phrases that will ultimately lead you more deeply into the available supporting materials on your topic.

Key Concepts	Alternative Words (Synonyms) for Key Concepts
Employment	job, career, vocation, work
Education	instruction, knowledge, learning, literacy, pedagogy, teaching
Ethics	morality, morals, principles, standards

FIGURE 7.2
Sample Lists of Synonyms

Search Information Sources

There are a number of sources of information available to public speakers including library catalogs and databases, newspapers, reference works, government documents, the Internet, and interviews.

Library Catalogs   Information-literate individuals understand that libraries contain valuable information that, in many cases, cannot be found elsewhere. Although your campus likely has a program in place to orient you to the resources available in your library, we will briefly overview the major types of information sources generally available in many college and university libraries. Most libraries have an *online catalog system* for accessing all of their holdings.

Finding books on your topic offers several advantages. For example, books generally provide a much deeper investigation of the topic compared to magazine articles, journals, or websites. In this way, books are likely to provide you with useful quotes and lead you to new ideas on the topic.

In addition, because books usually contain extensive reference lists, they make excellent sources of additional information on the topic. You sometimes can access entire books through electronic catalogs; however, once you have the call numbers for the books you are interested in, take the time to locate the volume and then search nearby sections of the stacks. You may find additional books relevant to your topic area using this strategy.

Electronic Databases   Most libraries have licenses to *electronic databases* that index selected periodicals. *Periodicals* include publications such as magazines and journals. Given that periodicals may be published weekly, biweekly, monthly, or quarterly, they are an excellent source of timely information on your topic. A periodical may also be the best source of information for your speech if the scope of the topic is so narrow or specific that it is not covered in other formats such as books.

Newspapers   *Newspapers* are exceptional sources of recent information on a myriad of topics. In addition, it is a good idea to get in the habit of monitoring your local and campus newspapers for topic ideas.

General References   There are a number of *general references* available to you that contain collections of facts and information. These materials are often shelved in a special section of the library and include dictionaries, encyclopedias, and collections of quotations. These references are often a good starting point for the most basic information.

Government Documents   Most colleges and universities have government depositories containing *government documents*. These documents cover every important public policy issue and include such items as congressional deliberations, research studies, and reports. If your topic is related to public policy, consult the librarian in charge of government periodicals for help in accessing the wealth of information contained in government documents.

Internet   You can also find a substantial amount of information related to your topic on the *Internet*. You can locate this information by using search engines, accessing related links between pages, or directly accessing a specific site.

Search engines identify websites by their Uniform Resource Locators or URLs. A number of search engines are available on the web, including:

- Yahoo!: http://www.yahoo.com
- Dogpile: http://www.dogpile.com
- Google: http://www.google.com
- Alta Vista: http://www.altavista.com
- Lycos: http://www.lycos.com

Using the same procedures for generating research questions and synonyms discussed previously in this chapter, you can use search engines to scan the web. Keep in mind, however, that each search engine uses different criteria for searches. As a result, each search engine will likely generate a different list of websites. It is advisable to use a combination of search engines to increase the likelihood that you will broadly cover the information on the web related to your topic.

As you peruse through various websites, you can find additional material by following links to related information. Alternatively, if you already know the URL, you can use your web browser to go directly to a specific site. For example, if you want to know how many EF5 tornadoes have been recorded in the United States in the last year, you could visit the Tornado Project Online website: http://www.tornadoproject.com.

Although you should always carefully scrutinize the information you retrieve from all of the sources discussed in this chapter, you should be particularly careful with information you locate on the Internet. Anyone, regardless of educational background or training, can develop and publish a website. Unlike other sources of information, material found on the web is rarely subject to peer review. In some instances, information found on the web is clearly slanted in the direction of a particular perspective. Political candidates, for example, construct websites that promote their own political agenda while trying to make opponents look bad.

As you evaluate information you retrieve from the web, start by considering the purpose and intended audience for the site. Does the site focus on information, news, advocacy, sales, or a mixture of all of these? By examining the domain of the site, you can pick up clues as to whether it is affiliated with an educational institution (.edu), government agency (.gov), organization (.org), or commercial products (.com).

You might be able to access additional information about the site by locating an "about the website" or "contact us" page. Look through the site for an author biography, philosophy, or other background information. Also, look for sponsors of the site. Does the site use banner sponsors? Are the sponsors well-known organizations or companies? What are the sponsors selling?

Another clue about the timeliness of the information on the site is the copyright date. You should check to see when the page was originally published and how often it is updated (this information may be at the bottom of each page or on the first page of the website).

Interviews   One of the best sources of information is people who have personal experience or who are recognized experts on your topic. In fact, on any college or university campus, you are likely to find at least one person who is an expert on your speech topic. As you might suspect, the effectiveness of *interviewing* depends on both selecting the best person to interview as well as developing a good list of interview questions.

In terms of selecting an individual to interview, start by creating a list of people on your campus who have experience with your topic. In many cases, you can identify such individuals by simply searching your university website. You can also work closely with your communication instructor to develop a list of potential interviewees. Once you have decided whom to interview, make an appointment to visit with the person and state clearly why you wish to speak with him or her. Be sure you go into the session already well informed on your topic. Doing so will allow you to craft better interview questions and increase the likelihood that potential interviewees will be willing to talk with you. This means that you need to have a broad understanding of both your topic area and the interviewee's experiences related to the topic before you conduct the interview.

As you develop a list of potential interview questions, carefully consider what information you think the person can provide. For example, one of our students wanted to give an informative speech on artificial intelligence and identified a philosophy professor who had been conducting research in the area for several years. She developed the following questions:

- How long have you been researching artificial intelligence?
- What is the current state of artificial intelligence research at this university?
- How many professors and students are currently involved in research on artificial intelligence at this university?
- Why should students take an interest in artificial intelligence research?
- What types of topics will artificial intelligence researchers be exploring five years from now?
- How can students get involved in the artificial intelligence research projects at this university?

As you design the interview questions, try to use a mix of limited response, "yes" or "no" questions as well as questions that encourage a longer response. This questioning strategy will allow you to cover a wide range of issues in a limited time and will provide an opportunity for the expert to elaborate on her or his opinions.

Preparing to Participate 7.2
Research Strategies

Knowledge
Describe the three main steps in developing a successful research strategy.

Application
How does each step help you to develop your speech topic?

Types of Supporting Materials

As you research your topic, you will have access to a number of different types of supporting materials. The most effective presentations incorporate a mix of supporting materials. It is easy to imagine how frustrated an audience might become with an unending barrage of statistics. Using multiple types of support adds vitality to the speech and keeps the audience interested. For example, a speaker might use statistics and personal examples together to both establish the scope of the topic and provide a real-world situation that deepens the audience's understanding of the issue. The types of supporting materials available to you include statistics, analogies, facts, examples, and testimony.

Statistics

Statistics provide a numerical method for summarizing data and can take such forms as means, medians, ratios, and percentages. Although statistics can provide substantial support for your claims, they can also be confusing, overwhelming if overused, and misleading.

Your chances of using statistics successfully improve dramatically if you follow a few practical guidelines. Initially, given the potential for information overload, you should not rely on statistics as your only form of supporting material. Keep in mind that your audience will have only one chance to hear your speech, so use statistics sparingly.

Consider creating a data graphic so that your audience can both hear and see the information (see Chapter 12). Similarly, you should round off statistics to help your audience understand and retain key statistical information. For example, it will be much easier for your audience to remember that the United States spent over $700 billion to bail out financial institutions in 2008 compared to $700,200,050,000.18. It is also important that you translate difficult-to-understand numbers into immediately comprehensible terms. One speaker translated statistics related to world hunger in the following way:

> According to recent statistics posted on the Hearts and Minds website, one of the leading advocacy groups for the elimination of world hunger, 40 million people die every year from hunger and hunger-related illnesses. This number is equivalent to more than 300 jumbo jet crashes every day with no survivors. 💻

Learn about Statistics

To get a quick background in statistics, visit this website:
http://www.robertniles.com/stats/[o]

1. According to this website, what should every writer [speaker] know about statistics? Why?
2. How can consumers avoid getting "duped" by numbers?

Analogies

Analogies are useful if you want to compare the defining characteristics of one concept to another. You can also use analogies to compare the similarities in things that are alike. Consider the following example of a **literal analogy**, which is based on a comparison of actual events:

The tactics used to control illegal immigration in Arizona worked, so the same tactics should also be successful in Texas.

For the audience to accept this analogy, the speaker would have to establish that the two states are similar in a number of relevant ways including population base, geography, financial resources, and so on.

Figurative analogies draw upon metaphors to identify the similarities in two things that are not alike. For example, in our Coliseum speech, the speaker compares our modern-day facilities to the Roman Coliseum:

> Just as we look down from gymnasium bleachers, spectators would look down upon the wooden arena floor. However, the Coliseum's floor was covered with sand, which served to soak up large quantities of blood.

Used this way, analogies can help clarify complex situations by comparing them with situations more familiar to the audience.

Facts

A **fact** is a statement that is verifiable as true. "A megabyte is 1,048,576 bytes"; "the Fujita Scale is the official classification system for tornado damage"; and "the Big 12 conference has 12 schools playing football" are all factual statements that can be verified. You might think that last one was a "no brainer," but the Big 10 conference actually has 11 schools! The point is that virtually all presentations are supported to some extent by facts. As you might imagine, facts are most effective when the audience has no trouble accepting them as true. Unless a factual claim is common knowledge, be sure to give the source of your information.

Examples

Examples are specific instances developed at varying lengths and used by speakers to make an abstract idea concrete. You can use brief, extended, or hypothetical examples to support your claims.

A **brief example** is a specific case used to support a claim. If you want to support the claim that the Federal Emergency Management Agency (FEMA) is not responsive enough to natural disasters, you might cite as an example FEMA's slow response to the victims of Hurricane Katrina in 2005.

Extended examples, also referred to as narratives, stories, or anecdotes, are substantially more developed compared to brief examples. Extended examples are especially effective at getting the audience to visualize and relate to your topic.

If your topic is the slow response of FEMA to natural disasters, you might tell a story about someone's grueling struggle to survive several days in the aftermath of Katrina. You could describe the rancid water conditions faced by those in New Orleans as well as the violence people had to endure because nobody was there to restore law and order after the storm. Such an extended, engaging story puts a human face on the issue and would go a long way toward helping your audience relate to your topic.

A **hypothetical example** describes an imaginary situation that could conceivably take place in the way it is described. Although hypothetical examples are fictitious, you should take great care not to exaggerate or distort the scenario if it is to be effective. The advantage of hypothetical examples is that they allow the audience to imagine themselves in a specific situation. You might say:

> Suppose that you woke up in the middle of the night only to find your house completely full of water. Now imagine spending more than a week in toxic water without food, water, or electricity. How would you feel about that?

Providing Examples. A vivid and relevant story such as the Hurricane Katrina disaster can lend support to the claims you are making.

Listeners are likely to conjure up images of scraping for food and water, the difficulties of communicating with loved ones, or even the possibility of becoming very sick after being exposed to polluted water. You could then use this example to help the audience understand the importance of reforming FEMA to prevent prolonged delays in responses to future storm victims.

Our Coliseum speaker uses the following hypothetical example to capture the audience's attention:

> Imagine yourself being ushered up a dark hallway and into a huge, outdoor theatre. Here you are greeted by 50,000 screaming spectators and one man—crazy for your death, hungry for the thought of ripping you apart limb from limb. You and Blood Thirsty are the only ones inside an arena encompassed by a 15-foot wall, and the 50,000 people are waiting for you to die.

Testimony

Speakers use **testimony** when they quote or paraphrase an authoritative source. When you use testimony, you are relying on someone else's judgment and expertise. For example, in our Blues speech, the speaker uses the testimony of a well-known musician:

> Keith Richards of the Rolling Stones said that when he was a young man trying to learn music from [Robert] Johnson's records, he was flabbergasted to find out that it was just one person playing.

When used effectively, testimony can help prove your point and bolster your credibility. Of course, relying on testimony from

Using Testimonials. Guitarist Keith Richards of the Rolling Stones was used as expert testimony in our Delta Blues speech.

sources that your audience finds unreliable or incompetent has negative implications for their assessment of your credibility.

Preparing to Participate 7.3
Types of Supporting Material

Knowledge
List and define five types of supporting material.

Application
What types of sources have you used in the past? What sources would you like to consider now? What sources seem to be the best for your topic?

Evaluating Supporting Materials

As a critical consumer and producer of information, it is essential that you never accept supporting materials at face value. You also have an ethical responsibility to ensure that the information you present is reliable and credible. ⌣ Consider the following questions as you select and incorporate supporting material for your speech.

Evaluating Websites

Access the following website and evaluate the content you find there:
http://www.dhmo.org/

1. Would you use this website for a source in your speech? Why or why not?
2. Is this source timely, credible, and free of bias? Why or why not?

Are the Statistics Representative? A **representative sample** is a critical measure of the reliability and validity of statistics. To be representative, a sample must be similar to the population from which it was taken. Think for a moment about the other students in your speech class. To what extent do they represent the entire population of students on your campus? Do they reflect the proportion of men and women on your campus? Are they representative of the wide range of majors available at your institution? Do the students in your class accurately reflect other demographic features of the general population at your institution like age, race, cultural background, and religious affiliation? Unless all of the students in your class were drawn randomly from the entire student body, you cannot know for certain that they are a representative sample.

Are the Items Being Compared in Analogies Similar? The analogies you use to support your ideas should compare cases that share similar characteristics. As already mentioned, the argument that immigration control should work in Texas because it worked in Arizona rests on the assumption that the two states are essentially alike. If the two items being compared are not similar, the conclusion is unacceptable.

Are the Facts Verifiable? As you collect facts for your speech, you should be concerned with whether the information is verifiable. Can you find the same fact in more than one source? An excellent way to verify whether the information is factual is to check it with another source on the same topic.

Are the Examples Relevant, Typical, and Vivid? Initially, any example you use should be relevant to the claim it is supporting. If the link between the example and the claim is unclear, it simply will not be effective. Although many in your audience may appreciate surfing stories, they likely will not be convincing if your topic is reforming FEMA.

You should also apply the test of typicality to the examples you use. **Typicality** assesses the extent to which your example is normal. Your audience will easily recognize atypical examples and your credibility is likely to suffer as a result. Indeed, exceptional cases are rarely persuasive to audience members. Finally, the examples you provide should vividly illustrate the claim you are advancing. Simply stated, the more vivid your examples are, the more likely they are to have a lasting impact on your audience. For example, one of the strengths of the Coliseum speech is the vivid imagery the speaker creates as she describes the horror of the games:

> The mornings began with fights between wild animals. One battle involved a bull and a panther, each at the end of a chain. They could barely reach, and they were forced to tear each other apart piece by piece.

Is the Source Identified and Credible? The rest of your classmates are privy to the same information on evaluating sources in this chapter as you are. This means that they, too, will be evaluating the credibility of the sources you use. If they doubt your sources, they may doubt you.

Suppose you were doing research on the global effects of climate change. Would someone who had no specialized training in climatology or meteorology be a good source to consult on models of climate change? Chances are that your audience would not give much credence to a music professor's assessment of recent climate models. In addition, relying on such sources is likely to damage your credibility, as it may cause the audience to question your knowledge of the topic as well as the quality of research you have conducted. As you select supporting materials for your speech, keep the following questions in mind: What special qualifications does the author possess that allow her or him to speak on this topic? Is the author a recognized authority on the subject? If you cannot answer these questions or if you cannot identify the author of the information, look for other, more qualified sources on the topic.

Is the Source Biased? A source is **biased** when it provides an opinion that is so slanted to one perspective that it is not objective or fair. Imagine for a moment that you are researching the effects of carbon dioxide on the environment. Suppose you come across testimony stating that there is no evidence that the global climate is warming. In addition, assume you find further testimony, from the same source, indicating that increasing

Comic 7.1

1. How does Jeffy's information violate one of the tests of evidence?

Family Circus

"I think I heard that on TV."

Family Circus ©Bill Keane, Inc. King Features Syndicate

levels of carbon dioxide are actually good for the planet. Setting aside other questions about the verifiability of this testimony, can you think of any reason that individuals would make such claims?

One possible explanation is that they have been given money by large oil companies to undermine consensus in the scientific community that humans are causing global warming. In other words, some oil companies actively seek out and pay for this kind of testimony in order to lobby politicians to limit expensive restraints on the production of carbon dioxide.[5] As a result, these claims are biased, given that the authors who advance them are doing so not on the basis of sound reasoning, but for profit. To determine if a source has bias, you might ask yourself, "Does this person/s have anything to gain or lose by advancing this claim?" If the answer to that question is "yes," then there's bias. Find another source.

Is the Information Timely? The information you incorporate in your speech should be **timely** enough to account for the laws, regulations, attitudes, and so on that currently exist. For example, a speaker advocating action in response to avian influenza (also known as bird flu) would have to know exactly what actions have already been taken in order to propose a novel solution.

How might the audience react to a speaker who advocates that the Centers for Disease Control (CDC) issue an immediate warning about the dangers of avian influenza if they know that the CDC has already issued such a warning? Again, the audience is likely to question both the speaker's credibility and her or his ability to conduct thorough research.

It is important to recognize that some topics require less timely information than others. Our Blues speech, for example, is based on the roots of popular American music in highlighting the three men who epitomized Mississippi Delta Blues before World War II. Our Tornado speech, on the other hand, required the latest data on tornado activity.

As you evaluate your supporting materials, you should also carefully consider the extent to which you have answered the research questions you posed at the beginning of the research process. Do your materials answer your research questions and address the needs of your audience? If they meet the evaluation criteria discussed here, answer your research questions, and address the needs of your audience, you are ready to incorporate the supporting materials into your speech.

Source Citation:
[5] Mooney, C. (2005, May/June). Some like it hot. *Mother Jones*, 36–49.

Preparing to Participate 7.4
Evaluating Supporting Materials

Knowledge
What should you consider when selecting and incorporating support material for your speech?

Application
What are the implications for using support material that may violate one of these considerations?

Incorporating and Documenting Supporting Materials

In your speeches, you have the responsibility to *orally document* the sources of your supporting materials. A complete **oral citation** consists of information about who authored the material you are using, a statement about the credibility of the author, the date the information was published (or the date you conducted the interview), and relevant information about the source (e.g., title of the journal, magazine, or website). To do this accurately, you need to photocopy the source information and/or take careful notes as you conduct your research. In your notes, be sure to make distinctions between materials that are directly quoted and those that are paraphrased.

The proper documentation of sources is important for a number of reasons. Initially, documenting your sources shields you against charges of plagiarism. As mentioned in Chapter 3, plagiarism is a serious ethical offense that could result in a failing grade for the course or expulsion from the college or university. Another important reason for fully citing your sources orally is to establish the credibility and reliability of your supporting material. It is important that you provide an oral citation in the speech at the time that you introduce your supporting materials. To illustrate this point, take note of the way that we provide source citations in the margins of this text. Rather than providing the references at the end of each chapter or the end of the book, you see them at the point at which the supporting material is provided. In this way, you can evaluate the credibility of the source in terms of the information that is used.

Consider the following sample oral citations.

Internet Source with No Author

In fact, according to *Tornado Project Online!* (source), a website hosted by a company that gathers tornado information for tornado researchers (credibility), accessed earlier this month (date), the deadliest tornado in U.S. recorded history occurred in Murphysboro, Illinois. In 1925 a violent tornado killed 234 people in this Southern Illinois town.

Book

According to renowned weather historian (credibility) Dr. David Ludlum (author), author of the 1997 (date) edition of the National Audubon Society's *Field Guide to North American Weather* (source), tornado researchers use a scale, known as the Fujita-Pearson Tornado Intensity Scale (named after its creators) to rate the intensity of tornadoes.

Journal Article

In addition, astrogeophysicist (credibility) Dr. Robert Davies-Jones (author) notes in a 1995 (date) edition of *Scientific American* (source) that most tornadoes have damage paths 150 feet wide, move at about 30 miles per hour, and last only a few minutes.

Magazine Article

Environmental activist and lawyer (credibility) Robert F. Kennedy, Jr. (author) argues in a 2007 (date) edition of *Vanity Fair* (source) that "More

Oral Citations. Robert F. Kennedy, Jr. is orally cited as an environmental activist and lawyer in our credibility statement.

than 100 representatives from polluting industries occupy key spots at the federal agencies that regulate environmental quality."

Movie Clip

The best attraction was saved for the afternoon: gladiatorial combat. The following video clip is taken from the Oscar-winning (credibility) 2000 (date) epic film, *Gladiator* (source), starring Russell Crowe. As stated earlier, notice the concealed trapdoors in the arena floor.

In addition to citing your sources orally, the outline you develop for your speech should contain a list of references you consulted in preparing your speech (a sample reference page can be found in Chapter 9).

Preparing to Participate 7.5
Oral Citations

Knowledge
What information should be included in an oral citation?

Application
Why is it important to include the oral citation in addition to the reference page? What might be the consequences if you don't include the oral citation?

SUMMARY

As you have learned in this chapter, giving a speech requires carefully chosen information that supports the ideas you want your audience to understand or accept. *Competent speakers* know how to access, evaluate, and incorporate high-quality information.

This chapter introduced you to the basic *information literacy* skills necessary to develop a research strategy, search multiple sources of information, and evaluate and incorporate supporting materials into your presentation. We hope that you agree that this process is a little more rigorous than finding the first four hits on Google. This process takes time as well as *ethical* and *critical* reflection—certainly not something that can happen a day or two before you make your presentation.

In the next chapter, we will discuss how to organize the ideas you will present in your speech.

KEY TERMS

information literacy (98)

research questions (100)

statistics (104)

analogy (104)

literal analogy (104)

figurative analogy (105)

fact (105)

example (105)

brief example (105)

extended example (105)

hypothetical example (105)

testimony (106)

representative sample (107)

typicality (108)

bias (108)

timely (109)

oral citation (110)

ADDITIONAL ENGAGEMENT OPPORTUNITIES

Now that you have finished reading the chapter, it is also important to make connections between the course content and your own experiences. These activities will help you understand, apply, analyze, evaluate, or synthesize course concepts. You can use these activities to provide evidence of your preparation for participation in class as well as to plan additional contributions to class discussion. The Civic Engagement Opportunities (CEOs) are designed to help you become more engaged in campus and community life and apply course concepts to important social issues.

1. Think back to a speech you have heard in the past (in person, on television, or in a movie). Provide a summary of a piece of supporting material in that speech that was especially effective and describe why you think so.

2. Pick up a copy of your school newspaper. Find an article that interests you. What types of supporting materials did the author(s) use?

Were they effective? Why? What was the article lacking? How would you suggest the author fix the holes? Write a citation of the source as it would appear on the reference page. Next, write a summary of the source you might use in your speech, using the proper oral citation style.

3. Visit the Annenberg Political Fact Check website located here: http://www.factcheck.org/. Factcheck.org is a project of the Annenberg Public Policy Center of the University of Pennsylvania. The goal of this project is to reduce the level of deception and confusion in U.S. politics. The project tracks the accuracy of statements by U.S. political players in various media including TV ads, debates, speeches, interviews, and news releases. Select one of the stories they are following currently and read their analysis. After reading this analysis, did you learn anything new about the politician? Did this report change your mind about the politician? If so, why? Did you find the information on this site useful? How might you use the information on this site to better prepare yourself to make informed political decisions?

8

Organizing Ideas

There are no secrets to success. It is the result of preparation, hard work, and learning from failure.
—Colin Powell

CHAPTER OBJECTIVES

After reading this chapter, you should be able to:

- Understand the importance of organizing ideas clearly.
- Understand the importance of organizing ideas strategically.
- Identify and use four patterns of organization: chronological, spatial, topical, and causal.
- Incorporate transitional devices into your speeches.

George Clooney

C hapter 7 introduced you to information literacy skills required to locate supporting materials for your speech. Once you have completed the research process and gathered support for your thesis statement, your next task is to organize your ideas.

Think for a moment about a presentation you witnessed recently in which the speaker was highly unorganized. How did you feel about the presentation? How did you feel about the speaker? If you are like most people, you probably found the presentation very frustrating and your evaluation of the speaker was likely less than positive.

In this chapter, you will learn why effective organization is essential to clear communication, how to organize your ideas strategically, and how to incorporate transitional devices into your speech that will make your organization obvious to the listener.

Importance of Organizing Your Ideas Clearly

As you begin the process of organizing your speech, you should consistently remind yourself that your goal is to put ideas and supporting materials together in a way that will make sense to listeners. There are a number of reasons why logical organization will help both you and your listeners as you present your ideas.

First, a number of communication scholars have found that listeners perceive well-organized speakers to be much more credible compared to poorly organized speakers.[1] There is a reason for this that we'll elaborate on in Chapter 11. But for now, it is important that you understand that listeners will find you to be more credible if they are able to follow your message.

Second, because speeches are delivered orally to an audience, speakers must present their message in a way that helps the listener to make sense of the speech as it happens. Your audience does not generally have access to your notes or your outline, and if the structure of your message is not clear, your audience may be lost and your goal (and credibility) may be in jeopardy.

A well-organized speech also benefits the speaker in other ways. For example, you are much more likely to feel confident in your ability to deliver a speech effectively if you have taken the time to carefully prepare a logical organization than if you recklessly slap ideas together at the last minute.[2]

In addition, the effective organizational skills you learn in this course will benefit you in every other course you take in college, as well as in your future career. For example, a better understanding of the logical relationships among ideas (e.g., how ideas are related in time and space) will improve your ability to organize and think critically about the information you encounter in readings, lectures, and discussions in other courses. Developing better organizational and outlining skills will also improve your note-taking abilities.

Source Citation:
[1] Sharp, H., & McClung, T. (1966). Effects of organization on the speaker's ethos. *Speech Monographs, 33,* 182–183.

See Also
Titsworth, B. S. (2001). The effects of teacher immediacy, use of organizational lecture cues, and students' notetaking on cognitive learning. *Communication Education, 50,* 283–297.

[2] Greene, J. O. (1984). Speech preparation processes and verbal fluency. *Human Communication Research, 11,* 61–84.

Preparing to Participate 8.1
Organize Ideas

Knowledge
Discuss why it is important to organize your ideas clearly.

Application
How is the oral style of speaking different from the way the information is presented in written style?

Organizing Ideas Strategically

In Chapter 5 we discussed narrowing your speech topics according to time, location, or subtopic. In this chapter we will discuss some **oral organizational strategies** that will allow you to devise an effective structure for your speech and your audience to better follow and comprehend your message. As you conduct research, you will get some idea about the way others have organized their thoughts on your topic. This will help you narrow even further the main ideas that you want to talk about.

Once you know which main ideas you will cover, you have enough information to write your thesis statement. The thesis statement you write will dictate the organizational pattern you will use. This organizational pattern will determine the arrangement of your main points. Figure 8.1 shows the relationships among the supporting material, main points, and thesis of the tornado speech. Again, the thesis is directly supported by the main points in the body of the speech, which are bolstered by supporting material.

In this section we explore several strategies for organizing the main points in the body of the speech. Given that the main points will form the core of your speech, you must carefully select the key ideas you will focus on and arrange them in a logical fashion.

One of the first questions we hear from students about organizing the body of the speech regards the appropriate number of main points that should be included in the body. Most of the speeches you deliver in a typical public speaking classroom will contain between two and five main points. Addressing more than five main points can be difficult or impossible, given the time constraints most often placed on classroom speakers.

In addition, if you have too many main points, your audience may become confused and have a difficult time sorting out what you are trying to say. Indeed, a simple speech design that limits the number of main points makes it easier for the audience to remember and retain your key points.[3]

After you have established your main points, you should turn your attention to ordering them strategically. There are several factors that will influence your choice of an organizational pattern. Initially, you should pick a method of organizing the speech that is consistent with your purpose, your topic, and your audience. As you develop the body of the speech, carefully consider whether or not the ideas you are advancing are clear, compelling, and well-substantiated. Also, consider how the main points and supporting material support your thesis.

Source Citation:
[3] Caplan, S. E., & Green, J. O. (1999). Acquisition of message-production skill by younger and older adults: Effects of age, task complexity, and practice. *Communication Monographs, 66*, 31–48.

FIGURE 8.1

Organizational Diagram for Tornado Speech

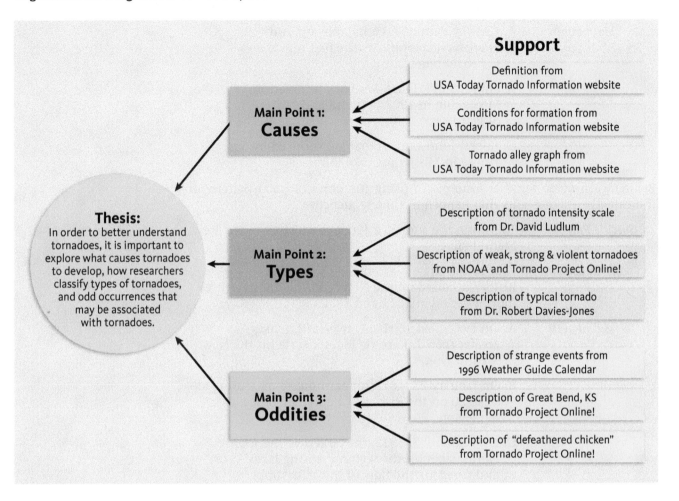

If your general purpose is to inform your audience, there are four basic methods for organizing your main points.

Chronological Order

If you use a **chronological pattern**, your main points will follow a time sequence. This pattern is appropriate if you want to inform your audience about a series of events as they occurred. For example, in our Blues speech, the order of the musicians matters because the earlier musicians influenced those who came later in terms of their contributions to the Mississippi Delta Blues:

Specific Purpose:	To inform the audience about the Delta Blues.
Thesis Statement:	To really understand the roots of popular American music, it's necessary to journey back

to the early 20th century and examine the music of three men who epitomize Mississippi Delta Blues.

Main Points: A. Charley Patton was a flamboyant and charismatic performer (the first in the area to record blues music).

B. Eddie "Son" House was born in Riverton, Mississippi in 1902 (a friend and protégé of Patton's).

C. Robert Johnson was that kid (noticed by Son House in Mississippi juke joints).

Below, we provide another example of using the chronological pattern to indicate a series of events that happen in time sequence:

Specific Purpose: To inform the audience about the history of the New Madrid fault.

Thesis Statement: Four of the largest earthquakes in recorded history occurred on the New Madrid fault in a three month period in 1811 and 1812.

Main Points: A. On December 16, 1811, two earthquakes greater than 7.0 on the Richter scale hit the New Madrid fault.

B. On January 23, 1812, an earthquake measuring at least 8.0 on the Richter scale flattened homes in the region.

C. On February 7, 1812, the largest of the four earthquakes hit the region draining lakes and reversing the flow of the Mississippi river.

It should be noted that you can organize your main points chronologically by either addressing events in time from present to past or from past to present. You can also use the chronological pattern if your goal is to demonstrate how to do something or explain a process. For example:

Specific Purpose: To inform the audience about how to develop a research strategy for their next speech.

Thesis Statement: The steps in developing a research strategy include selecting a topic, creating research questions, generating a list of synonyms, and selecting information sources.

Main Points: A. The first step in developing a research strategy is selecting and narrowing a topic.

B. The second step in developing a research strategy is creating research questions.

C. The third step in developing a research strategy is generating a list of synonyms for key concepts.

D. The fourth step in developing a research strategy is selecting appropriate information sources.

Spatial Order

Ideas can also be organized based upon spatial relationships. Specifically, the **spatial pattern** arranges ideas according to place or position. For example, you would use the spatial pattern for an informative speech demonstrating the location of various parts on a guitar (e.g., headstock, fret board, bridge, pickups, etc.). This pattern is especially useful if your topic is geographical or involves the discussion of multiple physical spaces.

Specific Purpose: To inform the audience about East Coast, West Coast, and Southern hip hop.

Thesis Statement: Modern hip hop features various styles including East Coast, West Coast, and Southern hip hop.

Main Points:
A. East Coast hip hop originated in New York City.

B. West Coast hip hop originated in California.

C. Southern hip hop, or Dirty South hip hop, originated in Miami.

Topical Order

The **topical order** pattern organizes your speech by breaking your overall topic into smaller subtopics. If you choose the topical pattern, each main idea you identify in writing and researching your speech becomes a main point of the speech. In other words, each main point is a subtopic of a larger topic.

Specific Purpose: To inform the audience about why the World Trade Center towers collapsed after the terrorist attacks on September 11, 2001.

Thesis Statement: The exterior structure and use of trusses in the construction of the World Trade Center, combined with intense heat resulting from burning jet fuel, contributed to the collapse of the towers.

Main Points:
A. The exterior structure of the World Trade Center made it vulnerable to collapse.

B. Trusses were used to save money, but they became unstable quickly when exposed to fire.

Ordering Your Main Points. When using a spatial pattern on a speech about Hip Hop, OutKast, a duo from Georgia, could be used as an example of the Dirty South style.

      C. Jet fuel created an intense fire that compromised the structural integrity of the World Trade Center towers.

Causal Order

Speeches using the **causal pattern** highlight the cause-effect relationships that exist among the main points. In this format, one of the main points is devoted to establishing causes and the other main point describes the effects.

Specific Purpose:	To inform the audience about the causes and effects of communication apprehension.
Thesis Statement:	Communication apprehension is caused by such variables as heredity and lack of speech training and can have several effects, including shortness of breath, sweaty palms, and use of filler words.
Main Points:	A. There are several causes of communication apprehension, including heredity and a skills deficit.
	B. Communication apprehension has several effects, including shortness of breath, sweaty palms, and the use of filler words.

Given the versatility of this organizational pattern, you may also choose to proceed from effect to cause. Although we discuss organizational patterns unique to persuasive speaking in Chapter 15, it is worth noting here that the causal pattern can be used both for informative and persuasive speeches.

In this section, we have provided information on four organizational patterns available to use in informative speeches. We have also provided examples for each. Based on the structure of the main points in our running speech topic on the Blues, we identified the use of the chronological pattern of organization. What about the other two running topics?

The process of organizing the body of a speech does not stop at selecting an organizational pattern. Your next task is to develop and incorporate transitional devices.

Preparing to Participate 8.2
Choose an Organizational Pattern

Knowledge

The text mentions three factors that influence your choice for an organizational pattern. What are they?

List and explain the four organizational patterns mentioned in this chapter.

Application

What happens when a speaker's organization is not clear?

Critical Interaction 8.1
Organizational Patterns

Based on what you have learned about four types of organizational patterns (chronological, spatial, topical, or causal), can you identify which type is used in each of our example speeches? See the full outlines for the speeches in the appendix.

Tornadoes: Thesis statement:

In order to better understand tornadoes, it is important to explore what causes tornadoes to develop, how researchers classify types of tornadoes, and odd occurrences that may be associated with tornadoes.

Pattern:

Coliseum: Thesis statement:

To truly understand the historical impact the Coliseum has had on civilization, it is important to learn of the architectural wonders of the Coliseum, the terror of the Roman Games, and the present plans for its restoration.

Pattern:

Delta Blues: Thesis statement:

To really understand the roots of popular American music, it's necessary to journey back to the early 20th century and examine the music of three men who epitomize Mississippi Delta Blues.

Pattern:

Incorporating Transitional Devices

Unlike a written text where a reader can go back over confusing passages, your audience will only have one opportunity to digest the information you present in your speech. You can use **transitional devices** (e.g., transitions, internal previews, internal summaries, and signposts) to link claims throughout the speech, provide a sense of organization, and ultimately make it easier for your audience to follow and remember the ideas you present.

Transitions

Transitions are words or phrases that demonstrate key relationships among ideas and also indicate a speaker is leaving one point and moving on to another. Transitions are critical to effective communication because they allow listeners to understand and follow the development of the speaker's ideas. Transitions link the introduction to the body, each of the main ideas, and the body to the conclusion. Consider the following examples, taken from the Coliseum speech in the appendix.

Transition from the Introduction to the Body:
> To begin, we will lay the foundation by describing its design and construction.

Transitions Between Main Points:
> Now that we have laid the foundation of the Coliseum's construction, let us live through a day at the Roman Games.

> Now that we have lived through the terror of the Roman games, let us learn of the present plans to restore and renovate this ancient monument to its original glory.

Transition from the Body to the Conclusion:
> Once restored, it will encompass, as historian Dr. Alison Futrell states in her 1997 book, Blood in the Arena, "all the glory and doom of the Roman Empire."

Transitions also provide the audience with information about the relationships among the ideas you are discussing. For example, terms such as "similarly" clearly indicate a comparison of ideas, whereas phrases such as "on the other hand" indicate that the speaker is contrasting ideas. A more detailed list of key transitional words and phrases is provided in Figure 8.2. In addition, several examples of transitions are provided in the sample outline presented in Chapter 9 as well as the sample speech outlines in the appendix.

Coliseum Speech. A film clip of Russell Crowe starring in *The Gladiator* is used to illustrate a day of competition at the Roman games.

Internal Previews

An **internal preview** is a very brief statement of what the speaker will discuss next. Whereas the preview statement in the introduction serves to outline the main points of the speech, an internal preview highlights ideas to be discussed within the body of the speech. For example:

> The two causes of communication apprehension that I will discuss are heredity and skills deficit.

This preview clearly establishes what the audience should be listening for in this main point. Internal previews should be brief and to the point so they draw the attention of the audience to your main points without interrupting the flow of the speech.

Internal Summaries

An **internal summary** offers a review of what has just been discussed before moving on to the next point. Internal summaries are especially useful

Function	Typical Words and Phrases
To indicate a reason for a claim.	for because
To show a causal or time relationship.	as since then
To signal an explanation of ideas.	for example in other words more specifically that is
To add ideas.	also and again in addition moreover
To qualify your position or return to an earlier claim.	although but however no doubt on the other hand while yet
To summarize ideas.	all in all and so finally in short on the whole

FIGURE 8.2
Functions of Transition

if you have just finished discussing a complicated point. Instead of immediately moving from difficult material to the next point, you may choose to provide a quick summary of the key points just discussed. For example:

> So, as we have seen, both heredity and a lack of training in speaking may contribute to public speaking apprehension.

Internal summaries help the audience remember key points in your speech and signal that you are moving on to another point. Like internal previews, internal summaries should use brief statements to highlight the main points.

Signposts

Signposts signal the next point to be made. In a sense, signposts provide an oral roadmap of the main points in the speech. Signposts are often numerical:

> The first step in preparing a resume is to develop your employment objectives.

Critical Interaction 8.2
Transitions

Now that you understand how to use transitional devices, try writing your own transitions between the main points for each of our thesis sentences. See the full outlines for the speeches in the appendix.

Tornadoes: Thesis statement:

In order to better understand tornadoes, it is important to explore what causes tornadoes to develop, how researchers classify types of tornadoes, and odd occurrences that may be associated with tornadoes.

Transition A:

Transition B:

Transition C:

Coliseum: Thesis statement:

To truly understand the historical impact the Coliseum has had on civilization, it is important to learn of the architectural wonders of the Coliseum, the terror of the Roman Games, and the present plans for its restoration.

Transition A:

Transition B:

Transition C:

Delta Blues: Thesis statement:

To really understand the roots of popular American music, it's necessary to journey back to the early 20th century and examine the music of three men who epitomize Mississippi Delta Blues.

Transition A:

Transition B:

Transition C:

The second step in preparing a resume is to gather relevant information about your education.

The third step is preparing a resume is to generate a list of any special academic or nonacademic awards you have received.

Signposts can also include words such as "next," "another," and "finally":

The next cause of this problem is high tuition rates.

Another contributor to global warming is carbon dioxide.

Finally, the mismanagement of funds by local officials has contributed significantly to the deterioration of infrastructure.

Speakers may also use signposts to help listeners focus on particularly important ideas. Consider the following examples:

The most important point to remember is that your vote does count.

It is critical that you understand the implications of higher student fees for your financial situation.

In the end, it is essential that you sign your driver's license to indicate you are willing to donate your organs to those in need.

If you don't remember anything else I said today, remember that "no" means "no."

In these examples, the bold phrases prompt the audience to recognize that you are about to make an important point.

Preparing to Participate 8.3
Transitional Devices

Knowledge
List and explain the four transitional devices described in the text.

Application
How does a speaker help the listener by using effective transitions?

SUMMARY

Effective organization is essential to the speech-making process. After reading this chapter, it should be clear that organizing a speech requires a great deal of strategic and *critical thinking*.

The process of organization builds on your *information literacy* and *critical thinking* skills, as it requires you to integrate information into your speech in a logical fashion. As the speaker, you need to think critically about how a particular organizational pattern will best meet your speech objectives. In other words, you must decide which pattern best fits your purpose, your topic, and the needs of your audience.

You should take great care not to overwhelm your audience with too many main points. Instead, focus on the key ideas of the topic and relate them clearly. You should also incorporate transitional devices that help your audience understand and remember the ideas you present. *Ethical communicators* are prepared, and competent communicators are organized.

In the next chapter, we will discuss how to move from an organizational pattern to an outline.

KEY TERMS

oral organizational strategies (117)

chronological pattern (118)

spatial pattern (120)

topical pattern (120)

causal pattern (121)

transitions (122)

transitional devices (122)

internal preview (123)

internal summary (123)

signpost (124)

ADDITIONAL ENGAGEMENT OPPORTUNITIES

Now that you have finished reading the chapter, it is also important to make connections between the course content and your own experiences. These activities will help you understand, apply, analyze, evaluate, or synthesize course concepts. You can use these activities to provide evidence of your preparation for participation in class as well as to plan additional contributions to class discussion. The Civic Engagement Opportunities (CEOs) are designed to help you become more engaged in campus and community life and apply course concepts to important social issues.

1. Watch your favorite television show. Determine if the particular episode was organized using chronological order, spatial order, topical order, or causal order. Give a brief synopsis of the program (give the date and time you watched) and why you believe it is organized in that way. Also, discuss if that particular organization was effective.

2. Watch a political figure express his/her thoughts on C-SPAN or a similar channel. Discuss which pattern of organization was used. Did the speaker use transitional devices? If so, how did the speaker transition to a new topic

Outlining the Presentation

In making a speech one must study three points: first, the means of producing persuasion; second, the language; third, the proper arrangement of the various parts of the speech.

—Aristotle

CHAPTER OBJECTIVES

After reading this chapter, you should be able to:

- Understand the importance of developing an effective outline.
- Develop an effective preparation outline.
- Develop an effective speaking outline.

Colin Powell

By now, if you have been working on your speech as these chapters progressed, you should have a topic, a thesis sentence, relevant supporting material, and an idea of how you will organize your speech. Now, how will you put all of that together?

The importance of developing an effective outline cannot be overstated. The process of outlining allows you to organize your ideas logically, giving you a better picture of the relationships among your ideas. In addition, this process allows you to use your critical thinking skills to refine your ideas, identify where you need additional support, and determine if the body of the speech is balanced. For example, as you write the outline, you can examine the arrangement of your points to determine if they are presented logically. Similarly, the process of outlining allows you to strategically integrate transitions and clearly link the introduction and conclusion. Abbreviated outlines are also useful as memory and delivery aids when you present the speech. A well-developed outline will also reduce your public speaking anxiety. As you learned in Chapter 2, the more prepared you are for the speech, the more confident you will be in presenting your speech to a live audience.

Source Citation:
[1]Kobayashi, K. (2006). Combined effects of note-taking/reviewing on learning and the enhancement through interventions: A meta-analytical review. *Education Psychology, 26,* 459–477.

Another good reason for improving your outlining skills is that doing so can help you earn better grades.[1] For example, for the messages you receive from your reading and study, outlining will help you form a clear picture of the major claims, supporting material, and conclusions offered. In addition, outlining can help you organize and synthesize lectures in an efficient way and help you better prepare for exams. The ability to efficiently organize and synthesize material will also benefit you in whatever career you choose.

As you produce your message, you will develop a detailed preparation outline and a condensed speaking outline.

Preparing to Participate 9.1
Importance of Outlining

Knowledge
Why is outlining important?

Application
Think of a time when you have heard someone present a lecture or a speech. Could you identify the parts of the speech? Was the outline structure clear? If not, how could outlining help the speaker?

Developing a Preparation Outline

In our experience, students are often unsure about when to begin outlining their speech. Simply put, you should begin outlining at the time you start building the speech. Again, this process will allow you to carefully reflect on the relationships among the ideas you will discuss and to identify specific areas for refinement. The outline you develop as you prepare your speech is called a **preparation outline**. The preparation outline is a tool that helps you prepare your speech. It consists of a detailed outline that includes the title, general and specific purpose, organizational pattern, introduction, main points and subpoints, transitions, and references used in the speech. Use the following guidelines as you develop your preparation outline.

Label the Introduction, Body, and Conclusion as Separate Elements

The **introduction**, **body**, and **conclusion** should be labeled as separate elements in your outline. Separating these elements will allow you to see if they are serving their intended functions. Doing so will also help you identify whether you have included all of the elements required by your instructor. In addition, you will be better able to look holistically at your speech to ensure that the introduction leads clearly into the body and that the conclusion effectively brings the speech to a close.

Use a Consistent Pattern of Symbols

A common approach to outlining is to use Roman numerals to identify the introduction (I), body (II), and conclusion (III) so that the outline is organized around the three major parts of the speech. In this system, you identify main points with capital letters (i.e., A, B, C) and subpoints with numbers (i.e., 1, 2, 3). Depending on how you develop your claims, you may even include sub-subpoints (identified with lower case letters, a, b, c). In this approach to outlining, you use subpoints and sub-subpoints to elaborate on your main points. As a result, main points, subpoints, and sub-subpoints move from general to specific content. As you outline these elements, make sure to use a consistent pattern of indentation. For example:

I. **Introduction**
   A. Attention getter
   B. Relevance statement
   C. Credibility statement
   D. Thesis statement
   E. Preview statement

II. **Body**
   A. Main point
      1. Subpoint
         a. Sub-subpoint
         b. Sub-subpoint
      2. Subpoint
   B. Main point
      1. Subpoint
      2. Subpoint
         a. Sub-subpoint
         b. Sub-subpoint

III. **Conclusion**
   A. Summary of main points
   B. Action statement (persuasive speech only)
   C. Memorable close

Keep in mind that the outline presents a visual image of the relationships among the ideas in your speech. Notice that this outlining format uses the principle of **subordination**, which is the ranking of ideas from the most to the least important. As a result, the relative importance of your ideas can be determined by examining the structure of the outline (the importance increases as you move to the left).

You should also notice that the points are organized with the principle of **coordination** in mind. When you follow the process of coordination, you arrange the points of the speech into successive levels, with the points on the same level having the same importance and grammatical structure. Examining the structure of your speech this way will help you determine whether your ideas fit together in a logical fashion.

It should be noted that there are many formats available for outlining. Therefore, you should check with your instructor to determine the format you are to follow for this class. 🖳 In Media Interaction 9.1, you can see how the main ideas of the speech can be enumerated with Roman numerals rather than the three parts of the speech (Introduction, Body, Conclusion) as we illustrate in this text with our example speeches. It is important to note that both approaches are acceptable, but that for clarity, consistency of approach is crucial.

Include Transitions

As noted in Chapter 8, *transitions* are critical to effective speech making. Include transitions throughout the outline where appropriate (e.g., between the introduction and body, between main points, as well as between the body and conclusion). As you will see in the sample outline included in this chapter, transitions are labeled and inserted into the outline where they will be used during the speech. One advantage of writing out your transitions is that you can quickly determine if you have overused a word or phrase (e.g., "My next point is"). You should also carefully examine the outline to determine which claims you could clarify by adding an internal summary and/or preview.

Integrate Supporting Material

Once you have established your main points, you can then integrate relevant *supporting materials* as subpoints and sub-subpoints. As you insert supporting materials, carefully balance the types of support used for each claim (e.g., statistics, testimony, personal examples, and so on). If you find you are relying too much on a particular type of support or not using enough support for your claims, you can easily modify the presentation.

Provide a List of References

It is important that you follow the *information literacy* guidelines (presented in Chapter 8) for citing your sources orally in the speech. Citing sources accurately boosts your credibility and increases the likelihood that your audience will take your claims seriously. Your outline should contain a list of references you consulted in preparing your speech. Two of the more popular formats for citing sources in the communication discipline are those developed by the Modern

Language Association (MLA) and the American Psychological Association (APA). It is your responsibility to check with your instructor to determine the format she or he prefers. A sample of how to cite sources using the APA style is provided in Figure 9.1.

Use Complete Sentences

State your ideas in the preparation outline in complete sentences rather than as questions or short phrases. Fully stating your ideas will help you and your instructor evaluate the overall merits of the speech. In addition, using complete sentences to introduce your supporting material will allow you to assess the credibility of your sources and determine the extent to which you are fully citing them. In Chapter 7, we talked about including key information in an oral citation such as author credentials, source, and date of publication. For example, in our sample speech, the first oral citation states, *The author Alan Baker, in his book,* The Gladiator, *published in 2001, makes the connection between the ancient Roman games and our culture today.* This citation is included in the outline so that the speaker remembers to cite it orally in the speech.

Media
Interaction 9.2

Style Wizard

Log on to the Internet and visit the following website: http://www.stylewizard.com/

1. What do these various styles have in common?
2. How are they different?
3. Why is it important to follow one of these styles?

The sample reference list provided below should be used as a guide. It contains examples of the most common sources used in speeches. Notations are provided in the right-hand margin to point out features in each entry. Students who wish additional background should purchase a copy of the *Publication Manual of the American Psychological Association*, Sixth Edition.

References

Baxter, L. A. (1987). Cognition and communication in the relationship process. In R. Burnett, P. McGhee, & D. Clarke (Eds.), *Accounting for relationships: Explanation, representation, and knowledge* (pp. 192–212). London: Methuen.

Conville, R. L. (1991). *Relational transitions: The evolution of personal relationships.* New York: Praeger.

Brown, P., & Levinson, S. (1987). *Politeness: Some universals in language usage.* Cambridge: Cambridge University Press.

Fidelity Investments. (1993). *Fidelity Brokerage Services handbook* (5th ed.). Boston: Author.

Cappella, J. N. (1994). *The management of conversational interaction in adults and infants* (2nd ed.). Thousand Oaks, CA: Sage.

Chapter in edited book
- Last name of author, then initials
- Initials of editors, then last names
- No quotation marks
- Only first word in chapter is in caps
- First word and word following a colon are capitalized for book title

Book by one author

Book by two or more authors
- Ampersand between names
- Place of publication before publisher

Corporate author

Book edition other than the first

(continued)

FIGURE 9.1
APA Style Guide

Journal article, one author
- No quotation marks around title
- No pp. for pages

Bekerian, D. A. (1993). In search of the typical eyewitness. *American Psychologist,
50*, 574–576.

Journal article, two or more authors

Klimoski, R., & Palmer, S. (1993). The ADA and the hiring process in organizations.
Consulting Psychology Journal: Practice and Research, 45(2), 10–36.

Editor or Compiler

Fox, R. W., & Lears, T. J. J. (Eds.). (1993). *The power of culture: Critical essays in
American history.* Chicago: University of Chicago Press.

Encyclopedia entry

Bergmann, P. G. (1993). Relativity. In *The new encyclopedia Britannica* (Vol. 26, pp.
501–508). Chicago: Encyclopedia Britannica.

Online journal
(When electronic and print versions are identical)

Heimlich, R., & Anderson, W. (2001, August). Development at and beyond the
urban fringe: Impacts on agriculture. [Electronic version]. *Agricultural Outlook, 5,*
15–18.

Online journal
(When electronic and print versions differ)

Haskins, R. (2001). Giving is not enough: Work and work supports are reducing
poverty. *Brookings Review, 19*, 13–15. Retrieved August 10, 2001, from http://www.
brook.edu/PUB/REVIEW/REVDES.HTM

Online journal
(Not otherwise available in print)

Fine, K. (2001, June). The question of realism. *Philosopher's Imprint, 1*, Article 0001a.
Retrieved August 10, 2001, from http://www.umich.edu/~philos/Imprint/
browse.html

Articles or abstracts from
Electronic databases
- Used to cite full-text articles or abstracts from fee-based article databases such as Academic Universe (Lexis-Nexis), JSTOR, and PsycINFO

Brown, S. G., & David, S. (2000). Putting on a new face on self-sufficiency programs. *American Journal of Public Health, 90*, 1383–1384. Retrieved August 10,
2001, from PsycINFO database.

Daily newspaper, no author

New drug appears to sharply cut risk of death from heart failure. (1993, July 15). *The
Washington Post*, p. A12.

Daily newspaper,
discontinuous pages

Schwartz, J. (1993, September 30). Obesity affects economic, social status. *The
Washington Post*, pp. A1, A4.

Weekly newspaper article, Letter
to the editor

Berkowitz, A. D. (2001, November 24). How to tackle the problem of student drinking [Letter to the editor]. *The Chronicle of Higher Education*, p. B20.

Magazine article

Posner, M. I. (1993, October 29). Seeing the mind. *Science, 262*, 673–674.

Television broadcast

Crystal, L. (Executive Producer). (1993, October 11). *The MacNeil/Lehrer news hour*
[Television broadcast]. New York and Washington, DC: Public Broadcasting
Service.

Motion Picture

Scorsese, M. (Producer), & Longergan, K. (Writer/Director). (2000). *You can count
on me* [Motion picture]. United States: Paramount Pictures.

Audio Recording

Costa, P. T., Jr. (Speaker). (1988*). Personality, continuity, and changes of adult life*
(Cassette Recording No. 207-433-88A-B). Washington, DC: American
Psychological Association.

Unpublished paper

Felmlee, D. H., & Greenberg, S. F. (1996, August). *The couple as a dynamic system:
A formal model.* Paper presented at the annual meeting of the American
Sociological Association, New York, NY.

Brochure

Research and Training Center on Independent Living. (1993).*Guidelines for reporting and
writing about people with disabilities* (4th ed.). [Brochure]. Lawrence, KS: Author.

Interview

B. Nelson. (personal communication, May 6, 1996).

Internet Source
- Use n.d. (no date) when a publication date is not available

Vogler, E. (n.d.). *Using technology in the classroom.* Retrieved October 1, 2001, from
www.tech.com/swiz/htm

As you look over your outline, make sure that you have adapted your material for your specific audience. In other words, build in phrases, claims, supporting materials, etc. that your audience can easily understand and relate to in order to engage them fully. These audience relevance points will provide a compelling reason for listening and maintain their interest throughout the speech (see examples in the sample preparation outline).

Preparing to Participate 9.2
Preparation Outline

Knowledge
What is a preparation outline?
List the seven guidelines for developing a preparation outline.

Application
Why is it important to use a consistent pattern of labeling and symbols?
Why do you think it is important to write the preparation outline in complete sentences?

Sample Preparation Outline with Commentary

The following outline for an eight-minute informative speech illustrates how to apply the principles just discussed. The comments in the margin are presented to help guide you through the essential steps in outlining a speech.

Coliseum Speech. Because of the ravages of time, the Coliseum is just a shell of what was probably the greatest arena of the ancient world.

Roman Coliseum

I. Introduction

A. *Attention Getter:* Imagine yourself being ushered up a dark hallway and into a huge, outdoor theatre. Here you are greeted by 50,000 screaming spectators and one man—crazy for your death, hungry for the thought of ripping you apart limb from limb. You and Blood Thirsty are the only ones inside an arena encompassed by a 15-foot wall, and the 50,000 people are waiting for you to die.

B. *Relevance Statement:* From professional football and basketball games to the sporting events at ISU's Redbird Arena, much of our culture is influenced by the success of one great sports arena built nearly 2000 years ago. The author Alan Baker, in his book, *The Gladiator*, published in 2001, makes the connection between the ancient Roman games and our culture today. Our own athletes, he states, " . . . are merely the pale echoes of the ancient fighters . . . [they] display their skill and aggression before thousands of screaming spectators, with millions more watching on television. This is exactly what happened in the ancient world."

C. *Credibility:* As a history major focused on Roman studies, I have always been enamored with the stories surrounding the Coliseum. Further, a tour of Ancient Rome this past summer intensified my horror and fascination with this great monument.

D. *Thesis:* To truly understand the historical impact the Coliseum has had on civilization, it is important to learn of the architectural wonders of the Coliseum, the terror of the Roman Games, and the present plans for its restoration.

E. *Preview:* Therefore, [show transparency] we will first lay the foundation by describing its design and construction; next, live through a day at the games; and finally, learn of the present plans to restore and renovate this ancient monument to its original glory.

Transition: To begin, we will lay the foundation by describing its design and construction.

II. Body

A. First, the Coliseum's construction will be discussed.
   1. According to John Pearson, acclaimed historian and author of *Arena: The Story of the Coliseum*, published in 1973, the Emperor Vespasian, to curry the favor of the Roman people, commissioned the construction of the Coliseum.
   2. Considering the games were held 1900 years ago, the construction was considered pure genius.

   a. The outdoor theatre boasted 80 entrances, with a design so incredibly pragmatic that each was equipped with a numbered staircase, ensuring the simultaneous exit of about 50,000 individuals in three minutes flat. Our sports stadiums today cannot even accomplish this feat.

b. Just as we look down from gymnasium bleachers, spectators would look down upon the wooden arena floor. However, the Coliseum's floor was covered with sand, which served to soak up large quantities of blood. The floor also concealed a labyrinth of tunnels, trapdoors, and a complicated system of chains and pulleys, similar to our modern-day elevators.

Transition: Now that we have laid the foundation of the Coliseum's construction, let us live through a day at the Roman Games.

B. A Day at the Games can be compared to a day watching football at the Redbird Arena.

1. As ISU students, part of our tuition pays for Redbird Arena. However, at the Coliseum's inception, it was a Roman citizen's right to attend the games free of charge. And just as we are treated to semesters of games, it was not uncommon for emperors to treat their subjects to many months of games.

2. The mornings began with fights between wild animals. One battle involved a bull and a panther, each at the end of a chain. They could barely reach other, and they were forced to tear each other apart piece by piece. Lions would be matched against tigers and bears pitted against bulls.

3. Lunchtime executions followed. The scholar Baker, as cited earlier, states that the infliction of pain was an essential part of punishment in ancient Rome. Therefore, common methods included crucifixions, being burned alive, and being thrown to wild beasts. In fact, Emperor Constantine would order molten lead to be poured down the condemned's throats.

4. The best attraction was saved for the afternoon: gladiatorial combat. The following video clip is taken from the 2000 epic film, *Gladiator*, in which Russell Crowe stars. As stated earlier, notice the concealed trapdoors in the arena floor. [Show video clip.]

Transition: Now that we have lived through the terror of the Roman games, let us learn of the present plans to restore and renovate this ancient monument to its original glory.

C. The present life of the Coliseum is undergoing change.

1. After 300 years of this publicly accepted entertainment, a monk named Telemachus ran into the arena, screaming for them to stop. However, the mob was not to be cheated of their entertainment, and he was torn to pieces.

   a. Although gladiatorial combat was subsequently banned, the battles and executions involving wild beasts took another 100 years to end.

   b. Stones were taken from the Coliseum to construct other buildings during the Middle Ages, and the inner arena, as shown here [show transparency] became overgrown with weeds and vegetation.

2. Recently, [show transparency] the National Geographic website reported in July of 2001 that a restoration project is underway to reinstate the Coliseum, which is located near the center of modern Rome.

   a. It will take eight years and cost 18 million dollars.

   b. It will also allow international tourists to attend Greek plays and gladiatorial exhibitions.

Subpoints and sub-subpoints are shown by Arabic numerals and lower case letters.

This transition indicates that the speaker is moving from the first to the second main point.

Again, notice how the speaker attempts to relate the topic to the audience's experiences.

Notice the speaker's shortened oral citation for this source.

Video clips often make for excellent presentation aids. Given the time constraints of this speech, this clip is approximately 45 seconds long.

Take a closer look at the pattern of subordination in this section. Subpoint 1 establishes a key historical event leading to the demise of the games.

Because sub-subpoints a and b expand that idea, they are subordinated to subpoint 1.

Again, the speaker uses a presentation aid to help the audience visualize what she is discussing.

Notice how the speaker uses a quote to transition from the body to the conclusion.

Transition: Once restored, it will encompass, as historian Dr. Alison Futrell states in her 1997 book, *Blood in the Arena*, "all the glory and doom of the Roman Empire."

III. Conclusion

A. Thesis/Summary: In many ways, the Coliseum has influenced the development of civilization and will likely do so for years to come. The Coliseum's construction was truly genius, bearing witness to the wealth of the Roman Empire. The games, unlike those at Redbird Arena, served bloodshed and agony, in the form of wild beasts, executions, and gladiators. Hopefully, the restoration of the Coliseum will see much less bloodshed.

B. Memorable Close: To quote the 7th century historian and monk, the Venerable Bede, in his famous *Ecclesiastical History of the English People*, "While the Coliseum stands, Rome shall stand; when the Coliseum falls, Rome shall fall; when Rome falls, the world shall fall."

Summarizing the main points of the speech will help your audience remember what you said.

A compelling quote is one of the rhetorical devices you can use to conclude the speech in a memorable fashion.

This is the speaker's list of references. Often, the references are listed on a separate page. Notice too that the speaker used APA style to cite her sources. Make sure to check with your instructor to determine what format you are required to use for references

References

Auguet, R. (1998). *Cruelty and civilization: The Roman games*. New York: Barnes & Noble.

Baker, A. (2001). *The gladiator: The secret history of Rome's warrior slaves*. New York: St. Martin's Press.

Bede, V. (1849). *The Venerable Bede's ecclesiastical history of the English people*. London: H. G. Bohn.

The Coliseum on Eliki. (n.d.) *The Coliseum*. Retrieved July 20, 2002 from http://www.eliki.com/coliseum/

Core Tour Europe 2003. (2002). *Coliseum. Sponsored by Saint Joseph's College*. Retrieved July 22, 2002 from http://www.saintjoe.edu/~mjoakes/europe/images/photos_01/coliseum.jpg

Futrell, A. (1997). *Blood in the arena: The spectacle of Roman power*. Austin: University of Texas Press.

National Geographic News. (2001, June 29). *Rome Coliseum being restored for wider public viewing*. Retrieved July 22, 2002 from http://news.nationalgeographic.com/news/2001/06/0625_wirecoliseum.html

Pearson, J. (1973). *Arena: The story of the Coliseum*. London: Thames & Hudson.

Wick, D. (Producer), & Scott, R. (Director). (2000). *Gladiator* [Motion picture]. United States: Dreamworks Pictures and Universal Pictures.

Previewing Your Main Points. Carla previews the main points of her speech about the Roman Coliseum with the help of a presentation aid

Developing a Speaking Outline

One challenge that many beginning public speakers face is how to convert the preparation outline into an effective **speaking outline**. A speaking outline is a brief outline that helps you remember

Critical Interaction 9.1
Outline Formats

How would our preparation outline on the Roman Coliseum look different if it followed the format (using Roman numerals for each main point) provided in Media Interaction 9.1 for this chapter? How would the main points be enumerated? How would this change the subpoints? Would this format change the content of the speech?

key points as you are speaking. The speaking outline also frequently contains **delivery notes** that remind you when to adjust your rate, tone, movement, and so on. Although this skeletal outline may seem difficult to use initially, with practice you will become very adept at using these brief notes. Using a speaking outline might also benefit your speech grade because you will not be as tempted to simply read to the audience—as might be the case if you speak from a full-sentence preparation outline.

As you prepare your speaking outline, keep the following suggestions in mind:

- Initially, you should follow the same framework used in the preparation outline. This will allow you to track exactly where you are in the speech at any given moment.
- In addition, it is important that your outline be legible. Trying to speak from messy, hard-to-read notes can be extremely frustrating. We instruct our students to type out the outline using large fonts and generous margins to ensure the document is readable from a short distance.
- It is also advisable to keep the outline as brief as possible. As previously mentioned, this will force you to establish eye contact with your audience and will prevent you from reading to your audience. The speaking outline should incorporate key words that capture the essence of your ideas and help prompt you for full thoughts when you are looking down at your notes.
- Finally, you can include delivery notes in the speaking outline. These notes will provide cues that will help you control the tempo, emphasis, and overall pace of your speech. Delivery cues are words and phrases such as *pause, eye contact*, and *gesture* that cue you to alter your verbal and/or nonverbal delivery of the speech at specific points. As you practice the speech, pay particular attention to places where altering the delivery might enhance the effectiveness of the presentation. Your speaking outline might also contain delivery cues that help you pronounce difficult words or names. These cues will help you ensure that you deliver the speech the way you want while maintaining connection with the audience.

Although at first you may feel that you will give a better speech by using a full-sentence preparation outline, our experience suggests otherwise. Indeed, we find that the most dynamic and compelling speakers are those who actively engage the audience rather than read directly from manuscript. As you gain more speaking experience, you will become more comfortable using a speaking outline, and you will discover exactly what types of comments you need to include in your outlines and what elements you can leave out. As you prepare for your speech, make sure to practice with the speaking outline.

Preparing to Participate 9.3
Speaking Outline

Knowledge
What is a speaking outline?
List the four suggestions from the text for developing a speaking outline.

Application
What is the difference between a speaking outline and a preparation outline? Why is it necessary to do both? What happens if you put too much information in your speaking outline?

Sample Speaking Outline with Commentary

The following outline for our Coliseum speech illustrates how to transform a preparation outline into a speaking outline. The comments in the margin are presented to help clarify this process.

It is critical that you establish eye contact with the entire audience as you begin your speech. This note reminds the speaker to do just that.

I. Introduction

EYE CONTACT

A. AG: Imagine yourself . . .
B. Rel: Redbird Arena/Today's athletes (Baker, 2001)
C. Cred: History major/Tour of Rome
D. Thesis: To truly understand . . . architecture, terror, restoration
E. Preview: [Transparency #1] Lay foundation, live through day, learn present plans

Notice the speaker's use of abbreviation for key phrases. You should develop your own shorthand for key ideas. Again, these notes should be designed to help jog your memory and you should be speaking rather than reading to the audience.

The inclusion of transitions in the speaking outline ensures that you won't forget them.

PAUSE

Transition: To begin, we will lay the foundation by describing its design and construction.

II. Body
A. Construction
  1. Vespasian (Pearson, 1973)

Your speaking outline should contain delivery notes specifically tailored to your needs. In this case, the speaker felt it important to pause before launching into the first main point of the speech.

2. Construction "pure genius"
   a. 80 entrances/numbered staircase simultaneous exit
   b. Sand floor soak up blood/labyrinth/pulleys

PAUSE

Transition: Now that we have laid the foundation of the Coliseum's construction, let us live through a day at the Roman Games.
  B. Redbird Arena
  1. Free of charge
  2. Wild animals (Lions v. tigers, bears v. bulls)

HAND GESTURE

  3. Lunchtime executions (crucifixion, burned alive, wild beasts, molten lead) (Baker, 2001)
  4. Gladiator combat [Video clip]

PAUSE

Transition: Now that we have lived through the terror of the Roman games, let us learn of the present plans to restore and renovate this ancient monument to its original glory.
  C. Present life
  1. Telemachus
     a. 100 years to end
     b. Stones taken/overgrown with weeds and vegetation [Transparency #2]
  2. Restoration project (National Geographic, 2001) [Transparency #3]
     a. 8 years/18 million dollars
     b. Greek plays and gladiatorial exhibitions

PAUSE

Transition: Once restored, it will encompass, as historian Dr. Alison Futreall states in her 1997 book, *Blood in the Arena*, "all the glory and doom of the Roman Empire."

III. Conclusion

EYE CONTACT

  A. Thesis/Summary: Influenced civilization/truly genius/bloodshed and agony

HAND GESTURE—BE SUBTLE

  B. Memorable Close: Venerable Bede – "While the Coliseum stands, Rome shall stand; when the Coliseum falls, Rome shall fall; when Rome falls, the world shall fall."

As with the preparation outline, the speaking outline is clearly divided into an introduction, body, and conclusion. The speaking outline also uses the same numbering system as the preparation outline.

Notice how the speaker includes key source information in the speaking outline. Your instructor may allow you to include complete quotes in your speaking outline. Make sure to check with your instructor to ensure that you are meeting all of her or his requirements.

The visual representation of fights between wild animals is something this speaker wanted to stress. You can see that she included a note to make a specific hand gesture as she explained this concept.

Notice the speaker's notes regarding the use of presentation aids.

Although abbreviated, the speaking outline contains enough detail to include all essential elements of the speech.

Again, the speaker includes a reminder to maintain eye contact with the audience during the conclusion.

Using a Speaking Outline. In her speaking outline, Carla gave herself a reminder to use a hand gesture at the appropriate time.

Critical Interaction 9.2
Speaking Outlines

From the preparation outline for either the Tornado or the Delta Blues speech found in the appendix, write a speaking outline on note cards. Be sure to follow the guidelines provided in this chapter. Use the following template to help you write your notes.

I. **Introduction**
   A. Attention Getter
   B. Relevance of topic to audience
   C. Credibility
   D. Thesis/Central Idea
   E. Preview

Transition

II. **Body**
   A. First Main Point
      1. Development/Support
      2. Development/Support
      3. If necessary

Transition

   B. Second Main Point
      1. Development/Support
      2. Development/Support
      3. If necessary

Transition

   C. Third Main Point
      1. Development/Support
      2. Development/Support
      3. If necessary

III. **Conclusion**
   A. Thesis/Summary
   B. Memorable Close

SUMMARY

It should be clear that an outline is important in both preparing and delivering a speech. The process of outlining pulls together the *information literacy* and *critical thinking* skills discussed throughout this text, allowing you to carefully scrutinize both the ideas and the supporting materials you are discussing. As you develop the preparation outline, remember to identify key elements of the speech, use a consistent pattern of symbols, include transitions, integrate supporting materials, and provide a list of references. The preparation outline should be written in complete sentences and should include clearly identified sections for the introduction, body, and conclusion.

A speaking outline should be used as a memory and delivery aid when you present the speech. The speaking outline follows the same general form and principles as the preparation outline, but is written in key words rather than complete sentences. In addition, the speaking outline may include delivery notes that cue you to control the tempo, emphasis, and overall pace of your presentation. In the next chapter, we will discuss strategies for beginning and ending the presentation.

KEY TERMS

preparation outline (130)

introduction (131)

body (131)

conclusion (131)

subordination (132)

coordination (132)

speaking outline (138)

delivery notes (139)

ADDITIONAL ENGAGEMENT OPPORTUNITIES

Now that you have finished reading the chapter, it is also important to make connections between the course content and your own experiences. These activities will help you understand, apply, analyze, evaluate, or synthesize course concepts. You can use these activities to provide evidence of your preparation for participation in class as well as to plan additional contributions to class discussion. The Civic Engagement Opportunities (CEOs) are designed to help you become more engaged in campus and community life and apply course concepts to important social issues.

1. The text gives many suggestions for constructing an outline. Pretend that you are the teacher for the day. Create an outline of this chapter (or choose another chapter from the book) that will aid in your lesson.

2. Outlines are used in various academic settings. Think of a time when you use or will use outlines outside of academia. Provide an explanation.

3. Select an article on an important civic or political issue in a recent campus, local, or national newspaper. Construct a speaking outline of the article using the guidelines discussed in this chapter.

Beginning and Ending the Presentation

It's quite simple, say what you have to say and when you come to a sentence with a grammatical ending, sit down!

—Winston Churchill

CHAPTER OBJECTIVES

After reading this chapter, you should be able to:

- Understand the importance of introductions and conclusions.
- Develop an introduction by planning an effective attention getter, relevance statement, credibility statement, thesis, and preview.
- Develop a conclusion by planning an effective summary statement and memorable close.

Michelle Obama

Source Citation:
[1] Buzan, T. (1976). *Use both sides of your brain.* New York: E. P. Dutton.

See also

Crano, W. D. (1977). Primacy versus recency in retention of information and opinion change. *The Journal of Social Psychology, 101,* 87–96

Lund, F. H. (1925). The psychology of belief: IV. The Law of primacy in persuasion. *Journal of Abnormal and Social Psychology, 20,* 183–191

Trenholm, S. (1989). *Persuasion and social influence.* Englewood Cliffs, NJ: Prentice-Hall.

Your roommate, whose car is in the shop, calls you on your cell phone as you leave school and asks you to stop by the grocery store to pick up a few items. You are instructed to get Gatorade, frozen pizza, toothpaste, Ramen Noodles, deodorant, peanut butter, shampoo, and bread. You don't have pen or paper handy, but you think you'll remember the things on the list. When you get to the store, you can remember only a few of the items. Which ones do you think you are most likely to remember?

Chances are, you will remember the first and last items on the list, but not the ones in the middle. This is known as the **primacy/recency effect**, which explains that people pay more attention to and remember information that is presented first and last.[1] Additionally, we tend to remember things that are most relevant to our needs. For example, as you enter the grocery store, you realize you are hungry and are not likely to forget the pizza. This tendency to remember the first, last, and most relevant items is a compelling reason for producing effective introductions and conclusions in your presentations.

Importance of Introductions and Conclusions

It is important that speakers prepare their audience to listen to and remember their message. As listeners or consumers of information, we often have a great deal on our minds and can easily become distracted if we are not prepared or motivated to listen to another speaker. Newscasters know this all too well. Before going to a commercial break, they often "tease" the audience with what news or information is coming up next. This allows you, the consumer, to decide whether you want to stay tuned.

As speakers, we need to realize that the first and last impressions we make on our audience will ultimately determine whether we accomplish our goals. We need to understand what it takes to prepare an audience to listen to and remember our presentations.

As we discussed in Chapter 6 (Analyzing Your Audience), there are several ways to connect content to the needs and interests of an audience. Learning about constructing effective introductions and conclusions will also help us to make connections with the audience so that they learn from or are influenced by our message. We'll start with how to begin the presentation.

Preparing Your Audience to Listen.
Journalists such as CNN's Campbell Brown use a technique called a "tease" to keep the attention of their audiences.

Preparing to Participate 10.1
Importance of Introductions and Conclusions

Knowledge
Discuss why introductions and conclusions are important.

Application
In what ways does the introduction prepare your audience to listen to your speech?
What are the implications if you do not prepare them to listen?

Beginning the Presentation

The beginning of your presentation—the introduction—is an opportunity for you to prepare your audience to listen to your topic. Have you ever been frustrated by an instructor who dives into a lesson before you are ready to listen? Perhaps you are upset by something that happened just before class and your mind is not ready to hear specific details about the American Revolution just yet. Remember the communication process model from Chapter 1? This scenario is an example of internal interference. If, as a speaker, you realize that this is likely to happen, you can develop strategies to overcome the interference.

What could your instructor have done to help you transition from your distractions to your lesson? There are several easy ways to prepare an audience to listen. It is important to know that audiences will want answers to the following questions:

- What's in it for me?
- Why should I listen to you about this topic?
- What can I expect to hear about the topic?

An effective introduction will answer these questions, motivating the audience to listen. Thus, an introduction should accomplish the following goals:

- Capture the audience's *attention*
- Establish the *relevance* of your topic to your audience
- Confirm your speaker *credibility*
- *Preview* the body of the presentation

Capturing Attention

The first task you must accomplish in your introduction is to convince your audience to listen to you. To accomplish this, begin with an **attention getter**. An attention getter is a strong opening statement that uses some kind of creative device to capture your audience's attention and motivate them to listen. It is the very first thing that you say in the presentation. In other words, you would not want to get up in front of your audience and say, "Hi my name is ___, and my speech is about ___" even though as you look at your outline, this information is most likely included at the top of the page. The first words you say should follow some strategy to get your audience to stop thinking about their evening plans or the test they just took. There are several creative strategies to choose from.

Ask a Rhetorical Question A **rhetorical question** is one that is posed for the purpose of getting your audience to think about, but not state, the answer. An effective rhetorical question will instantly get the audience to consider how they would answer the question. In doing so, you have prepared your audience to listen to your speech. Some rhetorical questions are, of course, more effective than others. It is not as easy as asking, "Have you ever thought about (insert your topic)?" You need to give your audience something more specific to think about. For example, you could get your audience to imagine a hypothetical situation ("What would happen if . . . ?") to prepare them for your topic. You could also ask a series of questions to lead the audience in the

direction you will take with your topic. For example, the following questions are used in our tornado speech outline:

What can hurl automobiles through the air, rip ordinary homes to shreds, defeather chickens, and travel at speeds over 60 mph?

Providing a series of rhetorical questions serves to arouse your audience's curiosity without revealing the topic. With each question, your audience will wonder where you are headed. Perhaps, you could pose a riddle such as, *"What do the following three things have in common?"* Of course, the answer would relate to your topic and command attention.

Provide a Quotation You could also start the presentation with a famous or profound quotation that relates to your topic. ⬚ When attempting to capture attention with quotations, it is important to decide whether to start with the quotation itself or with the name of the source. You have to consider which way would have the strongest impact on the audience. Remember, the goal is to capture attention immediately. For example, in our speech about the blues, the quotation comes first and is followed by the source:

Using Quotations. Sam Phillips, who opened Sun Studios in Memphis, TN in the early 1950s, provides a memorable quote in our Delta Blues speech.

"This is where the soul of man never dies." So says Sun Records founder Sam Phillips . . . the man who discovered and first recorded Elvis Presley, Jerry Lee Lewis, and Johnny Cash.

Start with a Startling Statement Surprise your audience by making a claim that is unimaginable, unusual, or unknown. A dramatic statistic can startle your audience, enticing them to listen. For example, if your topic is communication apprehension, you might begin your speech by saying:

More people are afraid of speaking in public than they are of dying.

As you conduct your research, what claims stand out to you? You might incorporate this information into an attention getter.

Stimulate the Audience's Imagination You could use "imagine if" scenarios to get your audience to put themselves in a position to think about your topic. You could provide descriptive details of what it looks, feels, smells, sounds, or tastes like to be in the context of a situation involving your topic. Our Coliseum speech accomplishes this nicely:

Imagine yourself being ushered up a dark hallway and into a huge, outdoor theatre. Here you are greeted by 50,000 screaming spectators and one man—crazy for your death, hungry for the thought of ripping you apart limb from limb. You and Blood Thirsty are the only ones inside an arena encompassed by a 15-foot wall, and the 50,000 people are waiting for you to die.

Tell a Story We all love a good story. An effective story will use words to evoke a certain emotion (e.g., happy, sad, excited, fearful, angry) in your audience. Your story can be based on something that actually happened, or it could be hypothetical. Real stories could involve a personal connection that the speaker has with the topic and would describe actual events that have taken place. In fact, sharing a personal story can enhance your credibility (which we'll discuss more in just a moment). For example, in a persuasive speech urging audience members to consider becoming live organ donors, the fact that you donated a kidney to a family member would make you qualified to speak on the topic. Your personal experience would compel the audience to listen.

To be effective, hypothetical stories should at least be possible in the minds of the audience. Always reveal to your audience whether your story is truth or fiction. Be sure to tell only those details that are relevant to the topic of your speech. In other words, keep it short but meaningful.

Use Humor Although your audience may find elements of humor in any of the previous strategies, you could tell a joke or begin with a funny statement. Whatever the joke or statement, it must be relevant to the topic and appropriate for the audience and occasion. Humor is risky—what is funny to you may be offensive to your audience. As a result, timing and delivery are quite important if humor is to be effective. There's a reason Tina Fey makes a lot of money.

Refer to a Recent Event Perhaps there is something happening in your community or school that requires that your audience give their attention to your topic. You could also consider national or world events that might have an impact on your audience's motivation to listen to your topic. In this sense, you are taking into account the context (as discussed in Chapter 1—Introduction to Communication) of your presentation to draw attention to your topic.

In short, attention getters should hook your audience immediately and get them to start thinking about your topic. You may even find examples of these strategies as you conduct research for your topic. Be on the lookout for possible attention getters as you look for evidence to support your claims in the body of your speech. Another way to generate ideas for an attention getter is to consider what piques your interest. When watching television, surfing the web, or reading a newspaper article, make note of what captures your attention. Use a similar strategy with your audience.

Incorporating Humor. Comedian Tina Fey is well known for the humorous roles she has played. Humor can be used to engage your audience.

Calvin and Hobbes

CALVIN AND HOBBES ©1989 Watterson. Dist. By UNIVERSAL PRESS SYNDICATE. All rights reserved.

Comic 10.1

1. How does Calvin start his introduction?

2. Is this effective?

3. What rhetorical strategy does Calvin use in the second frame?

Establishing the Relevance of Your Topic to Your Audience

Recall from Chapter 6 on audience analysis that most listeners pay attention if they find the topic personally *relevant*. In other words, a listener wants to know, *"What's in it for me?"* Once you capture an audience's attention, you need to maintain it by answering this concern. This is a two step process. You should indicate to members of the audience why they should listen to your topic. As we discussed in Chapter 5, you should choose a topic that is of general importance—one that is worthy of the time and attention of your audience. At this point in the introduction, you have the burden of clarifying your reason for choosing the topic. Why is it important or relevant? In our example speeches, the speakers assert that tornadoes are deadly and that the blues and the Coliseum have both influenced modern culture.

Once you establish the overall relevance of your topic, you now need to provide a specific **relevance statement** to your audience. Your topic may be of general importance, but how does it relate specifically to your audience or classmates?

As you chose your topic, you were asked to consider your audience's needs and interests. This is where you should address those considerations. You may use information from your audience analysis to connect the topic to your listeners. Be very specific. Ask yourself, *"Does my relevance statement apply to all audiences or specifically to the people I will be addressing?"* For example, if you are giving a persuasive speech on promoting the right to vote, you could say, *"As American citizens, we should all honor our right to vote."* Or, to be more specific to your classmates, you could say, *"As college students between the ages of 18 and 22, this election will be our first opportunity to express our voice in the democratic process. Additionally, in a time of war, we should understand the implications of how the results of this election will ultimately affect our lives."*

Our example outlines make specific references to the intended audience in the following ways. Recall that the audiences for these speeches were composed of first-year college students enrolled in a communication course at a large midwestern university.

Tornado

Illinois rests on the boundary of what tornado researchers call Tornado Alley. This is the area of the country that receives the most tornadoes every year.

Coliseum

From professional football and basketball games to the sporting events at ISU's Redbird Arena, much of our culture is influenced by the success of one great sports arena built nearly 2000 years ago.

Blues

I know many of you are from the Chicago-land area. Through the many books and magazine articles I've read, I've discovered that the world-famous "Chicago Blues" sound owes its origins to Mississippi Delta Blues—since many of those players migrated to Chicago in the 40's and 50's. In fact, the blues classic "Sweet Home Chicago" was written by a Delta musician.

Establishing Speaker Credibility

So now your audience knows why your topic is important, but why should they listen to you? What, if any, personal experience or connection do you have with the topic? Why did you choose it? What makes you an expert worthy of your audience's attention? These were concerns that we asked you to consider as you selected a topic. Now you must provide a **credibility statement** that explains your connection to the topic. For example, our tornado speaker grew up in the heart of Tornado Alley, our Coliseum speaker is a history major, and our blues speaker is a dedicated fan.

Aside from explicitly telling the audience, there are other, more subtle, ways to establish speaker credibility. **Competence** and **character** comprise credibility.[2] If your listeners see that you are prepared, organized, and knowledgeable, you will be considered competent. You will be perceived as possessing good character if you are honest, trustworthy, and have your listeners' best interests in mind. In other words, your audience has to believe not only what you say but how you say it.

If you say you are a fan of the blues, but act like you are bored during your presentation, your credibility will suffer. We'll discuss in more detail how delivery affects your message in Chapter 13.

If you claim expertise in weather phenomena, but are ill prepared or disorganized, you will not be perceived as knowledgeable about tornadoes. (See Chapter 8 on organization strategies.)

Source Citation:
[2] McCroskey, J. C., & Teven, J. J. (1999). Goodwill: A reexamination of the construct and its measurements. *Communication Monographs, 66*, 90–113.

Previewing the Presentation

You have your audience's attention. They know why they should listen. They're convinced that you know what you're talking about. Now, what can they expect to hear? The last part of the introduction is an overview of the content of your presentation. This includes both the *thesis* and *preview statements*. The first step toward accomplishing this goal is to state your thesis.

We have already talked about how to write a thesis statement, which is a major part of your introduction, in Chapter 5. Recall that the **thesis statement** is the framework for the body of your presentation. It reveals the purpose, topic, direction, and main points of your presentation. In doing so, it provides the audience with a preview of what's to come. Once you have stated your thesis, you can then elaborate on the direction of your main points with a **preview statement**. In other words, the preview statement provides a little more detail about each of the main claims before you delve into them. This further allows your audience to anticipate the direction of your speech. For the communication apprehension topic, your preview might look like this:

Thesis Statement:
Communication apprehension can be treated using systematic desensitization, cognitive restructuring, visualization, and skills training.

Preview Statement:
Specifically, I will discuss the mental and physical relaxation techniques used in systematic desensitization, common ways to restructure your negative

thoughts and think more positively about public speaking, and how to master the necessary steps to plan and present a speech.

Here's another example from our Delta Blues Speech:

Thesis Statement:
The Mississippi Delta Blues was epitomized by the music of three men: Charley Patton, Son House, and Robert Johnson.

Preview Statement:
First, we'll examine Charley Patton, one of the earliest Delta musicians; next Son House, his friend and protégé; and finally Robert Johnson, a man shrouded in myth and legend.

Preparing to Participate 10.2
Goals of an Introduction

Knowledge
Name and explain the four goals for an introduction.

Application
Is it always necessary to include each element of the introduction? What might happen if a speaker leaves out the attention getter, the relevance statement, or the credibility statement?

Recommendations for Integrating Elements of the Introduction

So, how does this all fit together as you prepare or produce your message? Here are our recommended steps:

- The *thesis sentence* is the first one you write.
- The *body* of the presentation is the first section you develop.
- The *introduction* is developed after the body.
- The *attention getter* is the first thing you say.
- The thesis sentence provides the framework of the presentation and comes right before the *preview.*
- The preview is the last sentence of the introduction, provides further direction with the speech, and leads into the body of the presentation.

Our final suggestion is that you refer to our example introductions provided in our tornado, Coliseum, and blues speeches, which can be found in the appendix. These will allow you to see how all of these elements flow together and prepare an audience to listen.

Ending the Presentation

In the last few chapters, we have talked about the steps in the speech-writing process. We've provided information about choosing topics, locating support, and organizing and outlining your ideas. Once you have constructed the body of your presentation and have written your introduction, you are ready to finalize your speech. You're almost there, but to make your audience remember your message, you need a strong ending. Remember the primacy/recency effect? We have a tendency to remember the most recent thing we hear. Thus, an effective conclusion will summarize the key points of the presentation as well as provide a memorable close. The next sections will address the goals of the conclusion in an informative speech. There is one additional step for persuasive speeches, the action step, which we will address in Chapter 14.

Providing a Summary

In the introduction, you prepared your audience to listen by previewing the content of your message. Once you present your information or argument, you need to prepare your audience for the end of your message. This is accomplished by providing a **summary**, or review, of your main claims.

You will want to give your audience a hint that the summary is coming by **signposting** the end of your presentation using terms such as *finally, in closing,* or *to summarize.* At this point, you will rephrase your thesis statement using the past tense. If the information you presented is complicated, you might also want to go over the key points you want your audience to remember. This is your final opportunity to summarize the most important information in your presentation. In doing so, ask yourself, *"What specifically do I want my audience to get out of my presentation?"* keeping in mind the purpose (to inform or persuade) of your speech. This should be included in the summary. Here are the example summaries for our tornado and Coliseum speeches.

Tornadoes

In this speech I have explored the key factors that cause tornadoes to develop, how researchers classify types of tornadoes, and odd occurrences that may be associated with tornadoes.

Coliseum

In many ways, the Coliseum has influenced the development of civilization and will likely do so for years to come. The Coliseum's construction was truly genius, bearing witness to the wealth of the Roman Empire. The games, unlike those at Redbird Arena, served bloodshed and agony, in the form of wild beasts, executions, and gladiators. Hopefully, the restoration of the Coliseum will see much less bloodshed.

Providing a Memorable Close

The last statement you make indicates in a powerful way that your presentation is complete and should be remembered. How would you do that?

Anything you can use as an attention getter can also be used as a **memorable close**. You could refer back to your attention getter at this time. If you provided a quote at the beginning, you might want to wait until this point to reveal who said it. You might want to refer back to the consequences of your startling statement. You could answer your riddle. You could disclose information about your story. You could reveal the punch line to your joke. In other words, the attention getter and the memorable close could serve as the *bookends* of your speech. For example, our blues speech makes reference to the attention getter as the audience is reminded of the soul of man.

Delta Blues

If you keep your eyes and ears open you may hear one of your musical heroes cover a Delta Blues song or list these musicians as an inspiration. The roots of modern American music run deep. Muddy Waters once sang, "The blues had a baby and they named it rock and roll." Charley, Son, and Robert may no longer be with us, but they left us a great musical legacy— where the soul of man never dies.

Our Coliseum speech, on the other hand, uses a new strategy altogether by quoting the Venerable Bede.

Coliseum

To quote the 7th century historian and monk, the Venerable Bede, in his famous Ecclesiastical History of the English People, "While the Coliseum stands, Rome shall stand; when the Coliseum falls, Rome shall fall; when Rome falls, the world shall fall."

The purpose of this last statement is to emphasize the end of your speech. If done effectively, your audience will know with certainty that you are finished without your even having to tell them so. In other words, if you feel compelled to say, "Thank you, I'm through!" then perhaps your close was not as strong as it should have been.

Preparing to Participate 10.3
Goals of a Conclusion

Knowledge
Name and explain the two goals for a conclusion.

Application
How does the conclusion help the audience to understand and remember the speech?
How might the audience feel if the speaker neglects to provide an effective conclusion?

Critical Interaction 10.1
Matching Outline

Directions: Match each of the following statements to the appropriate goal of an introduction or conclusion. (Speech adapted from Greg Fairbank, Com 110 student at Illinois State University.)

Attention Getter _____

A. *I've read many books on war, from novels to memoirs, and have been a fan since I was a kid. I was first introduced to this genre by reading* All Quiet on the Western Front, *and since then I've read many more. Also, I've seen several of the movies that are based on the books, as well as many Hollywood war films.*

Relevance Statement _____

B. *As you can see, J.R.R. Tolkien's horrific experiences in World War I affected him very deeply. He never forgot the "animal horror" of what he saw, and his memories would be represented in the fantasy books that he would go on to write. In addition, the aftermath of the war Tolkien created in his books is closely related to the outcomes that he himself felt following World War I.*

Credibility Statement _____

C. *First, we'll look at Tolkien's experiences in war; next, we'll discuss how his memories of war are present in his writing; and finally, how the outcome of war in the stories Tolkien created parallel the outcomes he saw following World War I.*

Thesis Statement _____

D. *Imagine yourself cowering inside a filthy trench that was meant to shelter the living, but instead houses the dead and dying. You haven't eaten or slept for days, and the only thing that you can do to cope with all of this misery is to pray that you will live to see the next day. This is the life of a soldier during one of the most horrific wars ever fought: World War I.*

Preview Statement _____

E. *To understand the everlasting impact war has on a soldier, we can look at World War I veteran J.R.R. Tolkien and examine how his experiences in war influenced his writing.*

Summary _____

F. *From films like* Full Metal Jacket *to Picasso's* Guernica, *war has influenced countless individuals to make statements about their thoughts on warfare. The Gulf War led to the*

(continued)

> *writing of such books as* Black Hawk Down *and* Jarhead, *both of which became films. For our generation, we can easily look to the films and books that have been made over the Iraq War, such as* Fahrenheit 9/11. *And with the war's end nowhere in sight, more works are bound to be written.*

Memorable Close _____

> G. *Tolkien summarized his own views on war when he wrote in* The Lord of the Rings: *"I do not love the bright sword for its sharpness, nor the arrow for its swiftness, nor the warrior for his glory. I love only that which they defend"* (280).

SUMMARY

Finally, by providing a strong introduction and a powerful conclusion, you are providing audience members with a well-rounded presentation that they are likely to listen to and remember. In preparing presentations this way, you are using repetition (preview in the introduction; review in the conclusion) to get your audience to understand and remember the main points of your message. (The previous is an example of a summary.) Thus, as you produce the introduction, body, and conclusion of your message, you:

- Tell them what you're going to tell them.
- Tell them.
- Tell them what you told them.

Chances are, they'll remember! How's that for a memorable close?

KEY TERMS

primacy/recency effect (146)

attention getter (147)

rhetorical question (147)

relevance statement (150)

credibility statement (151)

competence and
   character (151)

thesis statement (151)

preview statement (151)

summary (153)

signpost (153)

memorable close (154)

ADDITIONAL ENGAGEMENT OPPORTUNITIES

Now that you have finished reading the chapter, it is also important to make connections between the course content and your own experiences. These activities will help you understand, apply, analyze, evaluate, or synthesize course concepts. You can use these activities to provide evidence of your preparation for participation in class as well as to plan additional contributions to class discussion. The Civic Engagement Opportunities (CEOs) are designed to help you become more engaged in campus and community life and apply course concepts to important social issues.

1. Think of the last time you met someone. How did you introduce yourself? Did you capture his or her attention, bring relevance to your conversation, establish credibility, etc.? How did you end the conversation? Do you think you made a favorable impression? Do you think you made a lasting impression? How do you think the listener perceived your personality?

2. Think back to the last telemarketing call you received. Did the speaker gain your attention to listen to his/her message, or did you hang up after the first sentence? If the speaker held your attention, what was it about the introduction that made you want to listen? If not, what could the speaker have done to sustain your attention?

3. Analyze a recent public speech by the President, Provost, or a Dean of your college or university (such speeches are typically available on institutional websites if you are unable to experience them live). What devices did she or he use in the introduction to capture the attention of the audience and establish credibility? Did the speaker provide a meaningful and memorable close? How does this speaking situation differ from classroom presentations? In what ways are the situations similar?

11
Using Appropriate Language

Good words are worth much, and cost little.
—George Herbert

CHAPTER OBJECTIVES

After reading this chapter, you should be able to:

- Understand the importance of language.
- Describe the three ways that written language is different from oral language.
- Incorporate four criteria effective speakers use when choosing language.
- Understand how to promote clarity with language.
- Describe the difference between denotative and connotative meanings.
- Understand how to incorporate vivid language.
- Define inclusive language.

Stephen Colbert

I f we asked you to write down the name of something that you dislike immensely, wad up the paper, and hurl it across the room, how would that make you feel? In addition to wondering what on earth we were thinking, you might also feel some sense of relief or pleasure in your task. Now, if we were to ask you to write down the name of the person in this world whom you love the most, place the paper on the ground, and STOMP on it, what would you do? Would you hesitate? Why? It's just a word on a piece of paper. What can it hurt? This exercise demonstrates the power of language.

As you have been working on producing your message, or presentation, you have considered how your audience will respond to you as the speaker, your topic, and the content of your message. You have been gathering information and evaluating the credibility of your sources, and you have considered how best to organize your message. Now, you need to consider carefully the words you will use to communicate your message to get a favorable response from your audience. In other words, you need to think about how you will use language in your speeches to either inform or persuade your classmates.

The Importance of Language

Before you can consider how best to use language, it is important that you understand why language, or *word choice*, is so important. There are a few characteristics of language that will help you understand the implications of the words we use to produce a message.

First, language is **symbolic**.[1] That is, words stand for or symbolize things. They are not the actual things they represent. Thus, words can have several meanings. For example, consider the word *fish*. What immediately comes to mind? Do you envision a large shark in the ocean or a tiny goldfish in a bowl? Or, do you see someone wading in a river casting a line? It can almost be guaranteed that one of your authors thought the latter. In this example, the word can function as a noun or a verb and represents multiple images, given your interpretation (or wishes).

Second, language is **arbitrary**.[2] Words have no meaning in and of themselves. They get their meaning from the people who use them. There is nothing inherent in a fish that necessitates calling it a *fish*. We could call it anything really. For example, the French word for fish is *poisson*.

Figure 11.1 helps us to understand the symbolic and arbitrary nature of words by demonstrating that words have a **triangle of meaning**. The *symbol* is the word (lower left-hand corner). The top of the triangle is the *thought*—the meaning you give the word. The lower right-hand corner is the *referent*—or the actual thing itself.

So, if you hear the word *fish*, and you are planning a trip to Hawaii, you might think of a shark, whereas if your goldfish just died, you might be lamenting your pet. As for your author, Figure 11.1 most closely represents his thoughts. From this triangle of meaning, we get the principle that *meanings are in people; not in words*.[3] To illustrate, one of your authors shares the following story:

> When my son was three, he attended an Easter worship service at his grand-parents' church. The Sunday school teacher asked the class, "Does anyone here know how to be saved?" Dylan raised his hand eagerly and said, "I do, I do!" The teacher asked Dylan to share with the rest of the class how to be saved. And he said, "You call 911!"

Source Citation:
[1] Meade, G. H. (1934). *Mind, self, and society.* C. W. Morris (Ed.). Chicago: University of Chicago Press.

Source Citation:
[2] Meade, G. H. (1934). *Mind, self, and society.* C. W. Morris (Ed.). Chicago: University of Chicago Press.

Source Citation:
[3] Berlo, D. K. (1960). *The process of communication.* New York: Holt, Rhinehart, & Winston.

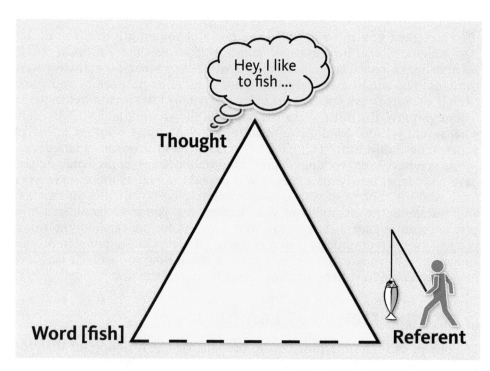

FIGURE 11.1

Triangle of Meaning

Now, in this example, the teacher and the student had two very different interpretations of the word *saved*. The teacher was thinking about a religious interpretation based on her experience and Dylan was thinking about a "search and rescue" interpretation based on watching entirely too much TV.

By considering these characteristics of language, you can understand why messages are often misunderstood or misinterpreted. As a producer of messages, if you recognize that meanings are in people, you will more carefully choose your words based on what you know about your audience's experiences.

Critical Interaction 11.1
Name Change

Think about the arbitrary and symbolic nature of words. Do these characteristics of language apply to our names? Try this! Take the letters of your name and write them in reverse order. For example, *Cheri* becomes *Irehc*, *Steve* becomes *Evets*, *Brent* becomes *Tnerb*, and so on. Now, say your new name out loud.

1. What if this were your name?
2. Would this change the kind of person you are?
3. Do you think other people would treat you differently?
4. What does this activity imply about the symbolic and arbitrary nature of names?

Comic 11.1   *Calvin and Hobbes*

1. How does Calvin interpret the word *snack*?

2. How is this different from his mother's interpretation?

3. How does each person's background affect these interpretations?

CALVIN AND HOBBES ©1987 Watterson. Dist. By UNIVERSAL PRESS SYNDICATE. All rights reserved.

Source Citation:
[4] Young, K. (1931). Language, thought and social reality. In K. Young (Ed.), *Social attitudes*. New York: Henry Holt.

But why should you care? Well, remember that your audience determines whether you are able to accomplish your goals—but there's still more. Language is important because, as many scholars agree, language creates a *social reality*.[4] What does this mean?

To illustrate, let's talk about the implications that word choice may have on reality. Years ago, people who protected our community were often referred to as *policemen* or *firemen*. During this time, a large percentage of that workforce was male. After all, why would a young girl grow up thinking she could be a policeman or a fireman? Now, we more accurately refer to the job they perform rather than the people they are and use words like *police officer* and *fire fighter*. Our current protective services now include more women in that workforce than when the job was described in male terms. Language creates a social reality because it tells us *what* and *whom* to value in society.

Preparing to Participate 11.1
Principles of Language

Knowledge
What are the characteristics or principles of language that serve to explain its importance?

Application
Think about a word that you typically use to describe something. Draw a triangle of meaning for this word.
How does language create a social reality? Provide an example to share.

Oral Style and Written Style

When you produce messages for a presentation, you do so with the *listener* in mind as opposed to the *reader*. A *listener* only gets one shot at your message, whereas a reader can go back over and review things that were complicated or unclear. So, when producing presentations, you need to write for the ear. This is known as **oral style**. When you say something aloud, it has the

Language Creates a Social Reality. The job title *firefighter* is much more descriptive of the work performed and is gender-neutral.

potential to have more of an impact because you can give it direction, volume, and intensity. Thus, spoken language is different from written language in several ways.

First, oral style uses *shorter sentences*. As a speaker, if you use long sentences, you may have difficulty catching your breath during the presentation because you tend to breathe during natural breaks in the sentence structure. To illustrate, try reading the previous sentence aloud. In addition, if you use long sentences, you may have your audience wondering where on earth the presentation is headed.

Second, oral style is *less formal*. When we speak, we tend to use more personal pronouns or slang to make connections with our audience. For example, one of your authors is well known for using positive slang to motivate his students in the classroom. It would not be uncommon to hear "You rock!" "I'm down with that!" or "Fire it up!" from this particular instructor.

Positive slang refers to informal language that a speaker utilizes to signal identification with the listener.[5] Of course, to be effective in a presentation, slang should be used sparingly and it must be appropriate to the audience. That is, you should know from your audience analysis whether your listeners would react favorably to certain kinds of language. Importantly, speakers should avoid using *negative slang*, or informal language that may be perceived offensive by the listener.

Beyond slang, we also use more contractions (e.g., I'm, you're, can't, doesn't) when speaking because they sound more natural to the ear. As such, oral style is much more conversational than written style. As

Source Citation:
[5] Mazer, J. P., & Hunt, S. K. (2008). The effects of instructor use or positive and negative slang on student motivation, affective learning, and classroom climate. *Communication Research Reports, 25*, 45–55.

See also

Mazer, J. P., & Hunt, S. K. (2008). Cool communication in the classroom: A preliminary examination of student perceptions of instructor use of positive slang. *Qualitative Research Reports in Communication, 9,* 20–28.

an example, your authors have attempted to write this text more like a conversation than a scholarly article in hopes of maintaining your interest as you read.

Third, oral style is more *repetitive.* Throughout this text, we have talked about organizing your ideas so that your audience can follow your message. This is why you are asked to provide an introduction (preview) and a conclusion (review) as well as signposts and transitions to your message. These oral strategies allow your audience to better follow and comprehend your message. Remember, a speech happens in time. You give it and then it is done. Your audience does not generally have access to your notes or your outline, and if the structure of your message is not clear, your audience may be lost and your goal in jeopardy.

Preparing to Participate 11.2
Differences Between Oral Style and Written Style

Knowledge
What are three differences between oral style and written style?

Application
Should your classroom speeches be more formal or informal in oral style?

Choosing Language

Now that you know the importance of language and the difference between speaking and writing, you can make better word choices as you produce your message. Taking into account the effect that words have on your audience demonstrates your ability to speak competently and ethically. Competent communicators make judgments about the appropriateness of language for a particular audience. Ethical communicators consider the impact that words have on their audience. Thus, effective speakers will work to assure that their presentations are clear, accurate, vivid, and appropriate.

Clarity

To be clear, you need to use words that are specific and familiar to your audience. As listeners, we do not get the opportunity to look up words we don't understand. Thus, it is the speaker's responsibility to choose words that when said the first time provide **clarity** for the audience. Unlike a classroom lecture, your audience members probably won't raise their hands to ask for clarification. There are several things you can do to promote clarity.

Use Specific Words Generally, speakers should try to make their explanations or descriptions as concrete as possible. **Concrete language** is specific, detailed, and tangible. The goal is that when a speaker describes a term or concept, the listener pictures the same thing. For example, in our Coliseum speech, the speaker describes the project to rebuild the Coliseum. She indicates the location *(near the center of Rome)*, the time it will take *(8 years)* and the cost of the renovation *(18 million dollars)*.

On the other hand, if a speaker explains terms or concepts using abstract language, the speaker and the listener may not share the same interpretations. **Abstract language** is general and vague. Unfortunately, we may not always be describing something as concrete as the Coliseum rebuilding project. Some of our ideas may be abstract. The challenge is to find a way to make them concrete and compelling.

For example, President Barack Obama, then a U.S. Senator from Illinois, spoke at the 2004 Democratic National Convention and, instead of speaking in abstractions about patriotism and the role of government, he told a personal story with historical references his audience understood:

Making Your Ideas Compelling. Many observers point to Barack Obama's speech at the 2004 Democratic National Convention as the point at which he became a national figure.

> The day after Pearl Harbor my grandfather signed up for duty, joined Patton's army and marched across Europe. Back home, my grandmother raised their baby and went to work on a bomber assembly line. After the war, they studied on the GI Bill, bought a house through FHA, and later moved west all the way to Hawaii in search of opportunity.[6]

Source Citation:
[6] Obama, B. (2004). Keynote to the Democratic National Convention on Wednesday, July 28th, 2004 [on-line transcript]. Available: http://www.democracynow.org/article.pl?sid=04/07/28/1313225 retrieved 11/14/06.

So, instead of saying, *"As everyone knows, Democrats often favor federal social programs, but what you may not realize is that we are often patriotic and not always opposed to war,"* he instead used concrete language to communicate abstract political views that his audience could more easily understand. *Abstract* terms are things such as *love, freedom,* or *democracy* that people can think of but not necessarily point to. For example, if a speaker claims that *"language is powerful,"* a listener might wonder what is meant by *powerful*. This term would need to be defined more specifically. Language is powerful because . . . (hopefully at the end of this chapter, you can complete this sentence).

The following example demonstrates how a speaker can go from *abstract* to *concrete* by providing a few descriptive details:

- Dog
- Small dog
- Small, gray dog
- Small, gray, poodle-schnauzer mixed (schnoodle) dog

Better yet, show a photo of the dog and eliminate unnecessary verbal detail. See Chapter 12 for more ideas about using visuals in your presentation.

Use Familiar Words Speakers should also use language that is familiar to the audience, given what they know about the audience's interests and knowledge of the topic. In doing so, they should avoid using **jargon**, which is language that is specific to a particular group. Jargon is generally unique to the people who use it in a specific field and is often unknown to outsiders. Speakers should be aware of this and be sure to define all terms unique to their topic for their audience. Sometimes jargon can come in the form of acronyms. **Acronyms** are used as first-letter abbreviations for longer terms.

For example, if you are giving a speech on dream states and use the term *R.E.M.*, you should explain that this means *rapid eye movement* at least the first time you use it. For example, do the following statements make any sense to you?

> I'll be presenting the results of my Com App research at NCA this year. I ran T-tests and found significance at the Oh-Five level on H1 and 2 but not 3. I'm worried because I heard the respondent wasn't a quantoid. Whose idea was it to get a rhet crit person anyway? It's not my fault Cicero couldn't count!

The preceding example illustrates why it is important to match your language choices to your audience. Believe it or not, there are some folks who would understand—and even be interested in—the results of the research mentioned in the example. However, as the example points out, the researcher was probably not going to find a sympathetic ear from the respondent at the NCA (National Communication Association) conference. The point is to match your word choice with the knowledge and interest levels of your audience. Jargon is useful and efficient with the right crowd, but it is downright boring and ineffective with general audiences.

Use Active Voice In **active voice**, the subject performs the action, whereas in **passive voice**, the subject is acted upon. For example, you could say, "It was decided by the voters of California that stem cell research should be funded," or, "California voters decided that stem cell research should be funded." In which sentence does the subject perform the action? Active sentences are more efficient, concrete, and clear to the listener.

Sometimes passive voice reveals a lack of knowledge or, at worst, downright deception. For example, take a look at this sentence:

> It is widely believed that Senator Smith has taken bribes.

Who exactly believes this? Is it just a rumor? In this case of passive voice usage, the doer of the action escapes notice. In researching your topic, did you find a source that verified your information? If so, tell your audience so that they can gauge the credibility of your source:

> The state's attorney general has announced she is investigating Senator Smith for allegedly taking bribes.

In this case, you have attributed the source of the information and you have clarified the state of affairs. However, as you no doubt realize, being accused and being guilty are two different things. In the worst case scenario, using passive voice can be deceptive. For example, what if your source was a tabloid newspaper? You could certainly say *"it is believed"* and hide your source and still be technically accurate, but it is probably unethical to do so. If you learn to identify passive voice in the messages you read and view, you will be able to better question the credibility of the source and become more media and information literate.

Avoid Clutter Keeping in mind the characteristics of *oral style*, speakers should also avoid long sentences that require multiple punctuation divisions. This makes it difficult for the listener to follow the presentation and maintain attention. **Vocalized pauses** such as *like, you know, um,* can also cause the

Critical Interaction 11.2
Active/Passive Voice

Indicate whether the following sentences are active or passive. If a sentence is passive, how can it be rewritten to make it active? Place an A or P after the sentence.

1. The contract was signed by the company president. _____
2. Professor Lee handed out the take-home final exam last Friday. _____
3. My favorite cousin was at my parents' house for the holidays. _____
4. It is known that all politicians are corrupt. _____
5. Our starting quarterback's knee surgery was performed by Dr. Hernandez yesterday. _____

listener to become distracted. Speakers are often fearful of silent pauses and use these filler words to help them get from one point to the next. The result, however, is that these vocalized pauses demonstrate a lack of concentration and may hurt a speaker's credibility. When you hear a presentation, what are your perceptions of the speaker who "hems and haws"?

Accuracy

Another issue that might affect your credibility is **accuracy**. Speakers should be sure that their presentation is grammatically and structurally correct. They should also be careful to use the right words at the right time. We can probably all recall a time when someone used an otherwise good word at a very inappropriate moment. For example, one of your authors recalls a time when a student was describing an anorexic patient as *emancipated* as opposed to *emaciated*. Let's face it, poor or inaccurate word choices may cause your audience to believe you have poor ideas.

When you write a paper, your word processing program provides you with grammar, thesaurus, and spelling hints. We have all seen those green and red squiggly lines under our text. They are there for a reason. You, of course, will want to monitor these as you prepare your presentation. However, these programs do not tell you if you are pronouncing a word correctly or using it in the right context. We suggest you "try out" your presentation in front of others to see if they can catch any oral inaccuracies—much like your word processing program catches written inaccuracies.

To be sure that you are using terms correctly, it is important to understand that words have different meanings. A **denotative** meaning is the literal dictionary meaning of the word, but your audience may associate a **connotative** or emotional response to the word. For example, if you look up the word *terrorist*, you will find similar definitions in most dictionaries. However, if you use the word in a speech, your audience may have an emotional response to the word because of what the connotative meaning suggests or implies to them about their national safety. We will not find such a connotative meaning in a dictionary.

In the political realm, the terms *liberal* and *conservative* have denotative meanings about how government and society should operate. Depending on your political views, you probably attach connotative meanings to the words. That is, you either respond negatively or positively (or perhaps indifferently!) to these terms. Speakers should be aware of this distinction as they choose words to gain a favorable response from their audience.

Vividness

Sometimes speakers will strategically use language to evoke a certain emotion or image from their audience. That is, they will use **vivid** language to appeal to the audience's senses. Toward the end of Barack Obama's speech at the 2004 Democratic National Convention that we mentioned earlier, he speaks of the election being one of hope. He could have said that "John Kerry, John Edwards, and Barack Obama are hopeful." Instead he said:

> It's . . . the hope of a young naval lieutenant bravely patrolling the Mekong Delta; the hope of a millworker's son who dares to defy the odds; the hope of a skinny kid with a funny name who believes that America has a place for him, too.[7]

Source Citations:
[7] Obama, B. (2004). Keynote to the Democratic National Convention on Wednesday, July 28th, 2004 [on-line transcript]. Available: http://www.democracynow.org/article.pl?sid=04/07/28/1313225 retrieved 11/14/06.

[8] Proverbs 26:11. King James Version.

[9] *Macbeth,* act 5, scene 5.

How can you use language more vividly to inspire your audience? There are several figures of speech available that will make any speech more descriptive, imaginative, and memorable to listeners.

Analogy   There are many ways speakers can make comparisons to help an audience relate to their topic. The objective is to get the audience to understand an unfamiliar concept by comparing it to something familiar.

A **simile** is a direct comparison of unlike things using the words *like* or *as.*

In the Bible, King Solomon is referred to as the wisest man in the world. In one of his proverbs, he said, "*As a dog returneth to its vomit, so a fool returneth to his folly.*"[8] How's that for vivid!

Metaphors are much like similes except that they are *implied* comparisons between two unlike things. In *Macbeth,* William Shakespeare compared life with a stage play:

> Life's but a walking shadow, a poor player, that struts and frets his hour upon the stage, and then is heard no more. It is a tale told by an idiot, full of sound and fury, signifying nothing.[9]

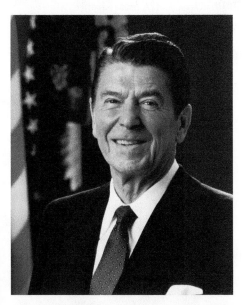

Powerful Language. As one of the twentieth century's most popular presidents, Ronald Reagan's optimistic speaking style connected with many Americans.

Ronald Reagan's 1984 reelection campaign was built around the metaphor *"It's morning in America."* Literally speaking, it is sometimes evening and sometimes night, but the metaphor poetically proclaimed hopefulness and underscored why President Reagan was called the "great communicator."

So, perhaps you think your situation is hopeless because you are not the wisest person in the world, the greatest writer of the English language, or a popular twentieth-century president. In all likelihood, you use similes and metaphors all the time when conversing with friends and family.

How often have you heard or used a sports metaphor? Maybe you made an "A" on a term paper and told your roommate that you *"knocked it out of the park."* Or, you refused to go out with your friends during finals week and stayed home to study because it was the *"fourth quarter and you were down by 10."* However, be careful. Analogies work best when they are not hackneyed and trite. Avoid clichés and strive for fresh, unique comparisons that will help your audience understand your message.

Extended analogies further explain metaphors in detail. So, instead of using one metaphor early in a speech and then shifting to another later on, an extended analogy can recall the previous example and extend it. This will also keep you from mixing metaphors.

For example, the Coliseum speech consistently refers to modern day sports stadiums and illustrates that the ancient Romans were not that much different from us in terms of their entertainment choices. Analogies are particularly useful in making the content relevant to the members of the audience by connecting it to their experiences. This is yet another reason for knowing and understanding your audience. In effect, you are reinforcing the relevance statement you made in your introduction.

Personification Personification occurs when a speaker gives human qualities to inanimate objects, ideas, or animals. This strategy is used to help the audience visualize and imagine what the speaker thinks or feels about a certain term or concept. It relies on the unexpected to get the audience to take notice and pay attention to the speaker. For example, in the Blues speech the speaker quotes an old Lynyrd Skynyrd song to vividly illustrate the way Son House sang. *"When that hound dog starts barking, sounds like old Son House singing the blues!"*[10]

Alliteration Speakers may choose to use **alliteration** for effect. Alliteration uses a repetition of sounds that are near each other. For example, the word *lollipop* repeats the consonants *l* and *p*, which gives it an *alliterative* sound.

Advertisers, campaign managers, and other persuaders often use alliteration for a quick and effective response from listeners. For instance, a lawyer once described his philandering client accused of murdering his pregnant wife as "a **c**reep, and a **c**ad, but not a **k**iller" in hopes that this phrase would stand out in the minds of the jurors during deliberation.

In *The Wizard of Oz*, the wizard states, *"Step forward, Tin Man. You dare to come to me for a heart, do you? You **c**linking, **c**lanking, **c**lattering **c**ollection of **c**aliginous junk . . . And you, Scarecrow, have the effrontery to ask for a **b**rain! You **b**illowing **b**ale of **b**ovine fodder!"*[11] Alliteration can be fun, but don't get too carried away with the technique. A little goes a long way. If overused, it might detract from, rather than enhance, your message.

Antithesis Sometimes, speakers may use **antithesis** to try to explain what something *is* by describing what it *isn't*. This strategy is used to show contrasting ideas and to create a memorable effect. For example, John F. Kennedy, in his Presidential Inaugural Address states, *Ask not what your country can do for you; ask what you can do for your country.*[12]

Source Citations:
[10] King, E., & Van Zant, R. (1974). Swamp music. On *Second Helping* [Record]. Universal City, CA: MCA Records Inc.

[11] LeRoy, M. (Producer), & Fleming, V. (Director). (1939). *The Wizard of Oz* [Film]. Century City, CA: MGM Studios Inc.

[12] Kennedy, J. F. (1961). Inaugural address on Friday, January 20th, 1961 {on-line transcript}. Available: http://www.bartleby.com/124/pres56.html

Using Alliteration. In *The Wizard of Oz* the wizard uses alliteration to address the Tin Man.

More recently, Barack Obama used the same device in his Inaugural Address when he refers to the efficiency of our government.

> The question we ask today is not whether our government is too big or too small, but whether it works—whether it helps families find jobs at a decent wage, care they can afford, a retirement that is dignified. Where the answer is yes, we intend to move forward. Where the answer is no, programs will end.[13]

Source Citation:
[13] Obama, B. H. (2009). Inaugural address on Tuesday, January 20th, 2009 {on-line transcript}. Available: http://www.bartleby.com/124/pres68.html

Onomatopoeia Speakers may use **onomatopoeia** to appeal to a listener's sense of sound. This strategy uses sounds that mimic the meaning of words such as *tick tock* or *snap, crackle, and pop*. There are many examples of onomatopoeia, and, if used appropriately, this device can be used to capture an audience's attention, making the speech more memorable.

Repetition Speakers may use **repetition** at the beginning or end of sentences to call attention to a particular point. When they hear a repeated phrase or word, audiences sit up and take notice of the sentences that follow.

A forceful example is from the movie *Field of Dreams* when James Earl Jones (as Terrence Mann) makes a speech on the baseball field telling Kevin Costner (as Ray Kinsella) that people will come to Iowa to watch games at his field, which will keep the bank (represented by Ray's brother-in-law Mark) from foreclosing on his farm. Notice the repetition:

Mann: Ray, **people will come, Ray.** They'll come to Iowa for reasons they can't even fathom. They'll turn up your driveway, not knowing for sure why they're doing it. They'll arrive at your door as innocent as children, longing for the past. "Of course, we won't mind if you have a look around," you'll say. "It's only twenty dollars per person." They'll pass over the money without even thinking about it; for it is money they have and peace they lack.

Mark: Ray, just sign the papers.

Mann: And they'll walk out to the bleachers, and sit in shirt-sleeves on a perfect afternoon. They'll find they have reserved seats somewhere along one of the baselines, where they sat when they were children and cheered their heroes. And they'll watch the game, and it'll be as if they'd dipped themselves in magic waters. The memories will be so thick, they'll have to brush them away from their faces.

Mark: Ray, when the bank opens in the morning, they'll foreclose.

Mann: People will come, Ray.

Mark: You're broke, Ray. You sell now or you lose everything.

Mann: The one constant through all the years, Ray, has been baseball. America has rolled by like an army of steamrollers. It's been

Calling to Your Main Points. In the film *Field of Dreams*, actor James Earl Jones uses repetition to convince Kevin Costner's character to keep his magical baseball field.

erased like a blackboard, rebuilt, and erased again. But baseball has marked the time. This field, this game, is a part of our past, Ray. It reminds us of all that once was good, and it could be again. Ohhhhhhhh, people will come, Ray. **People will most definitely come.**[14]

Appropriateness

Speakers should be sure that the language used in a presentation is appropriate to the topic, the occasion, and the audience. Recall that audiences may respond differently than anticipated to certain words or phrases.

An effective speaker will use **appropriate language** by considering the implications word choices have on the way the audience receives a presentation. Profanity is rarely, if ever, appropriate. There is nothing to gain by its use and everything to lose. Be assured that someone in the audience will be offended. Additionally, speakers should strive to use language that is inclusive.

Inclusive language considers and respects all types of people regardless of gender, race, sexual orientation, and so forth. In other words, inclusive language avoids excluding anyone for any reason. Inclusive language avoids making assumptions about who can and cannot engage in certain activities. Inclusive language respects listeners and helps speakers accomplish their goals. Following is a list of suggestions that will enable you to see if you are including all members of your audience in your message:

- Avoid using the generic "he" when referring to both sexes.
- Avoid using gender terms to describe what people do. Avoid making judgments about which gender should have certain jobs or social roles.
- Avoid linking personal traits that don't have anything to do with the topic. 🖳

Source Citation:
[14] Frankish, B. E. (Executive Producer), & Robinson, P. A. (1989). *Field of Dreams* [Film]. Universal City, CA: Universal Studios. Courtesy of Universal Studios Licensing LLLP.

Speech Analysis

Log on to the Internet and visit the following website: http://www.americanrhetoric.com/speechbank.htm

1. Find a speech that interests you.
2. Analyze a portion of the speech and determine if the language choices are clear, accurate, vivid, or appropriate language.
3. How effective or ineffective is the speaker's language in this passage?

Sample Speech Analysis—Language

Log on to MySpeechLab.com and access the sample "C" and "A" videos on Tornadoes and The Coliseum.

1. How does each speaker use language in the "C" speeches?
2. How does each speaker's language change in the "A" speeches?

Critical Interaction 11.3
Inclusive Language

Consider the following statements. Are they inclusive or exclusive? If you determine they are exclusive, how can they be rephrased to be inclusive?

1. Dr. Martin, a leading female psychologist, offers her insights into chronic depression.
2. The male nurse treated Adam in the Emergency Room.
3. All right, you guys, listen carefully.
4. I wonder if the mailman delivered the mail today.

Preparing to Participate 11.3
Effective Word Choice

Knowledge
What are four considerations for effective word choice?

Application
How do these considerations enhance a speaker's presentation? Can you think of a time when you heard a speaker neglect one of these suggestions? What happened?

SUMMARY

In this chapter we have discussed the importance of language and word choice in public speaking. In summary, if language really does create a social reality, then we as speakers should consider the impact of the words we use to produce messages. If our goal is to inform or persuade an audience, then the audience's response to the language we use is crucial to our meeting our goals. Why would you want to say or do anything in your presentation that might offend or exclude anyone in your audience? Rather, to achieve success in your presentation, you should strive to use language in a meaningful and powerful way. By considering the impact of your language choices, you are engaging in both *ethical* and *competent communication*. To use a metaphor, language can reel your audience in or it can cast them away. Language can make the difference between an average speech and an awesome speech.

KEY TERMS

symbolic (160)

arbitrary (160)

triangle of meaning (160)

oral Style (162)

clarity (164)

concrete and abstract language (164)

jargon (165)

acronyms (165)

active and passive voice (166)

vocalized pauses (166)

accuracy (167)

denotative and connotative meaning (167)

vivid (168)

simile and metaphor (168)

extended analogy (169)

personification (169)

alliteration (169)

antithesis (169)

onomatopoeia (170)

repetition (170)

appropriate language (171)

inclusive language (171)

ADDITIONAL ENGAGEMENT OPPORTUNITIES

Now that you have finished reading the chapter, it is also important to make connections between the course content and your own experiences. These activities will help you understand, apply, analyze, evaluate, or synthesize course concepts. You can use these activities to provide evidence of your preparation for participation in class as well as to plan additional contributions to class discussion. The Civic Engagement Opportunities (CEOs) are designed to help you become more engaged in campus and community life and apply course concepts to important social issues.

1. Check out your shampoo bottle. What positive and appealing language choices are displayed on the product itself? Do the marketers use vivid language? Give an example.

2. Think of five words/phrases/abbreviations that you use that are appropriate for one situation, but not another. For example, when you are writing to someone electronically, you would use Internet slang "LOL" to indicate that you are laughing out loud. However, if you were having a conversation with someone face-to-face, you would not say LOL if you found something funny; you would simply laugh.

3. In this chapter, we describe the important differences between denotative and connotative meaning. To further illustrate this point, provide the denotative (dictionary) and connotative (emotional) meaning of the term *citizenship*. Once you have developed your own understanding, ask your parents or grandparents for their definition of the term. Briefly describe any differences and similarities between the definitions.

12

Designing Presentation Aids

Graphical excellence consists of complex ideas communicated with clarity, precision, and efficiency.
—Edward Tufte

CHAPTER OBJECTIVES

After reading this chapter, you should be able to:

- Understand the benefits of visual literacy.
- Describe the types of presentation aids.
- Understand how to display presentation aids.
- Consider design principles in a presentation aid.
- Understand how to integrate presentation aids into the message of a speech.

Al Gore

Have you ever tried to describe a new or unfamiliar item to a group of people? It is likely that the images formed in their minds, based on your description, bear little resemblance to the thing you are describing. However, if you show them a picture, the information is communicated quickly, forcefully, and accurately. Such is the power of images.

Benefits of Visual Literacy

Source Citation:
[1] Heinich, R., Molenda, M., & Russell, J. (1982). *Instructional media and the new technologies of instruction.* New York: Wiley. (p. 62).

This chapter introduces you to the idea of **visual literacy**. What we're concerned with here is the *production* and *consumption* of visual messages. What exactly does that mean? Visual literacy is "the learned ability to interpret visual messages accurately and to create such messages."[1] From this definition, we can see that fully literate communicators must be able to not only interpret visual information but express themselves visually as well. Depending on the activity, Figure 12.1 shows us that there are two sides of literacy—one side describes what happens when we consume information (e.g., reading, listening, interpreting) and the other side describes what happens when we produce information (e.g., writing, speaking, creating).

In this class, you will be expected to produce messages that your audience can easily interpret. To do this, you will need to be able to consume messages critically by analyzing how, or if, the information helps you explain your topic. Additionally, you will interpret your classmates' speeches and make decisions about how this information is useful to you. By learning to *create* (produce) visual messages, you will increase your ability to accurately and critically *interpret* (consume) other speakers' visuals. This, in turn, will allow you to become more literate with images you encounter in the mass media.

Critical Interaction 12.1
A Picture Is Worth a Thousand Words

Find a photograph of someone in your family. Now, try to describe your family member to one of your friends at school (someone who does not know your family member). Try to include the following information in your description.

- What does your family member look like?
- What kind of clothes does he or she wear? What does your family member do?
- How does he/she feel about him/herself?
- How do other people feel about him/her?

Now, have your friend picture in his/her mind and then describe for you what your family member looks like. Show your friend your picture.

Were there any differences in the actual picture of your family member and what your friend described?

Consume	Produce
Read	Write
Listen	Speak
Interpret	Create

FIGURE 12.1
Two Sides of Literacy

So how can you use this particular view of literacy to help yourself as a public speaker? We will discuss this in terms of designing presentation aids for your speeches. In doing so, we will also provide you with tools for analysis and future use of visual forms.

Factors such as the situation, the audience, and the goals of the speech should guide your choice or design of an appropriate aid. You should not immediately assume that an electronic presentation full of fancy graphs is the answer. That is, before you begin designing your message and the aids that will help you communicate that message, you must first articulate the goal of your presentation.[2]

At this point you should have a clear idea about your purpose and the direction of your speech. Can you identify some areas where a presentation aid would be useful? In other words, is there content that would be easier to show than to describe? If so, there may be several solutions available to you. The next section describes different types of visual representations that can help you achieve your goals.

Source Citation:
[2] Tufte, E. R. (2001). *E. T. on technologies for making presentations* [On-line]. Available: http://www.edwardtufte.com/bboard/q-and-a-fetch-msg?msg_id=00001B&topic_id=1, retrieved 11/14/06.

Preparing to Participate 12.1
Visual Literacy

Knowledge
What are the two sides of visual literacy?

Application
Why is it important for public speakers to be visually literate?

Types of Presentation Aids

Let's take a look at the various ways you can represent your content and explore what may make a particular image a good choice. The most appropriate type of presentation aid really depends on your subject, your audience, and your overall goal.

Written Language

Spoken words are gone as soon as you say them. It is this impermanent quality that makes them hard to pin down and often hard to remember. How many times have you said, *"I didn't say that!"* while your friend swears that indeed you did (and vice-versa). For that reason alone, it is usually advantageous to give physical form to at least some portion of your presentation. That way, your audience knows that you mean business and that you are willing to be held accountable for what you say. This is one way to enhance ethical communication as well as speaker credibility.

Written language can take the form of bulleted lists, numbered lists, or tables that you can easily incorporate into a PowerPoint presentation. Note that this does not imply that your presentation aids should contain complete sentences. You should deliver complete sentences orally, and you should write them in reports and other printed materials, but most of the time, full sentences are inappropriate as visuals for your audience (a quotation is a possible exception).

As an example, a bulleted list would be a useful way to preview the main topics in your presentation (see Figure 12.2). Then, you can orally specify the important relationships and provide stories and context that make the lists meaningful. These bullets can serve as reminders for your audience of where you are in your speech and can provide a visual roadmap to help them follow what you are saying. However, because bulleted lists are one of the simplest visual aids to create, they are often overused and most of the time misused. Many presenters rely too heavily on bullet points by simply reading their slides to the audience. We advise that you only use them for what they do best—as organizational devices. Long, seemingly endless bulleted lists have become cliché and have rightly been criticized in many publications such as newspapers, trade magazines, and scholarly journals.[3] The problem is that too many presenters employ this "easy-to-create-visual" to deliver their content.

Source Citation:
[3] Hlynka, D., & Mason, R. (1998, September-October). PowerPoint in the classroom: What is the point? *Educational Technology.*

See also

Keller, J. (2003, January 5). Killing me Microsoftly. *Chicago Tribune Magazine,* pp. 8–12, 28, 29.

Edward Tufte especially takes PowerPoint to task in Tufte, E. R. (2003). *The cognitive style of PowerPoint.* Cheshire, CT: Cheshire Press.

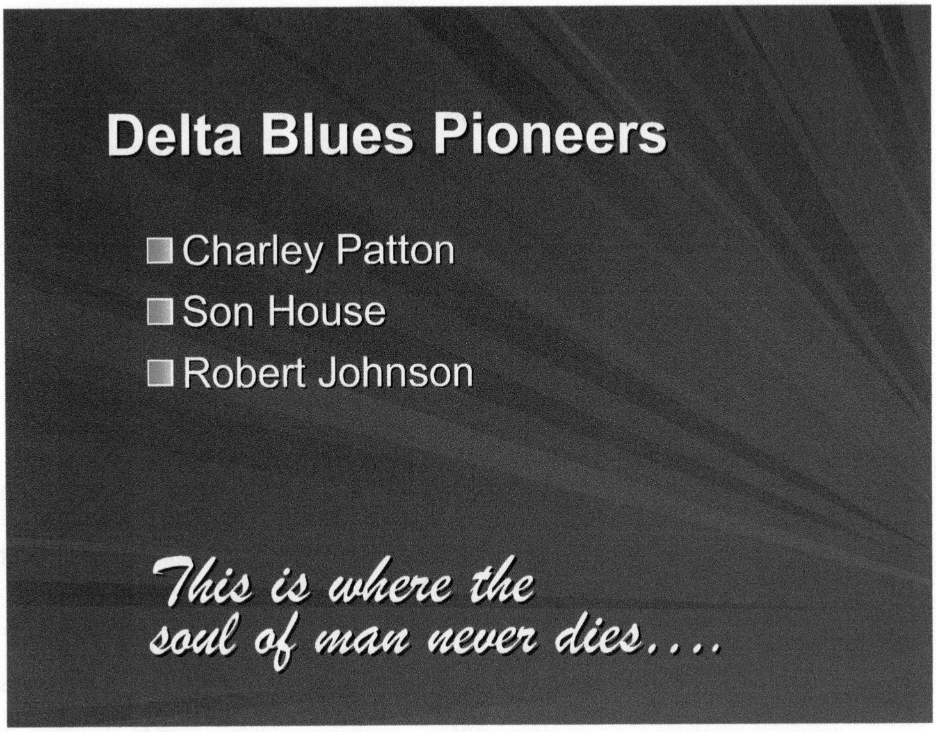

FIGURE 12.2
Sample Bulleted List:
Delta Blues Pioneers

A **numbered list** can display rankings or other ordered content, making it easy for your audience to grasp important relationships. According to 3M executive Gordon Shaw and his colleagues, lists can communicate three logical relationships: sequence, priority, and membership in a set.[4] For example, a *numbered* list might be used to communicate the proper order of steps in a process (**sequence**). Or, you may list what you believe to be the most important factors in choosing a new car (**priority**). Finally, a **bulleted list** may be used to communicate items that are related but are in no particular order, such as the parts of a motorcycle (**membership**). You may be tempted to merely read a list to your audience. Don't. Instead, specify the other critical relationships that exist among items in the list.

A **table** often includes numbers as well as words. In fact, it is often advantageous to create a table that includes numbers rather than writing all of the information out in sentence form (see Figure 12.3).

Source Citation:
[4] Shaw, G., Brown, R., & Bromiley, P. (1998, May-June). Strategic stories: How 3M is re-writing business planning. *Harvard Business Review, 76,* 42–44.

Hitting Statistics for the Top Four Home Run Hitters

	HR	3B	2B	Hits	Ave.
Barry Bonds	762	77	601	2,935	.298
Hank Aaron	755	98	624	3,771	.305
Babe Ruth	714	136	506	2,873	.342
Willie Mays	660	140	523	3,283	.302

FIGURE 12.3
Sample Table: Home Run Hitters

Notice how wordy a sentence would have to be just to indicate the information in the first item of the table:

As of the 2008 baseball season, Barry Bonds had hit 762 home runs, 77 triples, 601 doubles, and 1,495 singles for a total of 2,935 hits with a lifetime batting average of .298.

If your table contains more information than you can easily display for your audience, consider giving your audience handouts. Do not oversimplify a visual at the expense of accuracy. Many presenters in business and industry supplement their PowerPoint presentations with high-resolution printed visuals so that their audiences can further study complex information. Check with your instructor to see if using handouts would be an appropriate strategy in your particular setting.

Data Graphics

Think of **data graphics** as pictures of numbers.[5] Carefully chosen data displayed in an appropriate visual form can make complex information much easier to understand. Please note that different software used to create these visuals may use different terminology. For example, Microsoft PowerPoint and Apple Keynote refer to these visuals as *charts,* but Adobe Illustrator calls them *graphs.* By recognizing the various terms that different programs use, you will be less confused as you begin to create you own presentation aids.

The best data graphics help us understand data and guide our decisions about how to act on the information most effectively. They do this by making

Source Citation:
[5] Tufte, E. R. (2001). *The visual display of quantitative information* (2nd ed.). Cheshire, CT: Cheshire Press. (p. 9, Introduction)

the data visible and accessible. The numbers you include should help you communicate your main ideas and should mean something to your audience. If they don't, then a colorful graphic is not going to make your presentation any more successful. Data graphics can take many forms. Here are a few of the most common ones.

Pie Graphs   **Pie graphs** (also called *pie charts*) are constructed from small data sets and the values are reported as percentages. Therefore, all the pieces of the pie should add up to 100%. Pie graphs visually display how individual categories relate to the whole (see Figure 12.4) and are particularly useful when presenting budget information. However, these data graphics cannot usefully show more than six or seven categories without creating pie slices that are too small to see. Presenters often collapse smaller categories into an "other" or "miscellaneous" category to avoid that problem. For this reason, pie charts have limited usefulness. Reporting small data sets that are percentages could probably be done just as well and as forcefully in a table format. For example, it would require four pie graphs to represent the same data from the table back in Figure 12.2. Audience expectations should guide your decision about whether a pie graph or a table is more appropriate.

Line Graphs   **Line graphs** are also called *time-series plots* and are very common. Basically, one or more variables are plotted against a time interval (see Figure 12.5). Time can be measured in seconds, minutes, hours, days, etc. The other variable values are then plotted on a graph that allows viewers to see how that variable changes over the time period displayed. These graphics excel at making big data sets comprehensible and can really aid in understanding the measurements. By charting two or more variables along the same time dimension, thoughtful comparisons can be made about the data to enhance understanding. Typically the X (horizontal) axis represents time and is read from left to right with the far left representing the earliest point in time. The Y (vertical) axis represents the change in the other variables. By observing the rise and fall of the charted variable against time, viewers can note trends.

Bar/Column Graphs   A **vertical bar graph** (or *column graph*) can also be a time-series graphic, although the data set is usually not as large as the one you would use in a line graph (e.g., it would be very cumbersome to represent the data used in Figure 12.5 as a column graph). But it does allow for quick

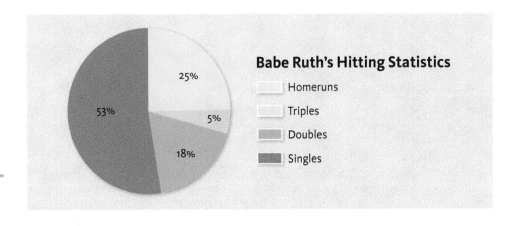

FIGURE 12.4

Sample Pie Graph: Babe Ruth's Hitting Statistics

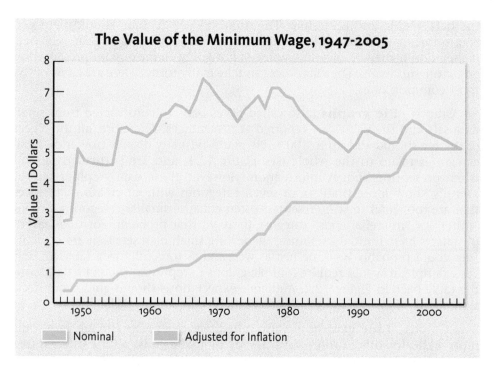

FIGURE 12.5
Sample Line Graph:
Minimum Wage

comparisons between groups. For example, a student organization might chart its fund-raising efforts over the course of a few years and compare the success of different tactics that were used (see Figure 12.6). By viewing the results graphically and historically, student members can make *policy* decisions about how to approach further fundraising events.

Bar graphs can also be used without a time-series element. Perhaps a local pizza franchise wants to look at how many pizzas it sold of different varieties

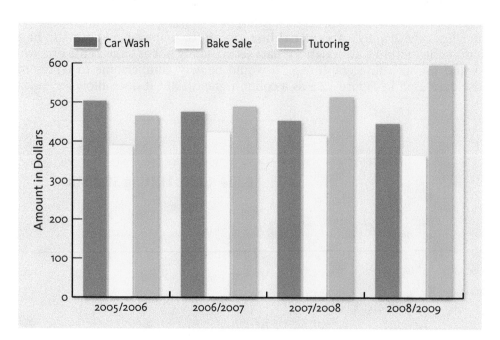

FIGURE 12.6
Sample Bar Graph:
Fundraising Efforts

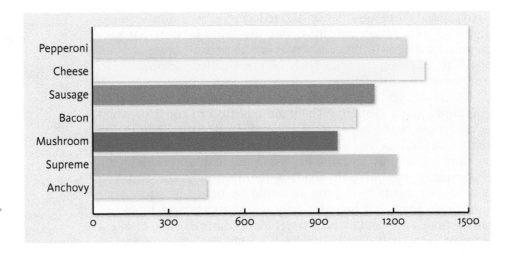

FIGURE 12.7
Sample Bar Graph:
Pizza Sold

during a one-month period so that the owners can determine which ingredients to purchase for the next month (see Figure 12.7).

Data Maps   **Data maps**, unlike time-series plots, are compared in space, not time. For example, in a persuasive speech, you want to argue for a change in traffic ordinances near your apartment. To illustrate your concerns, you could use a map of your community to plot the number of traffic accidents that took place during the year. By comparing accident-prone locations with other known data about those areas, you could determine possible causes for the accidents. City officials could then make *policy* decisions about speed limits on certain streets, number of traffic lights, police cruise routes, etc. Of course, this type of visual can be misused just like any other.

During presidential campaigns, there is usually lots of discussion about red and blue states in news coverage. Unfortunately, illustrating this graphically sometimes produces a kind of "us" versus "them" quality that is a form of either/or thinking that is also known as the *fallacy of the excluded middle* (see Figure 12.8). What if shades of purple were used to color how each county in the state voted within specified ranges? That is, if candidates were about evenly split, the county would be purple. If one candidate won handily in a particular county, the color would be a brighter blue or red. This kind of display

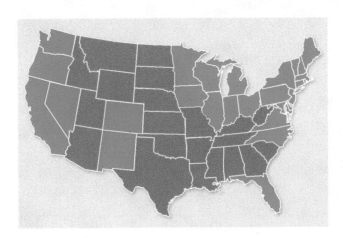

FIGURE 12.8
Sample Data Map: Red
and Blue States (2008
Presidential Election)

would reveal more information and reduce overly simplistic thinking. Also, population density is not the same in different geographic locations. In this country it is one person, one vote, not one acre, one vote. Special types of maps called *cartograms* can compensate for this fallacy. ⌁

Of course, you can use maps as visual support even if they do not contain data elements. The main question to consider when using a map is the appropriate level of detail to include in the visual. Depending on what you are trying to accomplish, less detail in a map may reveal more. For example, if you were giving a persuasive presentation about a fundraising event and you needed to provide directions, it would be better to show your audience a map that includes only major streets and highways rather than every single side street. Sometimes it might take a series of maps, with increasing detail, to accomplish your goal.

Diagrams

Perhaps you are planning to speak about something that has no physical referent that you can point to—a process, for example. It may be helpful to think of diagrams as pictures of verbs. A **diagram** is a visual representation that shows relationships between abstract ideas. However, unlike a data graphic, the information is not quantitative.

Typically, diagrams are composed of text, boxes, lines, and arrows that give form and direction to your topic. One type of diagram is a flow chart that reveals the steps in a process. A timeline is a common and familiar type of diagram that may use additional visual forms such as photos and illustrations (see Figure 12.9).

Media
Interaction 12.1

Red and Blue States

Log on to the Internet and visit the following website:
http://www-personal.umich.edu/~mejn/election/
Examine the relationship between the red and blue states in the 2008 Presidential Election.

1. What conclusions can you draw about the political divisions in our country based on each image?
2. How do the details of each image change your perceptions?
3. Which one best represents reality?

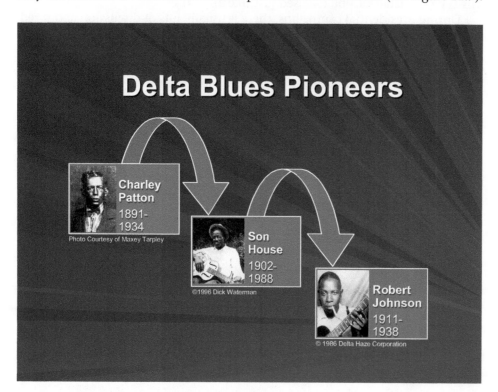

FIGURE 12.9

Sample Diagram: Flow Chart of Delta Blues Pioneers

Another type of diagram is an organization chart that shows the hierarchy, chain-of-command, and/or reporting process within an organization (see Figure 12.10). This particular organization chart is probably too complex to be used as a presentation aid that you display, but it might be useful as a handout. In this case, you could enlarge specific sections of the diagram as a presentation aid (see Figure 12.11). You could briefly display the whole diagram to your audience and then focus on the area that helps to explain your point (e.g., by using the zoom function on a document camera or a smart board).

Illustrations/Paintings

Illustrations and paintings are visuals that resemble what they represent (modern art notwithstanding!). Think of them as pictures of nouns. These are items that you can point to in the physical world. Illustrations and paintings may be humorous, nostalgic, or dark and threatening.

Clip art is a very common—and thus overused—form of illustration because it's plentiful and easy to use. For the most part, we don't recommend its use because it often does not advance the message. Many speakers tend to use clip art as a tacked on decoration, giving little thought to what impact it might have on the audience. If it detracts, it becomes a source of interference (remember the communication process?). And please, don't use humorous clip art during a serious presentation. Appearing insensitive, callous, or silly during a speech about a solemn topic is, at best, damaging to your credibility and, at worst, unethical.

Photographs

Photographs are also pictures of nouns. If you're making an informative presentation about a famous person, why not show your audience a photo of that person? If, during a persuasive presentation, you recommend that your audience study abroad in Paris next summer, why not show them pictures of when you studied there? Just be sure that you don't state the obvious. You don't need to say, "This is the Eiffel Tower." Rather, you could point out something that is not widely known or a particular location that you visited. This will enhance your credibility.

Today, with image editing software, photos can be manipulated easily. When you download an image from the Internet, you may not be able to tell if it's been changed. Ethical problems arise when you present images to your audience that you cannot vouch for.

We're sure you've seen images that made you smile from the Internet or in tabloid newspapers as you were waiting in the grocery store line. We all know the president didn't really speak about world affairs to an alien on the White House lawn. But, how about those images that claim to be true and we have no means of verification? One way to ensure authenticity is to take your own photos for use in your speeches. You can vouch for the integrity of your images, and your credibility is enhanced in the eyes of your audience. However, sometimes photographic special effects or "imagined" images may suit the topic and advance your message. It is important, though, to let your audience know if an image has been "doctored." Newspapers and news magazines that use these

FIGURE 12.10

Sample Diagram: Organization Chart of the U.S. Department of State

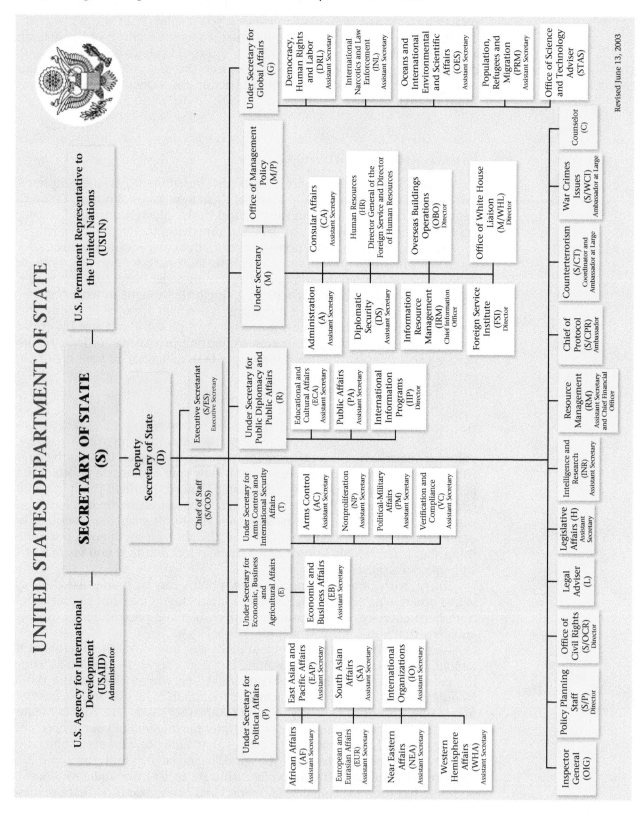

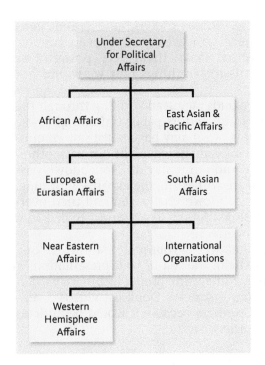

FIGURE 12.11

Sample Diagram: Organizational Chart for the Under Secretary for Political Affairs

strategies label the images as "photo-illustrations." You should do the same to ensure ethical communication.

You can use photos that you did not take in your presentations, but you must state the source of those photos, not only to give credit where credit is due but also so that your audience can gauge the image's (and the image maker's) credibility. Please be advised that you are able to use images that you do not own for educational purposes only. This is a provision in copyright law known as "fair use." Any commercial use of an image that you do not own the rights to is prohibited by law.

Films/Videos/Animations

All of the visual forms we have discussed so far have been two-dimensional. That is, they have height and width. Film, video, and animation include

Comic 12.1

1. What are the ethical implications of showing pictures that don't tell the whole truth?

2. How can you be sure the pictures you choose are ethical?

Calvin and Hobbes

CALVIN AND HOBBES ©1992 Watterson. Dist. By UNIVERSAL PRESS SYNDICATE. All rights reserved.

another dimension: time. Of course, films, videos, and animations may also include sound, but not necessarily. They may even involve manipulation of time and space, which make them very powerful as presentation aids because they allow us to see things that we would not ordinarily see.

Have you ever seen a film of storm clouds racing and boiling through the sky? How about a flower growing, opening, and its petals unfolding? These are examples of time compression. That is, what may have taken several minutes, hours, or days is sped up to reveal movement we might not have otherwise perceived. When you watch a slow-motion replay of a touchdown pass or a "photo-finish" at a horse race, you are witnessing the expansion of time. How many times have you seen the touchdown challenged and then overturned after the official watched the slow-motion replay and decided that what the referee saw on the field was incorrect?

So, should you use a video or an animation in your presentation? As long as the clip is short and it doesn't overwhelm the rest of your presentation, it may be a good choice. Of course, you must have the proper technology available to make it work. If in doubt, ask your instructor. Don't use videos or animations for their "whiz bang" effect. Use them because it would be difficult or impossible to get your point across otherwise.

Objects

The most concrete visual aid available is an object. Your audience will see exactly what you are talking about in three dimensions. Of course, it must be large enough to be seen by the audience and small enough to carry to your presentation. If you are presenting to just a handful of people in a meeting room, you can use a much smaller object than you could in front of hundreds of people in an auditorium. If an object is rare, fragile, valuable, or dangerous, it is probably not a good choice as a presentation aid. Playing paintball is a fine hobby and may make a good informative speech topic, but bringing a paintball gun on campus is a bad idea (and probably illegal). Use common sense and ask your instructor if you have any doubts about using an object in your presentation.

Preparing to Participate 12.2
Types of Presentation Aids

Knowledge
What are the types of presentation aids?

Application
Which types best suit your topic, audience, and classroom situation?

Display Technologies

When it comes to visual presentation there are basically two **display technologies**: screen or paper. There are some variations of these technologies available and they can be used together, depending on content, audience, context, and availability.

Screen

Screen presentations include the use of overhead transparencies, computer/video projectors, and computer/television monitors.

Overhead Transparencies The machine that projects overhead transparencies is sometimes called a *vu graph*. This technology has been around since right after World War II, but many schools, universities, government agencies, and large businesses still have these machines. As you know, there are newer technologies that are replacing the vu graph's use, but it's still a good idea to have familiarity with this device. For example, since vu graphs can be found just about everywhere, they make a good "plan B" backup option should another technology fail. The transparencies are easy to create with a personal computer and printer. Just load your printer with the proper material and hit print. Please make sure to get the right transparencies for your printer—laser printers and ink jet printers use different materials. In addition, using the wrong material can damage your printer.

Computer/Video Projectors Probably the most common type of display technology in use today in universities and businesses is the computer/video projector combination. Basically, either a computer or a video device (VCR, DVD player, etc.) is connected to an electronic projector to display information. Many classrooms, boardrooms, and meeting rooms are permanently wired with such technology, making it fairly simple to use. There are several small, portable projector models available for use with laptop computers that make giving electronic presentations anywhere a reality. Depending on brightness level of the projector, the room lights may or may not have to be lowered during the presentation.

Presentation software such as Microsoft PowerPoint and Apple Keynote are typically used in these situations. All of the visual forms discussed earlier (with the exception of objects) can be incorporated into these programs. You can also include animation, transitions, and sound. For more detailed instruction on the creation and use of PowerPoint, refer to the online appendix.

Monitors With the advent of extremely large flat panel television/video/computer monitors, some speaking rooms are outfitted with these instead of projectors. They are usually not as large as a projected image, but almost always can be used in normal room light and feature extremely vivid images with good color and contrast. Just make sure everyone in your audience can see the monitor.

Paper

You may not think of paper as a technology, but in fact it is. It has just been around for several hundred years. As such, it is a mature technology that has a long history of use and well-established design principles. The visuals you create to support your presentation can be printed as handouts for each person in the audience, or you can create large prints and posters to show from your speaking position. Remember to ask your instructor about his or her preferences for use of handouts during classroom presentations. The speaking/meeting room will have to be fairly small, with your audience sitting nearby to use printed materials such as posters as a display technology. Another way to present with paper is to use flip charts. Your visuals can be prepared in advance or you can solicit information from the audience and write on the pad as you speak. Flip charts are most useful in an interactive format such as a brainstorming session or business meeting, and may not be the best choice during a classroom presentation.

Preparing to Participate 12.3
Display Technologies

Knowledge Icon
What are the various ways you can display your presentation aid?

Application Icon
Which of these technologies will you have available to present your speech?
Which of these technologies do you think you might use in your profession?

Design Considerations

Visual communication and design is a topic/book/course/major/career all on its own. Before we talk about specific design principles, it is important to note that any presentation aid needs to be large enough to be seen by the entire

Critical Interaction 12.2
Analyzing Figures

There are several figures that serve to illustrate certain concepts in this chapter. Some would work well using display technology, whereas others would function better as handouts. Look at each visual offered in this chapter and decide *how* or *if* it should be used as a presentation aid. Is there anything that should be changed that would make these figures more effective as presentation aids?

audience. This usually means large font, photo, and graphic sizes if the aid is to be projected at the front of the room. In addition, some basic **design principles** including contrast, repetition, alignment, and proximity can help you create your presentation aids.[6]

Source Citation:
[6] For an expanded discussion of these principles, see Williams, R. (2004). *The non-designer's design book* (2nd ed.). Berkeley: Peachpit Press.

Contrast

To show **contrast**, you can vary the size of the visual elements you use. Information varies in terms of importance, and using contrasting sizes helps communicate this variability. Headings should be larger than table elements. Also use contrasting colors. Blue almost always makes a good background color because cooler colors seem to fade away from the viewer. However, black text on a dark blue background is hard to read because there is not enough color contrast. White text on blue is much easier to read.

Repetition

Be consistent. Once you have established a look or color scheme, stick with it by using **repetition**. If you change the background, the audience will start to wonder if the change means something and they will quit listening to what you say. If you are using a warm, nostalgic illustration style, don't switch to something cool and modern. If you pick a particular typeface for your headings, stick with it throughout your presentation. Unless you've been trained in typography we recommend using no more than two typefaces during a presentation. Of course, you can vary a typeface just by making it bold, larger, etc. Just because you have 200 typefaces on your computer doesn't mean you have to use them all at once.

Alignment

Novice designers tend to stick visual elements all over the place, trying to fill up all of the corners, and it tends to get a little messy. Visual elements (text, graphics, diagrams, illustrations, photos) can be **aligned** on their tops, bottoms, and sides. By creating some strong alignments and edges you can clean up a messy visual relatively quickly. Try to ensure that every element on the screen aligns with at least one other item. Try it—it works wonders!

Proximity

If two or more visual items are related, group them closely. Because of their **proximity**, your audience will immediately know to interpret them together. Conversely, if the visual items should be interpreted as separate elements, then space them further apart. By the simple act of careful placement, you can create relationships that help your audience comprehend the information.

These four principles are easy to understand and implement, but they will make your visuals look much better and will enhance your visual literacy.

Integrating the Presentation Aid into the Speech

The presentation aid must be gracefully integrated into the message of the speech. Before the presentation, you should inspect the room for lighting and general setup, assemble everything needed to display the presentation aid, and determine your position and the placement of the presentation aid. Practice is essential. Once you are comfortable with the content of your speech, you should practice incorporating the presentation aid. This means that you will have to *talk* and *do* at the same time. Rehearse your presentation until you are comfortable with the presentation aid and know how to handle it during the speech. By considering in advance what you physically need to do to display your aid and where you need to be to make this happen, you will enable the integration of the presentation aid to flow with the content of your speech.

You should be able to maintain eye contact with the audience and avoid talking *to* the presentation aid. If you glance briefly at the presentation aid, you can draw your audience's attention to it, but then you need to turn your attention back to the audience to explain the content of the aid. Be sure that your audience can see the aid and you at the same time. Timing is important. After you have used the aid, it should be removed. Do not display the next aid until you are ready to use it.

One more thing: Always be prepared to do without. Televisions can break, overhead projectors can burn out, computers can lock up, and transparencies can be left at home. After all, if used properly, presentation aids are not the presentation themselves. You and your message should always come first.

Using Presentation Aids

Log on to MySpeechLab.com and access the video on Using Presentation Aids.

1. What types of presentation aids will be appropriate to your topic, audience, or situation?
2. Are there any limitations to the types of presentation aids you can use in your classroom? Hint: Ask your instructor.

In the next chapter you will learn some strategies for effectively delivering your speech.

SUMMARY

To accomplish your communication goals, you often need to express yourself visually. In this chapter we introduced the idea of *visual literacy* and how this knowledge will help you create, as well as interpret visual messages. Beyond production of presentation aids for your speech, you need to correctly interpret the deluge of images that you encounter each day. Effective production and consumption of visual messages is one more skill needed to become a *confident* and *competent* communicator. You also learned about many types of visuals and the display technologies that are used to present them. We also discussed basic design considerations that will allow you to create attractive and effective visuals. Finally, we offered some tips about how to integrate the presentation aids into your speech.

KEY TERMS

visual literacy (176)

written language (178)

numbered list, bulleted list, and table (179)

sequence, priority, and membership (179)

data graphic (179)

pie graph (180)

line graph (180)

vertical bar graph (180)

data map (182)

diagram (183)

display technology (188)

design principle (190)

contrast, repetition, alignment, and proximity (190)

ADDITIONAL ENGAGEMENT OPPORTUNITIES

Now that you have finished reading the chapter, it is also important to make connections between the course content and your own experiences. These activities will help you understand, apply, analyze, evaluate, or synthesize course concepts. You can use these activities to provide evidence of your preparation for participation in class as well as to plan additional contributions to class discussion. The Civic Engagement Opportunities (CEOs) are designed to help you become more engaged in campus and community life and apply course concepts to important social issues.

1. Peruse a magazine to find examples of visual representations. What types of presentation aids are used? Are they appropriate to the audience? Would you need to alter these visuals to present them in the classroom?

2. Imagine the following scenario.

   Your roommate has failed to pay his/her part of the rent monies for your apartment for the second month in a row. You have agreed to meet at the apartment to discuss the issue.

   What presentation aids would you bring with you as support for your argument?

3. 🗨 On February 5, 2003, U.S. Secretary of State Colin Powell appeared before the United Nations Security Council and used visual aids to forcefully argue that Iraq possessed a number of weapons of mass destruction that threatened global security. For this CEO, first read the following article summarizing Mr. Powell's use of presentation aids: http://www.presentersuniversity.com/ visuals_visuals_being_persuasive.php. Do you agree with the author's assessment of the persuasiveness of Mr. Powell's presentation? Why was visual evidence so important in this situation? What did the visuals provide that verbal argument could not?

Delivering the Presentation

A good orator is pointed and impassioned.
—Marcus T. Cicero

CHAPTER OBJECTIVES

After reading this chapter, you should be able to:

- Understand the importance of delivery to effective public speaking.

- List and identify the methods of delivery.

- Distinguish between verbal and nonverbal aspects of delivery.

Elisabeth Hasselbeck

Effective delivery gives life to words. Ineffective delivery has the potential to make words meaningless. In the previous chapters, we discussed each step in the speech-making process including choosing topics, conducting research, organizing ideas, and choosing language. With each step, you have engaged in the process of becoming a critical producer of information. Now that you have considered *what* you will say, you need to think about *how* you will say it. The good news is that if you have followed the guidelines presented in this text as you produced your message and you have allowed yourself enough time to consider how you will deliver the message, your ability to communicate to your audience should be enhanced by the decisions you made.

For example, if you considered the difference between written and oral styles as you constructed your speech, your delivery will sound more conversational—that should be your goal. Effective delivery demonstrates your desire to communicate *with*, not *at* your audience. Effective delivery demonstrates your enthusiasm for the topic and confidence in the content. Effective delivery does not detract from the message in any way. As such, effective speakers "sound" natural, conversational, confident, and enthusiastic about the opportunity to share information with or influence their audiences in some way.

In this chapter, we will discuss the importance of delivery, the various methods of delivery, and how to enhance both your verbal and your nonverbal delivery.

Importance of Delivery

The delivery of your presentation will be the means by which you communicate your credibility as a speaker. Keep in mind one central tenet of nonverbal communication—*we cannot not communicate nonverbally.*[1] From the moment you approach the front of the room, you are communicating to your audience. They will not know of your efforts unless you communicate your preparation to them through your delivery. The first thing the audience sees is your actions before you ever speak a word. These actions should be consistent with the amount of time you spent in preparation for this moment and demonstrate your confidence in a well-produced presentation. This will enhance your speaker credibility.

Because your audience will most likely not have access to your outline or the content of your speech, they will be paying particular attention to your delivery. A recent study found that when asked to comment on student presentations, peer evaluators were much more likely to comment on the strengths or weaknesses of a speaker's delivery as opposed to the content of the speech.[2] Perhaps this is because it is easier to comment on what you see rather than what you hear. This certainly has implications for the amount of time you should set aside to practice your delivery and make a good impression on your audience.

Methods of Delivery

There are several ways to deliver a presentation, but one is most suitable to a classroom presentation. We'll discuss the other methods briefly

Source Citation:
[1] Watzlawick, P., Bevelas, J. B., & Jackson, D. D. (1967). *Pragmatics of human communication.* New York: W. W. Norton.

Source Citation:
[2] Reynolds, D., Hunt, S. K., Simonds, C. J., & Cutbirth, C. W. (2004). Written speech feedback in the basic communication course: Are instructors too polite to students? In B. S. Titsworth (Ed.), *Basic communication course annual* (Vol. 16, pp. 36–71). Boston: American Press.

Preparing to Participate 13.1

Importance of Delivery

Knowledge

What is the difference between effective and ineffective delivery?
Why is delivery important?

Application

Can you think of a public speaker that has effective or ineffective delivery?
What does he or she do that is effective or ineffective?

and end with a more thorough discussion of how you will present your speech. The four methods of delivery are impromptu, manuscript, memorized, and extemporaneous.

Impromptu

Impromptu speaking happens when you are called to talk "off the cuff." That is, you have little or no time to prepare your remarks. This happens on a daily basis. You may be asked to explain your actions, provide directions, defend an idea, participate in class discussions, or simply converse with a friend or classmate. You do not always plan in advance what you say, but you may think of ways that you can best convey your message. For example, in a class discussion, as you listen to your classmates provide contributions, you can begin to formulate your own. You can identify a key point you'd like to make, as well as decide how you will begin and end your comment. If you are asked to go to the front of the room to give an impromptu presentation, you can also think of key words or phrases you'd like to use. You can jot down key points and decide how you will support each point. As you walk to the front of the room, take a few deep breaths for confidence and be sure to speak directly to your audience. Additionally, as you are giving your class presentation, you may need to adapt your speech to your audience. For example, if you use a term that you are familiar with, but note some confusion on the face of one of your classmates, you may want to provide an impromptu definition of your term.

Manuscript

Some speeches are read word for word, and rightly so. If what you have to say needs to be precise and has limited time constraints, then you would want to speak from a **manuscript**. For example, if you are giving a television or radio address, you will need to give a clear and concise message in a short amount of time. Television newscasters speak from manuscripts through a teleprompter and do not have much leeway to stray from the script. They do this because they have strict time limitations and they are skilled in the practice of making the news sound conversational. Effective manuscript speakers will practice aloud to make their speech sound more natural. They will make advanced decisions on when to pause, emphasize a word, look at the audience, and so forth.

There may be instances where you will need to read a passage such as a brief poem or an excerpt from a piece of literature in your classroom presentation. However, as most beginning speakers don't sound conversational when reading, we do not advise that you read your entire class presentation to your audience.

Memorized

If your message is going to be somewhat brief, you may consider **memorizing** all or parts of the presentation. This might be a good strategy for special occasions such as introducing other speakers or making a toast at a wedding. Sometimes, speakers will memorize the attention getter and conclusion of their presentation to make sure they have a strong opening and a memorable close. Additionally, certain quotes may need to be memorized to ensure the accuracy of the citation. Even though you know exactly what you are going to say, you will want to rehearse the presentation in such a way that it does not sound like it is memorized. You can plan, in advance, how to emphasize certain words as well as determine times to look directly at the audience. You will want to be sure you can concentrate on the audience rather than remembering the words. Some apprehensive speakers think that they will feel much more comfortable if they memorize their speech, but this is not advisable. Most likely, your nerves will make you forget the exact wording you had planned and your audience will tend to perceive that you are talking *at* them instead of *to* them.

Extemporaneous

Simply put, **extemporaneous speaking** means that you deliver your presentation from a prepared outline or speaking notes. This method is often preferred in classroom presentations because it allows you to experience what it is like to communicate a message that is well-conceived and planned. Recall from Chapter 9, we discussed the difference between a preparation outline and a speaking outline. As you write your preparation outline and practice your speech aloud several times, you become confident enough to transfer the detailed information to a speaking outline that provides you with the notes you need to deliver your presentation. You know, in advance, what you plan to say, but you do not have it written out word-for-word. This allows you to better communicate with your audience.

Extemporaneous speaking allows you to gauge your audience's reactions (feedback) and adapt your message accordingly. For example, if you say a term and you notice that a member of the class looks confused, this may indicate to you that you need to define or more carefully explain that term. If you see someone in the back of the room struggling to hear you, you know that you need to adjust the volume of your presentation.

Extemporaneous speaking allows you to speak more conversationally. Your audience does not expect you to be flawless as they would if you were reading. In fact, audiences do not like being read to. This gives them the opportunity to get distracted and perhaps not pay attention to your speech. When you look up from your notes, you may even pause or stumble a bit, but this happens naturally in conversation. In fact, as instructors we often tell our students that we would much rather they stumble here and there than read to us (which is not natural at all).

It should be noted that in the course of an extemporaneous speech, there may be elements of the other delivery methods. For example, as discussed earlier, you may want to memorize the attention getter, memorable close, and exact quotes. You may want to read a passage from a source, or you may want to use impromptu communication to adapt to your audience.

You know *what* you want to say; now you need to consider *how* you will say it. In the following sections, we will discuss how you can use verbal and nonverbal delivery strategies to make your presentation sound more conversational, credible, and confident.

Preparing to Participate 13.2
Methods of Delivery

Knowledge
What are the four methods of delivery?

Application
Which one are you most likely to use in your classroom presentation? Think of an example of when you have heard someone use each of these methods. For example, when do politicians use each of these methods of delivery?

Verbal Delivery

How can you use your voice to make yourself appear credible and your message sound conversational? The trick is variety! To be perceived as credible, you will want to have clear articulation and pronunciation. To sound conversational, you will want to vary your volume, rate, and pitch. All of these characteristics make up your **verbal delivery**.

Articulation

Articulation is the clear formation of words. Your articulators are parts of your physical anatomy that allow you to form your words. To illustrate, try saying the following tongue twister:

> A tutor who tooted the flute tried to tutor two students to toot. Said the two to the tutor, "Is it harder to toot or to tutor two students to toot?"

Now, what did you physically have to do to say this? Did you use your mouth, tongue, teeth, and hard and soft palate? These are your articulators and they help you to form each sound in a word.

Sometimes people get lazy with their words and skip a few sounds. For example, has anyone ever asked you, "Yungry, lesqueet?" Did you understand what they were asking? Probably, but they were not clearly articulating. Lazy articulators say things like "gonna" instead of "going to," "din't" instead of "didn't," or "fishin" instead of "fishing." Lazy articulators lack a certain level of credibility in the eyes of their audience. As you practice your presentation, try loosening up those articulators to clearly form each and every sound of your words. Think about what you do when you use a mouth wash. The swishing motion you make as you rinse would be similar to loosening your articulators. When you are done rinsing, open and close your jaw as widely as you can. Taking a drink of water just before your presentation will allow you to become aware of your articulators and loosen them up. You may even consider warming up with a few tongue twisters.

Pronunciation

> you say tomato, i say tomahto
> you eat potato and i eat potahto
> tomato, tomahto, potato, potahto
> let's call the whole thing off

Many of you may be familiar with Fred Astaire and this song (or, maybe not!), but the difference between the ways in which *tomato* and *potato* are said is in pronunciation. Each language has an accepted standard for how a word should sound. Although many people can read or write a particular word, they may be less certain about how to pronounce it. **Pronunciation** is how a word is said and stressed. Which syllable is the strongest and which vowel sound is used? Is it a short *a* or a long *a*? Dictionaries provide information for how a word should be said. As you construct your message, be on the lookout for any words that you may not be sure how to pronounce. You will want to pay particular attention to how names of sources are pronounced, which can sometimes be tricky. For example, if you are talking about the German scholar, Max Weber, you will want to be sure to pronounce his name as Max *Veber*, which is the correct pronunciation. Incorrect pronunciation will also affect speaker credibility if the audience catches on.

Volume

The loudness or softness with which you speak should be varied to sound conversational. In natural conversation, no one really ever talks with the same amount of **volume** at all times. People tend to get louder when they want to stress a point and softer when they want to show effect. Try reading a passage from this chapter without varying your volume. It sounds monotonous, right?

Your volume should also be appropriate to the size of the room and the audience. Do you know anyone who is a loud talker? This can be quite annoying and detract from a person's message. On the other hand, if people can't hear the message, nothing can be communicated. Rooms with a lot of people require more volume than rooms with just a few people. Larger rooms require more volume than smaller rooms. Try practicing in the room where you will be speaking and get a classmate to sit at the back of the room. You will want to project your voice in such a way that the audience member in the back of the room can hear you comfortably without the people in the front of the room thinking you are shouting at them.

Rate

You will also want to vary the speed with which you speak, or your **rate**. This might include some well-planned pauses for emphasis or effect. We have all heard speakers who, once in front of an audience, start talking like a speeding bullet. This can be distracting. However, it is important to know that sometimes when you are nervous, you have a tendency to speak fast. You should look to your audience for clues that this is happening.

To find a comfortable rate and to help you relax, try taking three deep breaths before you speak. As you do, remind yourself to speak slowly. You should practice your rate so that you are saying about two words per second. This will give you a comfortable pace that sounds conversational and will also allow you to practice giving your speech within the allotted time limit. Remember, your audience needs time to grasp complex information and follow the organization of your presentation. On the other hand, speaking too slowly may bore audiences and ultimately decrease the amount of information they retain from your speech. In fact, research has generally found that moderate speakers are perceived as more intelligent, competent, confident, credible, socially attractive, and effective than slow speakers.[3]

Pause

One way to vary your rate is through the use of pauses. A well-timed moment of silence can speak volumes to an audience. **Pauses** can be used to emphasize a point, collect your thoughts, or transition to a new point. The use of pauses can also demonstrate poise and confidence, which will enhance your credibility with your audience.

The problem is, we have a tendency to want to fill our pauses with something. How many times have you heard speakers hem and haw during a presentation? You know what we're talking about because you've probably been annoyed by someone's overuse of *umm, ah, you know, like* . . . Or, maybe you're the culprit. We would recommend that you practice your speech in front of someone to have them check for these filler words. Once you realize you have a tendency to use them, it is much easier to learn to replace them with silence.

Pitch

Pitch is the highness or lowness of your voice. Have you ever known anyone with a particularly high voice? Again . . . annoying! On the other hand, someone

Source Citation:
[3] Simonds, B. K., Meyer, K. R., Quinlan, M. M., & Hunt, S. K. (2006). Effects of instructor speech rate on student affective learning, recall, and perceptions of nonverbal immediacy, credibility, and clarity. *Communication Research Reports, 23,* 187–197.

See also

Skinner, C. H., Robinson, D. H., Robinson, S. L., Sterling, H. E., & Goodman, M. A. (1999). Effects of advertisement speech rates on feature recognition, and product and speaker ratings. *International Journal of Listening, 13,* 97–110.

who attempts to speak in a low range can sound unnatural. Nervousness may also cause you to raise your pitch beyond what is comfortable for the audience to hear. Once you find a comfortable range or pitch, you should consider points in the presentation where you will want to vary it. When you vary your pitch, you are using **inflection** to help communicate your ideas. When you do not, your speech becomes **monotone**. Perhaps you have known someone who speaks in the same pitch at all times and you know exactly what we are talking about. A good example of a monotone voice comes from the ever-popular movie, *Ferris Bueller's Day Off*, where the teacher calls roll, lectures, and then asks questions he never really intends for anyone to answer. And yet he continues with his monotone lecture after no one responds to: *anyone?. . . anyone? . . .*

We generally raise our pitch at the end of a question and the audience knows it is a question without actually seeing the punctuation mark. For example, consider the following statements:

> Got the keys? (asking if someone else has the keys)
> Got the keys! (telling someone else you have the keys)

You may remember an episode of *Friends* where this caused confusion and the group was ultimately locked out of the apartment with Thanksgiving dinner waiting inside.

Vocal Variety

The way that you vary the last four vocal qualities (volume, rate, pauses, and pitch) will enhance your overall **vocal variety**. Vocal variety allows speakers to become more conversational and expressive. In other words, vocal variety will provide evidence of your communication competence. The next time you have a conversation with a family member or friend, see if you can identify when and how he or she varies in volume, rate, pause, and pitch. Whereas we have a tendency to do this in natural conversation, we also have a tendency to stiffen up in our presentations. The fact that you are standing in front of an

Altering Pitch. A former speechwriter for Presidents Nixon and Ford, Ben Stein later entered the entertainment field, where he became known for his monotone vocal delivery.

audience and being evaluated will most likely cause you to do this. Your concentration is on the content of what you have to say, but not necessarily on how you are saying it. That is why you need to practice your delivery. Think about ways to vary your voice so that the audience becomes more interested in what you have to say.

Preparing to Participate 13.3
Verbal Delivery

Knowledge
What are the aspects of verbal delivery?

Application
How can you vary each of these to enhance your presentation?
What happens when there is no variation in verbal delivery?

Nonverbal Delivery

Nonverbal delivery also gives meaning to your words. In fact, if your actions are inconsistent with your message, your audience is more likely to believe *how* you say it rather than *what* you say.[4] For example, if you say you are interested in your topic, but your face and body indicate that you are bored, your audience will not be motivated to listen. However, if you are able to demonstrate energy and enthusiasm for your topic, your audience will become interested as well. So, how do you do that? Through your eyes, face, body (posture and gesture), and movement (use of space).

Source Citation:
[4] Knapp, M., & Hall, J. (1997). *Nonverbal communication in human interaction* (4th ed.). Philadelphia: Harcourt, Brace, Jovanovich.

Critical Interaction 13.1
What Did You Say?

Say the following sentences out loud, emphasizing the words in bold. How does the meaning change if the words stay the same? How did your verbal and nonverbal delivery change the meaning of each sentence?

I didn't tell Maria that you were mad.

I **didn't** tell Maria that you were mad.

I didn't **tell** Maria that you were mad.

I didn't tell **Maria** that you were mad.

I didn't tell Maria that **you** were mad.

I didn't tell Maria that you were **mad.**

Eye Contact

Source Citations:
5 Napieralski, L. P., Brooks, C. I., & Droney, J. M. (1995). The effect of duration of eye contact on American college students' attributions of state, trait, and test anxiety. *Journal of Social Psychology, 135,* 273–280.

6 Richmond, V. P., McCroskey, J. C., & Payne, S. K. (1987). *Nonverbal behavior in interpersonal relations.* Englewood Cliffs, NJ: Prentice-Hall.

In many cultures, **eye contact** communicates to your audience that you are credible and that you care about how they are receiving your message;[5] however, this can vary from culture to culture.[6] In the United States, we value when someone looks at us while they speak. In fact, we may tend to disbelieve someone who cannot look us in the eye. In some Asian cultures, however, avoiding eye contact is a sign of respect in interpersonal contexts. However, in the public speaking context, eye contact establishes the connection between the speaker and the audience. When a speaker looks out at the audience, the audience is more likely to listen. When a speaker uses eye contact, he or she is able to gauge audience feedback to the message. In this way, eye contact is what allows speakers to actually communicate *with* their audiences as opposed to speaking *at* their audiences. Therefore, eye contact should be purposeful. You should look at your audience to determine how they are responding to your message. Many times, students think that if they just look up from their notes about half the time, this is considered good eye contact. But the purpose of eye contact is not to let your audience know that you have practiced enough to be able to look away from your notes from time to time. Rather, your eye contact should be directed to your audience for the purpose of determining their reactions to your message.

Face

As you look into the faces of your audience through the use of eye contact, they are looking right back at you. As they watch you present your message, they are looking at your face to determine if *what* you say is consistent with *how* you are saying it. If you say you are excited about your topic, does your face agree? If your topic is serious, does your face indicate this? If you are attempting to use humor, does your face help you with your punch line? A well-planned smile or even a frown can communicate more to your audience than perhaps your words alone. Speakers should learn to let their **facial expressions** compliment their message as opposed to contradicting it. Varying your facial expressions and making sure they match your verbal message will also enhance your credibility.[7] Try practicing with a close friend or in front of a mirror and see if your face actually demonstrates how you feel about your topic and message.

Source Citation:
7 Burgoon, J. K., Birk, T., & Pfau, M. (1990). Nonverbal behaviors, persuasion, and credibility. *Human Communication Research, 17,* 140–170.

Body

Your body communicates to your audience how you feel about your message. Through the use of posture and gestures, you can indicate your speaker credibility and confidence in your message. Let's first discuss **posture**.

In the chapter on communication apprehension, we discussed several strategies you could use to relax your body through tension and release exercises. These techniques will allow you to walk to the front of the room more relaxed and to appear more confident.

Once you get to the front of the room, you will want to stand with your weight distributed evenly on both legs and with your feet approximately shoulder width apart. This will keep you from swaying back and forth. You do not want your audience wishing they had taken their Dramamine before your speech! Indeed, swaying because one leg gets tired can become quite annoying and it certainly detracts from the content of your message. Be sure to begin your presentation with your arms resting comfortably at your side. This may indicate to your audience that you are relaxed and ready to present, which will certainly affect their perceptions of your credibility. When you are ready to speak, simply raise your speaking outline and begin (see Chapter 9 for information on speaking outlines). Try holding your notes with one hand so you can free your other hand to make gestures.

Gestures are the use of your body in some way to reinforce an idea. Most gestures are done with the hands or arms, but can also be accomplished with a shrug of a shoulder or the movement of a leg or foot. Gesturing is natural in communication. Most of us gesture without even thinking about it. Try talking to someone sometime without moving your body in any way. Difficult, right? After you have constructed your presentation and have begun practicing your delivery, consider where in the presentation is a good place to gesture. You can include your plans on your speaking outline (again, see Chapter 9). Gestures should be natural; it will take some practice to make them look comfortable as opposed to mechanical. Sometimes a small movement can communicate more than a large one. A simple raising or lowering of the hand can be used to indicate movement or direction with a concept.

Gesturing. As a former movie actor, President Reagan understood the value of good delivery and was called "the great communicator."

Gesturing can indicate size and relationship among ideas as well. But unintended and unplanned gestures, such as nervous fidgeting, fiddling with your notes, or repeatedly raising your hand for no apparent reason can also be distracting. As you practice your presentation, monitor your gestures to make sure they are effective.

We recommend using note cards as opposed to printed pages for your speaking outline because they are easier to use when gesturing and do not rattle when hands are shaky. We also recommend using just a few note cards, because if you have too many, they can become cumbersome and cause you some frustration as you speak. You should number your note cards and only use one side. Practice with your note cards. Don't assume this will be easy. As instructors, we have certainly seen our fair share of students becoming flustered because their cards get out of order.

Movement

It is not often that we see speakers stand in just one place unless they are behind a podium and cannot move because of the placement of the microphone. This will most likely not be the case for your classroom presentation, however. When you get out from behind a podium, you are indicating to your classmates that you are approachable and confident in your message. In fact, making use of your available space through **movement** may even help you to reduce your level of anxiety. Movement takes energy. Using energy releases the adrenalin that may cause nervousness. If you are using a presentation aid, you will want to plan where you are before, during, and after your demonstration of the aid. This is a very natural place in the presentation for movement.

Movement should be meaningful and well planned. Again, your audience may be wishing they had taken that Dramamine if you move aimlessly about the room. But, if you use movement for emphasis or to show transition, you can allow your use of space to support and enhance your message.

Media
Interaction 13.1

Analyzing Delivery in a Sample Speech

Log on to MySpeechLab.com and access the C and A sample videos on the Coliseum.

1. How does Carla use verbal and nonverbal delivery in the C speech?
2. How could she use delivery more effectively?
3. How does Carla use verbal and nonverbal delivery in the A speech?
4. How does this change the quality of her presentation?

Preparing to Participate 13.4
Nonverbal Delivery

Knowledge
What are the aspects of nonverbal delivery?

Application
What happens when your nonverbal delivery is not consistent with your verbal delivery?

Critical Interaction 13.2
Sarah Palin at RNC 2008

Sarah Palin, the 2008 Republican Vice Presidential Nominee, has been applauded for her ability to deliver an effective speech. Take a moment to view her acceptance speech at the Republican National Convention at http://www.americanrhetoric.com/speeches/convention2008/sarah-palin2008rnc.htm. How does she use the following verbal and nonverbal characteristics to enhance her message?

- Articulation
- Pronunciation
- Volume
- Rate
- Pitch
- Eye Contact
- Face/Body
- Movement

SUMMARY

Often, students think that once they construct their presentation, they are finished preparing for their speech. They are not! As you have seen in this chapter, there are many things to consider in the delivery of your presentation. Taking both verbal and nonverbal delivery into consideration will require much time and practice. You should practice alone until you become comfortable enough with your delivery to practice in front of a friend. As you practice for your friend, ask him or her to look for effective or ineffective uses of your voice and body. Remember, your delivery should be consistent with your content and not detract from your message. You may not be aware of any distracting mannerisms until they are pointed out for you.

A well-written speech and an effective delivery will lead to perceptions of you as a *competent communicator*. As your audience perceives you to be a competent communicator, you also become a more *confident communicator*. Have confidence in a well-written speech. This is how it works! You have spent much time selecting, researching, and organizing your topic. You are confident with your material and you still have time before the presentation to practice your delivery. This confidence should help with your performance, which will result in your audience having confidence in you.

This chapter marks the end of our second unit on message clarity. You should now be ready to present your informative speech. In addition to presenting your own speech, you will be listening to and evaluating the messages of others. For information on how to effectively evaluate or provide feedback to your classmates' speeches, please review the section on Evaluating Messages Using Critical Listening in Chapter 4.

KEY TERMS

impromptu speech (197)

manuscript speech (197)

memorized speech (198)

extemporaneous speech (198)

verbal delivery (199)

articulation (199)

pronunciation (200)

volume (200)

rate (201)

pause (201)

pitch (201)

inflection (202)

monotone (202)

vocal variety (202)

nonverbal delivery (203)

eye contact (204)

facial expressions (204)

posture (204)

gestures (205)

movement (206)

ADDITIONAL ENGAGEMENT OPPORTUNITIES

Now that you have finished reading the chapter, it is also important to make connections between the course content and your own experiences. These activities will help you understand, apply, analyze, evaluate, or synthesize course concepts. You can use these activities to provide evidence of your preparation for participation in class as well as to plan additional contributions to class discussion. The Civic Engagement Opportunities (CEOs) are designed to help you become more engaged in campus and community life and apply course concepts to important social issues.

1. Visit a speaker on campus. How did the person handle his/her delivery? What did he/she do that was effective? Ineffective?

2. Think about and respond to the following situation:

   a. You have a monthly review session with your boss in a few days. You have decided you will ask for a raise.

   b. What delivery skills will be important at your meeting with your boss? What are things you should avoid doing?

3. 🗩 Visit the History Channel's Great Speeches website (http://www.history.com/media.do?action=listing&sortBy=1&sortOrder=A&topic=GREAT%20SPEECHES)
   This site contains some of the most important political speeches in U.S. history. Select and view at least one speech and answer the following questions:

   a. What method of delivery did the speaker use? Why did the speaker select this method?

   b. Evaluate the speaker's verbal (i.e., articulation, pronunciation, volume, rate, pause, pitch, and vocal variety) and nonverbal (i.e., eye contact, facial expressions, body language, and movement) delivery. Overall, was the speaker's delivery effective? Why or why not? Are there changes in delivery that might have made the speech more effective?

c. Think broadly about the role of communication skills generally, and public speaking skills specifically, in the political process. How important are communication skills to the political process? How might you use the skills you are acquiring in this class to encourage political change in your own community?

14

Understanding Persuasive Principles

*Speech is power: speech is to persuade,
to convert, to compel.*

—Ralph Waldo Emerson

CHAPTER OBJECTIVES

After reading this chapter, you should be able to:

- Understand the nature of persuasive public speaking.
- Identify the burdens of proof and effectively organize persuasive speeches using claims of fact.
- Identify the burdens of proof and effectively organize persuasive speeches using claims of value.
- Identify the burdens of proof and effectively organize persuasive speeches on claims of policy.

Tim Gunn

In your daily activities, how often are you exposed to persuasive messages? You might use persuasive communication to challenge a grade with a teacher, reduce the price of that house or car you are purchasing, convince your parents to send more money to you at school, get your children to clean their rooms, and so on. These examples illustrate a very important point—persuasion is a central feature of every aspect of human communication. Persuasion happens wherever you find people communicating. In this chapter and throughout this final unit, you'll read about basic principles that will make you a more effective producer and consumer of persuasive messages. Also, you will learn a few theories that can be applied to your everyday interactions with others. You might even learn a few new ways to buy that car for less or get more spending money for school!

Why Should I Study Persuasion?

One very important reason to study persuasive communication is that you have been and will continue to be bombarded with attempts to influence your decisions. Take a look around your campus, residence, workplace, and classroom for evidence of persuasive communication. As you left your residence for class today, you likely encountered people on campus who solicited you for one thing or another. As you sit in the classroom, posters for credit cards, apartments, and travel destinations likely surround you. As you listen to your instructor, you are being persuaded, even if indirectly, to adopt a particular view of the world. As you watch television, you are saturated with advertisements for a whole range of topics. And this is simply a thumbnail sketch of some of the ways that others attempt to influence you on a daily basis. One benefit of better understanding persuasion is that you will become a more informed and critical consumer of persuasive messages.

The Importance of Persuasion. As consumers we face persuasive appeals every day.

Many students assume that they know all they need to know about persuasive communication because they've been practicing it all their lives. In reality, you probably have formed your own personal theories about how to persuade others and to respond to the persuasive attempts of others. You probably test such lay theories in different situations, adapting them as you learn from experience. The problem is that there is a limit to what you can learn from experience alone. In fact, there are times when you should not rely on this learning-from-experience approach. By familiarizing yourself with a few basic principles of persuasive communication, you can go a long way toward enhancing your own efforts to persuade others. In addition, a better understanding of these principles will help shield you against the persuasive attempts of others.

Think about the implications of making a mistake when using persuasive communication strategies in your negotiations to buy a car. Such a mistake could cost you hundreds or thousands of dollars. Fortunately, communication scholars have been studying persuasion for a very long time and have developed a great number of empirically tested persuasive techniques that can help you in every facet of your life—from influencing your friends and family, to buying a new car, to resisting the persuasive attempts of others. One thing to keep in mind, though, is that persuasion is not inherently bad or negative. In fact, critical thinkers are often persuaded—for the right reasons! That is, when presented with high-quality evidence and sound reasoning, ethical communicators change their minds and accept the conclusions and recommendations of the persuasive speaker.

Media Interaction 14.1
Deadly Persuasion

Visit the Media Education Foundation's *Deadly Persuasion* website (http://www.mediaed.org/videos/MediaAndHealth/DeadlyPersuasion) and view the video trailer.

1. According to this video, what persuasive strategies do manufacturers of tobacco and alcohol use to market their products?
2. Is the *Deadly Persuasion* video effective? Why or why not?
3. Who is the target audience for the *Deadly Persuasion* video?
4. How can you use your knowledge of persuasive strategies to shield yourself from the persuasive attempts of others?

Preparing to Participate 14.1
Persuasive Public Speaking

Knowledge
What reasons does the text mention for studying persuasion?
What is persuasive public speaking?
What are the goals of persuasive public speaking?

Application
How is persuasive speaking different from informative speaking?
How does the role of the audience change?

Calvin and Hobbes

Comic 14.1

1. How will understanding persuasive principles help us to become better consumers of information?

Persuasive Public Speaking

Source Citations:
[1] Aristotle. (1960). *The rhetoric of Aristotle* (L. Cooper, Trans.). New York: Appleton-Century-Crofts. (Original translation published 1932).

[2] Miller, G. R. (1980). On being persuaded: Some basic distinctions. In M. E. Roloff & G. R. Miller (Eds.), *Persuasion: New directions in theory and research* (pp. 89–116). Newbury Park, CA: Sage.

More than 2,000 years ago, the Greek philosopher Aristotle identified important elements of persuasion in his book *The Rhetoric*.[1] According to Aristotle, speakers can use particular appeals to persuade audience members. We discuss these appeals in much greater detail in the next chapter; however, in order to understand the elements of persuasive public speaking, it is first important that we define persuasive communication. **Persuasive communication** is any message that is intended to shape, reinforce, or change the responses of another, or others.[2] Unlike the informative speaker, the persuasive speaker is an **advocate** for a position, policy, or way of viewing the world. In terms of persuasive speaking, the speaker's goal is to influence the audience's attitudes, beliefs, or values. Therefore, effective persuasive speakers must conduct a thorough analysis of the audience in order to develop compelling arguments.

Analyzing the Audience

One of the first choices you'll have to make as a persuasive speaker is selecting a topic for your speech. You will also have to develop a very good understanding of your audience's position on your topic and carefully address their concerns throughout the speech. Does your audience agree with your position? Are they generally undecided? Does your audience oppose your

Advocating for Your Cause.
Senator Daniel Inouye has served continuously in the U.S. Congress since Hawaii became a state in 1959.

advocacy? The answers to these questions will necessarily influence your development of the speech. For example, if your audience is generally neutral about your position, your goal should be to shape their response in a way that is consistent with your advocacy. If your audience agrees with your advocacy, try to reinforce their position. If your audience opposes your advocacy, your goal will be to change their position. We offer several additional sections for crafting your advocacy in the remaining sections of this chapter.

It is quite likely that members of your audience will have differing opinions on your topic. As you analyze their positions, you should be able to identify a majority group or **target audience**. The target audience will become the focus of your persuasive efforts as they represent the portion of the whole audience that you most want to influence. You can use the same audience analysis techniques that you learned in Chapter 6 to determine the attitudes, beliefs, and values of your audience, which will inform how listeners will process your persuasive messages.

Attitudes   An **attitude** is a relatively enduring set of beliefs around a person, group, idea, or event that predispose an individual to respond in a particular way.[3] For example, suppose that you strongly disapprove of drilling for oil in Alaska's Arctic National Wildlife Refuge (ANWR). Further, suppose that you want to deliver a speech reflecting this opposition to an audience composed mostly of individuals who hold a positive attitude toward ANWR drilling. Although we cover a number of strategies for organizing persuasive claims later in this chapter, think for a moment about how you might select specific claims against drilling for a speech to a hostile audience. What types of arguments should you present to change the attitudes of this audience? In order to answer that question, you need to have an understanding of the specific beliefs that support the pro-drilling attitude.

Source Citation:
[3] Zanna, M. P., & Rempel, J. K. (1988). Attitudes: A new look at an old concept. In D. Bar-Tal & A. W. Kruglanski (Eds.), *The social psychology of knowledge* (pp. 315–334). Cambridge, UK: Cambridge University Press.

Beliefs   A **belief** is the acceptance that something is true even if we can't prove that it is true. For example, even absent any evidence, some people may hold positive attitudes toward drilling for oil in ANWR based on the belief that doing so will immediately lead to lower gasoline prices. A persuasive speaker seeking to change such beliefs faces the burden of presenting significant evidence to the contrary (for example, you might argue that drilling in ANWR would not significantly influence gasoline prices for many years)—especially in light of the fact that most people consider their beliefs to be facts.

Values   A **value** is a deeply held, stable conviction about what is good or bad, right or wrong with respect to human existence, including such concepts as fairness, justice, freedom, love, security, and honesty.[4] At this point you should have a sense that values are very difficult to change because they are much more stable than attitudes and beliefs. For example, an individual's positive attitudes and beliefs about drilling for oil in ANWR could be linked to the value she or he places on American security and independence. Rather than attempting to change the core values of your audience in a brief persuasive speech, your time might be more profitably spent highlighting how developing some alternative source of energy would also promote American security and independence. In other words, you could demonstrate how your advocacy fits in or is consistent with the values held by your audience. This discussion of attitudes, beliefs, and values clearly underscores just how important it is that persuasive speakers conduct a thorough analysis of their audience before developing any persuasive claims.

Source Citation:
[4] Johannesen, R. L., Valde, K. S., & Whedbee, K. E. (2008). *Ethics in human communication* (6th ed.). Prospect Heights, IL: Waveland Press.

Developing Persuasive Claims

As you develop your persuasive topic, it is important that you identify whether it is a claim of fact, value, or policy as the topic type has significant implications for determining both your **burdens of proof** and the organizational pattern you will use. We use the phrase *burden of proof* to refer to the obligation a persuasive speaker faces to provide sufficient reasons for changing what already exists and is accepted in the **status quo**. What is the status quo? This term refers to all of the laws, regulations, and attitudes that currently exist. If you are advocating change as a persuasive speaker, you must recognize and develop strategies to overcome the **status quo bias**. In other words, people are generally predisposed to favor what they currently believe as well as what currently exists.[5] As a result, you face the burden of providing solid reasons for changing the status quo.

Source Citation:
[5] Zeckhauser, R. J. (1988). Status quo bias in decision making. *Journal of Risk and Uncertainty, 1,* 7–59.

Advocating Factual Claims

When speakers address **claims of fact**, they are concerned with what is or is not true, what does or does not exist, what did or did not happen. In addition, these types of claims may focus on whether something did or did not happen in the past (*past fact*), whether something is true or not currently (*present fact*), or whether something will be true or not in the future (*projection*).[6] To be perfectly clear, speakers cannot really know with certainty whether something will be true in the future. Instead, speakers need to present evidence regarding the probability or likelihood of events occurring in the future. Examples of topics that address claims of fact include the following:

Source Citation:
[6] For more information about persuasive claims see Inch, E. S., & Warnick, B., Endres, D. (2005). *Critical thinking and communication: The use of reason in argument* (5th ed.). Boston, MA: Allyn & Bacon.

- Lee Harvey Oswald assassinated John F. Kennedy (past fact).
- Elvis died of a drug overdose (past fact).
- The 65 mile per hour speed limit saves lives (present fact).
- Marijuana usage leads to harder drugs (present fact).
- Seafood industry faces collapse by 2048 (projection).
- Social security will be depleted as greater numbers of baby boomers retire (projection).

As we've already noted in this chapter, one of the key considerations for speakers advocating factual claims is to pick a topic that is controversial enough to allow for a meaningful conversation. Some claims of fact are so narrow in scope or so widely accepted as truth that the audience will likely agree with them, leaving little room for persuasion. Consider the following statement of fact: "The United States currently has an all volunteer army." This statement is hardly debatable. Therefore, you should avoid such topics for your persuasive speeches.

Burdens of Proof

The persuasive speaker working with a factual persuasive claim faces the burden of proving that the facts support her or his position. It is essential that the speaker clearly define key terms. Consider the following factual claim: "There is life on Mars." In this case, the term *life* deserves clarification. Is the speaker referring to bacterial remains found in rocks collected on Mars or seven-foot high Martians with very long tentacles? Obviously, the speaker will have to define precisely what is meant by life on Mars.

Burdens of Proof. It is important to define terms when making claims of fact such as what constitutes life on Mars.

Organizing Speeches on Claims of Fact

The majority of claims of fact will be organized using the topical, spatial, or chronological organizational patterns that we discussed in Chapter 8. Consider the following topical organization of a persuasive speech on a claim of fact:

Specific Purpose:	To persuade my audience to believe that passive smoking negatively affects the health of non-smokers.
Thesis Statement:	Passive smoking is harmful because tobacco smoke contains dangerous chemicals that threaten the health of non-smokers.
Main Points:	A. Tobacco smoke contains over 4000 dangerous chemicals.
	B. Passive smoking causes several health problems.
	C. Passive smoking is especially dangerous to the health of young children.

As another example, suppose you are attempting to persuade your classmates that Lee Harvey Oswald was solely responsible for the assassination of John F. Kennedy. In this case, you might decide to present the facts chronologically:

Specific Purpose:	To persuade my audience to believe that Lee Harvey Oswald assassinated President John F. Kennedy.

Thesis Statement:	Witness accounts suggest that Lee Harvey Oswald was solely responsible for the assassination of President John F. Kennedy.
Main Points:	A. At 7:15 a.m., witnesses observed Lee Harvey Oswald carrying a long paper bag.
	B. At 9:45 a.m., witnesses observed Lee Harvey Oswald on the sixth floor of the Texas School Book Depository.
	C. At 12:30 p.m., Lee Harvey Oswald shot John F. Kennedy.
	D. At 1:50 p.m., Lee Harvey Oswald was captured by police.

It is also possible that you may choose to arrange a speech on a claim of fact spatially. For example:

Specific Purpose:	To persuade my audience to believe that terrorism is a serious international problem.
Thesis Statement:	Terrorists are developing and using deadly weapons that threaten innocent populations around the world.
Main Points:	A. In Spain, Islamic militants killed almost 200 people in the Madrid train bombings.
	B. In Japan, the Aum Shinrikyo cult used serin gas to kill several people in a subway.
	C. In Iran, terrorists may soon have access to nuclear materials.

In all of these examples, the speaker's intent is to persuade the audience to accept a specific view of the facts in question. Sometimes, however, persuasive topics are more appropriately addressed as a claim of value.

Advocating Value Claims

Should rehabilitation be valued above punishment in the U.S. criminal justice system? Is the war in Iraq moral? Are the rights of endangered animal species more important than the rights of indigenous human populations? Such questions go beyond a debate about the facts involved to a judgment about values. A **claim of value** concerns what you might consider to be right or wrong, moral or immoral, just or unjust, or good or bad. The following topics are developed around value claims:

- Capital punishment is justified.
- Product testing on animals is inhumane.
- The protection of the environment is more important than industrial growth.
- National security is more important than freedom of expression

As you can see, some claims of value examine one action (e.g., capital punishment), whereas others are comparative in nature (e.g., the protection of the environment vs. industrial growth).

Burdens of Proof

As is the case with factual claims, speakers advocating value claims also must clearly define key terms. Consider the following thesis statement: *"The right to a dignified death is morally justified."* Putting aside your own personal beliefs about this statement, can you imagine a scenario where members of an audience are likely to hold vastly different definitions about the term *dignified death*? They absolutely will have different denotative and connotative meanings for these words. As a result, the speaker in this case must clearly define what constitutes a dignified death.

In addition to defining key terms, speakers who advance value claims face the specific burden of identifying some **criterion**, or standard, by which the value judgment is to be made.

Consider the following claim: *"Protecting the environment is more important than economic growth."* How could the speaker come to the conclusion that one is more important than the other? More important in terms of what? The speaker could argue that survival of the earth is the most important value we could hold. (Obviously, if you're not alive, other values such as justice or liberty become meaningless.) In this case, the speaker is likely to pit this value against the benefits of economic growth such as job creation. Ultimately, in order to successfully defend her or his thesis that protection of the environment is the most important consideration, the speaker would have to prove that industrial growth risks survival of the planet. Put simply, the criterion is the measuring stick by which the value judgment is made.

Preparing to Participate 14.2
Fact, Value, and Policy

Knowledge
What are claims of fact, value, and policy?
What are the burdens of proof for each?

Application
How do you know whether your speech topic needs to be argued from fact, value, or policy?

Organizing Speeches on Claims of Value

Claims of value are typically organized topically. However, the speaker may choose either to weave the criteria into the main points of the body of the speech or to separate them into different subpoints. The following speech illustrates how you can weave your criteria into the main points:

Specific Purpose:	To persuade my audience to believe that human genetic engineering is morally wrong.
Thesis Statement:	Human genetic engineering violates the values of human equality and societal welfare.
Main Points:	A. Human genetic engineering opens the door to genetic discrimination and therefore violates principles of human equality.
	B. Human genetic engineering is dangerous and therefore risks societal welfare.

When you advocate value claims, you may also consider devoting your first main point to setting forth the criteria for your value judgment and the second to applying those criteria to your topic. Consider the following example:

Specific Purpose:	To persuade my audience to believe that the public's right to know ought to be valued above the right to privacy of candidates for public office.
Thesis Statement:	Placing the public's right to know above political candidates' right to privacy is justified because it decreases political corruption and produces an informed vote.
Main Points:	A. All actions that we take must meet two major criteria.
	1. Our actions must create the greatest good for the greatest number of people.
	2. Our actions must benefit the least advantaged members of society.
	B. Placing the public's right to know above candidates' right to privacy is justified.
	1. Infringing upon a candidate's privacy benefits society by reducing political corruption and therefore creates the greatest good for the greatest number of people.
	2. Infringing upon a candidate's privacy gives everyone an informed vote.

It should be clear to you at this point that claims of value have clear implications for our actions and behavior. A person who believes that human genetic engineering is morally wrong is likely to support legislation banning the activity. However, speeches that focus on claims of value don't advocate any specific action or policy. Once you move from setting a standard or criterion into the realm of questioning what should be done, you move from a value claim to a policy claim.

Advocating Policy Claims

Claims of policy concern what should be done, what law should be changed, or what policy should be followed. Policy claims can be easily identified by the word *should* as well as the existence of an **agent of action**, or the entity who is responsible for taking action. Consider the following policy claims:

- The University (agent of action) should double tuition.
- The United States government (agent of action) should institute a national system of health care.
- The NCAA (agent of action) should reorganize college athletics to optimize television revenue.

Burdens of Proof

As with the other topic types we've discussed, a speaker advocating a policy must clearly define key terms. Consider the following thesis statement: *"The United States federal government should establish stricter controls of immigration."* Initially, it is important that the speaker define the agent of action. For example, there are several arms of the federal government that could take action to strengthen immigration control, including Congress and the Citizenship and Immigration Services (CIS) bureau of the U.S. Department of Homeland Security. In addition, the speaker would need to carefully define what is meant by stricter controls of immigration. Among other options, this could mean shutting down our borders to all immigrants or adopting more restrictive measures for individuals from nations that sponsor terrorism.

In addition to defining key terms, the policy speaker faces several specific burdens of proof. From a policy-making perspective, a speaker advocating change in the status quo must prove that some **problem** or harm exists. First, using the previously mentioned thesis on immigration, a speaker might argue that immigration controls are currently so lax that we are at significant risk of future terrorist attacks.

Second, the speaker must also prove that the status quo won't or can't solve the problem. In other words, the speaker must establish that some **inherent barrier** exists that is preventing the status quo from acting to solve the problem. Again, it is important to think of these burdens from a policy-making perspective. Why would a legislator vote for legislation advocating stricter controls on immigration if such a policy already existed? This means that policy advocates must do their research to know what laws and regulations are currently in effect.

Third, the speaker must establish that her/his recommended course of action will *solve* the problem. Your audience is not likely to be persuaded to accept your policy recommendations unless they perceive that the plan you recommend can be feasibly implemented.

Persuasive speeches that advocate a change in policy should contain a well-developed **action statement**. An action statement indicates what you want your audience to believe or do. Then, you provide the audience with the means or information they would need to do so.

Seeking Agreement.
Politicians use their persuasive abilities in hopes of getting others to accept their policy positions.

As you develop your action statement, you need to consider whether your goal is to gain immediate action or passive agreement from your audience. If you want to gain **immediate action**, your goal should be to motivate the audience either to engage in a specific behavior or to take a specific action. For example, if you have given a powerful and emotional presentation on the needs of the homeless in your community, you would then provide the audience with information on how they could help your cause. You could also provide information on how the audience could contact representatives associated with your topic. You may want them to write or email local policy makers, and you could provide a form letter. You may want them to sign a petition. Keep in mind that your action statement should be reasonable for the audience to complete and as specific as possible. After all, if you have been successful, your audience will certainly be motivated by your message to make a difference. However, they are unlikely to act if you present them with only a vague plan of action (e.g., contact someone about homelessness) or an unreasonable request (e.g., volunteer at least 40 hours per week at the local homeless shelter).

If, on the other hand, you want to gain **passive agreement**, your objective is to persuade the audience to adopt a new attitude without asking them to engage in a specific behavior. Importantly, speeches that seek passive agreement include a solution to a problem; however, in contrast with immediate action, the speaker doesn't call the audience to action. For example, you might give a persuasive presentation about how the United States needs a national system of health care and then provide a solution for implementing such a system without ever asking your audience to do anything more than agree with your position.

Organizing Speeches on Claims of Policy

Although you can use any of the organizational patterns discussed in Chapter 8 when discussing a policy, the following are particularly useful for organizing persuasive speeches: problem-solution, problem-cause-solution, comparative advantage, and Monroe's motivated sequence.

Problem-Solution Order If you are advocating a change in policy, consider using the **problem-solution** format. In this format, the first main point is devoted to establishing the problem. In the second main point, you'll introduce your specific plan and explain how it solves the problem.

Specific Purpose:	To persuade my audience to believe that action is needed to deal with safety hazards posed by water scooters.
Thesis Statement:	Solving the safety problems of water scooters will require new legislation stipulating a minimum operating age and mandatory classes in water safety.
Main Points:	A. Water scooters are operationally hazardous to the people who use them.
	1. A recent newspaper article indicates that water scooter fatalities are on the rise.
	2. Because no regulations exist to govern the use of water scooters, operators are often inexperienced and untrained.
	B. The problem can be solved by government action.
	1. State governments should adopt legislation stipulating a minimum operating age for water scooter operators.
	2. Individuals who operate water scooters should be required to complete mandatory classes in water safety.

Problem-Cause-Solution Order If you want to focus on specific causes associated with a problem, you should consider the **problem-cause-solution** format. For example:

Specific Purpose:	To persuade my audience to believe that discrimination against gays is a real problem that requires immediate action.
Thesis Statement:	Discrimination against gays is a serious problem caused by discriminatory laws and personal attitudes that can be addressed by individual action.

Main Points: A. Discrimination against gays remains a significant problem.

    1. Research indicates that more than 90% of gays will experience some form of overt discrimination in their lifetime.

    2. Gay spouses don't receive the same benefits of heterosexual marriage partners.

B. There are several causes of gay discrimination.

    1. Many states have adopted legislation making it legal to discriminate against gays.

    2. Personal attitudes allow society to perpetuate myths about gays, which fosters discrimination.

C. There are several steps that you can take to help solve the problem.

    1. You can exercise your right to vote to defeat discriminatory initiatives and vote for political candidates that protect rights.

    2. You should face your own fears and ask yourself if your fears are based on rational experience.

Comparative Advantages Order If, during the course of audience analysis, you find that your audience already agrees that a problem exists in the status quo, you could use the **comparative advantages order**. In doing so, you could organize your speech around the advantages and disadvantages of at least two competing solutions. If you use this format, you'll present arguments throughout the main points and explain why your solution is preferable to other solutions.

Specific Purpose: To persuade my audience to believe that the United States should put greater emphasis on nuclear power as a way of generating electricity.

Thesis Statement: Nuclear power is friendlier to the environment and less costly compared to coal power.

Main Points: A. Nuclear power produces far less CO_2 emissions compared to coal power.

B. Nuclear power will result in cheaper energy prices compared to coal power.

Monroe's Motivated Sequence **Monroe's motivated sequence** is a five-step approach for arranging your main points.[7] The objective of this pattern is to gain immediate action by identifying the problem and solution as well as the consequences of implementing your plan. The five steps of this sequence are attention, need, satisfaction, visualization, and action.

Source Citation:
[7] Monroe, A. H. (1935). *Principles and types of speech.* Chicago, IL: Scott Foresman.

1. **Attention**—capture the attention of your audience
2. **Need**—demonstrate to your audience that serious problems exist that must be addressed
3. **Satisfaction**—offer your plan for solving the problem
4. **Visualization**—attempt to help the listeners visualize the advantages of adopting your plan or the disadvantages of not adopting your plan
5. **Action**—tell the listeners exactly what they should do and how they can do it

Monroe's motivated sequence is especially useful when you want to get your listeners to take action; however, keep in mind that you should specify action that the audience can reasonably take.

Monroe's motivated sequence is compatible with the method of outlining discussed in Chapter 9. Specifically, the *attention* step is accomplished in the introduction of the speech (attention getter), the *need, satisfaction,* and *visualization* steps are accomplished in the body of the speech, and the *action* step is accomplished in the conclusion. The following outline demonstrates how one speaker incorporated the sequence into a speech urging her classmates to become more involved in community service projects:

Specific Purpose: To persuade my audience to get involved by volunteering for community service.

Thesis Statement: Volunteering for community service can improve your self-esteem and satisfaction as well as benefit members of the community.

I. Introduction
Attention:
A. *Attention Getter:* "Be the change you want to see in the world." How many of you know what group on campus has adopted this quote as their motto? If you guessed the Student Volunteer Center, you're correct! Their philosophy is that each and every one of you has the ability and the opportunity to make a difference in the world.
B. *Relevance Statement:* Research indicates that many college students fail to take advantage of opportunities to get involved in meaningful social issues. In fact, my on-line survey of this class indicates that, while many of you expressed an interest in community service, less than 10% of this audience has ever participated in a community service project. The same survey indicates that more than half of you said you would like to become more active in making a difference in this community, but you're unsure of how to get involved.
C. *Credibility Statement:* In addition to conducting a great deal of research on this topic, I have personally participated in the University's Habitat for Humanity and alternative spring break programs. Also, I currently work in the Student Volunteer Center.
D. *Thesis Statement:* Volunteering for community service can improve your self-esteem and satisfaction as well as benefit members of the community.
E. *Preview:* In order to understand why you should volunteer for community service, it's necessary to explore the need for student volunteerism, the opportunities you have to volunteer, and the many benefits of volunteering.

II. Body

Need:

A. There is a significant need for college students to volunteer in their communities.

   1. Research indicates that far too few college students get involved in social issues in their communities.

   2. This apathy is a significant problem for both students and the community in which they live.

      a. Students' educational experiences are substantially diminished if they are uninvolved.

      b. A host of problems, such as homelessness, continue to go unaddressed.

Satisfaction:

B. Students have many opportunities to get involved thanks to campus volunteer centers.

   1. Campuses all over the nation, including this one, have established student volunteer centers to get students involved with social issues.

   2. You can volunteer to help with virtually any social issue you can imagine.

Visualization:

C. Volunteering will benefit you personally as well as members of your community.

   1. Engaging in community service projects will enhance your self-esteem and increase your satisfaction with your educational experience.

   2. You can make a difference in addressing the most significant social issues that confront your community.

III. Conclusion

Action:

A. *Restate Thesis:* Volunteering for community service can improve your self-esteem and satisfaction as well as benefit members of the community. So, I encourage each of you to register with the student volunteer center.

B. *Memorable Close:* By volunteering for community service you can indeed be the change you want to see in the world. You have the ability and the opportunity to make a difference in the world.

Preparing to Participate 14.3
Organizational Patterns

Knowledge
What organizational patterns are best for claims of fact, value, and policy?

Application
How do you decide which pattern is most appropriate for your topic?

Critical Interaction 14.1
Thinking Critically About Fact, Value, and Policy Claims

Identify whether the following topics are claims of fact, value, or policy. What organizational pattern(s) would be most appropriate for these topics?

1. Passive smoking affects non-smokers because of indirect exposure.
2. The rights of endangered animal species are more important than the rights of indigenous human populations.
3. The American judicial system has overemphasized the rights of the accused.
4. Smoking in public places should be banned.
5. The U.S. government should establish a national safety program for elementary school students.
6. Fastening seatbelts saves lives.
7. The current tax system favors the wealthy.
8. Organized college athletics should reorganize to optimize television revenue.
9. The U.S. government should significantly increase the exploration of space.
10. *Friends* is a better television program than *Seinfeld*.
11. Life evolved naturally from existing conditions on Earth.
12. American commercial broadcasters have sacrificed quality for entertainment.
13. Poodles make better pets than beagles.
14. Computer technology will change American education.
15. The U.S. government should establish a comprehensive AIDS policy.

SUMMARY

In this chapter, we have defined persuasive communication, noting that it refers to messages that are intended to shape, reinforce, or change the responses of others. We also noted that persuasion is not something to be taken for granted. Although many might assume that they are naturally effective communicators, such an assumption can get us into trouble when the persuasive strategy we employ fails. We also noted that it's important to study persuasion in order to become a more critical consumer of persuasive messages (from interpersonal interactions to our consumption of mass media messages).

As a persuasive speaker, making a decision about whether to formulate your thesis as a claim of fact, value, or policy has very important implications for what you have to prove in your speech as well as the organizational pattern you'll employ. As we noted in this chapter, any of these claims can be used to assist you in conceptualizing a thesis statement or in framing a major proposition. However, you should recognize that any given speech may involve claims of fact, value, and policy. For example, you might argue that the United States will not implement a national system of health care under the current administration (fact), the government has a moral responsibility to provide its citizens with health coverage (value), and therefore, the United States federal government should act immediately to establish national health care (policy). Understanding these principles will enhance your *critical thinking* skills.

KEY TERMS

persuasive communication (214)

advocate (214)

target audience (215)

attitude (215)

belief (215)

value (215)

burdens of Proof (216)

status quo (216)

status quo bias (216)

claims of fact, value, and
  policy (218)

criterion (219)

agent of action (221)

problem (221)

inherent barrier (221)

action statement (221)

immediate action (222)

passive agreement (222)

problem-solution order (223)

problem-cause-solution
  order (223)

comparative advantage
  order (224)

Monroe's motivated
  sequence (224)

ADDITIONAL ENGAGEMENT OPPORTUNITIES

Now that you have finished reading the chapter, it is also important to make connections between the course content and your own experiences. These activities will help you understand, apply, analyze, evaluate, or synthesize course concepts. You can use these activities to provide evidence of your preparation for participation in class as well as to plan additional contributions to class discussion. The Civic Engagement Opportunities (CEOs) are designed to help you become more engaged in campus and community life and apply course concepts to important social issues.

1. Think of a controversial topic that interests you. Create a fact, value, and policy claim with this topic in mind.

2. The governor of your state is coming to campus and will take a few minutes at the end of her talk to allow students to suggest issues and alternatives. Choose a social issue (health care, education, families and children, principles and values, etc.) that you have a passion for. Write a policy claim (thesis statement) for that issue and be

ready to present to the governor, just in case you get the chance. Remember that your policy claim (thesis statement) should parallel certain organizational patterns. Be sure to choose the correct one.

3. Select a problem of importance to you and your community (e.g., tuition increases, parking regulations, free speech zones, etc.). Using the persuasive principles discussed in this chapter, design a strategy to persuade key decision makers in your community to address this problem. How might the status quo bias present a barrier to motivating others to act on this problem? What persuasive strategies could you use to overcome the status quo bias? In formulating a solution to the problem, is your objective to gain immediate action or passive agreement?

15

Building Arguments

Use soft words and hard arguments.
—English Proverb

CHAPTER OBJECTIVES

After reading this chapter, you should be able to:

- Understand the importance of argumentation in persuasive speech making.

- Effectively incorporate six components of the argument model.

- Effectively incorporate three major persuasive appeals (logos, ethos, and pathos).

- Identify and understand common fallacies of reasoning.

Arnold Schwarzenegger

When was the last time that you had a spirited conversation about a controversial issue? What kind of evidence did you use to support your claims? How did you respond to the objections of others? What types of appeals did you find most persuasive? These questions address the essential components involved in building effective arguments.

Perhaps you find the term *argument* distasteful. For example, no one likes to get in an argument with friends or family. That's not what we're referring to here. We use the term **argument** to refer to the process of advancing claims supported by evidence and reasoning.[1] In this chapter you will learn how to structure arguments, incorporate effective reasoning, and avoid fallacious reasoning in your persuasive speeches. We begin by examining a model for constructing arguments.

Argument Model

British philosopher Stephen Toulmin has developed a model for understanding the critical components of effective arguments.[2] Our slightly modified version of his **argument model**, represented in Figure 15.1, contains the following six elements: claims, evidence, evidence credibility statements, warrants, qualifiers, and rebuttals. An understanding of these elements is an essential step in becoming a critical producer and consumer of persuasive arguments.

Claims

A **claim** represents the assertion or point that a speaker advocates. Persuasive speakers can advance claims of fact, value, or policy. Consider the following factual claim:

Source Citation:
[1] Toulmin, S. E. (2003). *The uses of argument.* New York: Cambridge University Press.

Source Citation:
[2] Toulmin, S. E. (2003). *The uses of argument.* New York: Cambridge University Press.

Comic 15.1

1. What is the difference between Leroy's definition of argument and ours?

The Lockhorns

©2006 WM. HOEST ENTERPRISES, INC.   Distributed by King Features Syndicate.

www.thelockhorns.com

D. PULLMAN MARRIAGE COUNSELOR

8-15

HOEST & REINER

"OF COURSE WE EACH HAVE SOME VALID POINTS ... THAT'S WHY WE ARGUE."

Lockhorns@ Wm. Hoest Enterprises, Inc. King Features Syndicate.

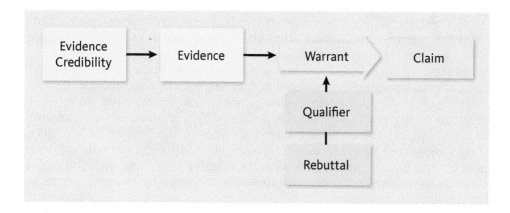

FIGURE 15.1
Toulmin's Argument Model

> Posting private information on social networking sites like Facebook poses significant security risks.

As you can clearly see, a claim by itself is hardly persuasive. Indeed, your audience will expect you to provide reliable evidence to support your claims.

Evidence

Evidence (also referred to as *supporting material*) is employed to substantiate a speaker's claim and, as noted in Chapter 7, may take several forms including statistics, analogies, facts, examples, and testimony. We'll consider how speakers can use evidence and reasoning in much greater depth later in this chapter, but for now, consider the following quote from the United States Department of Justice:

> Releasing private information like phone numbers, addresses and other contact information on social networking web sites is a major cause of identity theft and stalking in America.[3]

Is this good evidence to support the claim that *posting private information on social networking sites poses significant security risks*? The evidence certainly highlights the potential dangers of releasing private information on such sites. It is important to keep in mind that several external factors work together to influence the overall effectiveness of evidence, including the credibility of the speaker, message delivery, and the subject's familiarity with the evidence.

Importantly, evidence has relatively little impact when it is included in a speech that is delivered poorly and when the data presented are inconsistent with individuals' initial attitudes.[4] You can heighten the effectiveness of your evidence by providing the audience with a brief evidence credibility statement.

Evidence Credibility Statements

We have noted throughout this text that, as a critical producer of information, you have a burden of demonstrating that the evidence you use to support your claims comes from credible sources. **Evidence credibility statements** are brief statements that establish the quality of the information you are using to support your ideas. Indeed, your audience will likely find your arguments much

Source Citations:
[3] U.S. Department of Justice. (2008, October 8). *Computer Crime and Intellectual Property Section.* Retrieved November 1, 2008 from the Department of Justice website: http://www.usdoj.gov/criminal/cybercrime/index.html

[4] Reinard, J. C. (1998). The persuasive effects of testimonial assertion evidence. In M. Allen, & R. W. Preiss (Eds.), *Persuasion: Advances through meta-analysis* (pp. 69–86). Cresskill, NJ: Hampton Press.

See also

Reinard, J. C. (1988). The empirical study of the persuasive effects of evidence: The status after fifty years of research. *Human Communication Research, 15,* 3–59.

more compelling if you present a brief credibility statement for the evidence you use in the persuasive speech:[5]

> According to the Computer Crime and Intellectual Property web site developed by the Cyberstalking Division of the U.S. Department of Justice and accessed on September 6, 2008, "releasing private information like phone numbers, addresses and other contact information on social networking web sites is a major cause of identity theft and stalking in America."

Research by communication scholars indicates that evidence is more likely to change attitudes if it is of high quality, plausible, and novel rather than something the audience members have already heard several times before.[6] Importantly, the evidence you use in your persuasive speech should meet all of the tests for evaluating sources discussed in Chapter 7.

Warrant

A **warrant** provides the justification and reasoning to connect the evidence with your claim. In essence, a warrant explains how the evidence substantiates your point and demonstrates that making the mental leap from one to the other is rational. In other words, warrants are the general assumptions, principles, or rules that demonstrate to your audience that your evidence supports your claim. Consider the following example:

Claim:	Posting private information on social networking sites like Facebook poses significant security risks.
Evidence:	Releasing private information like phone numbers, addresses and other contact information on social networking web sites is a major cause of identity theft and stalking in America.
Warrant:	People value personal privacy and safety.

In this example, the speaker implicitly links the claim (posting private information is dangerous) and the evidence (the information from the *Department of Justice* website) through the unstated principle that most people value personal privacy and safety. Examining this argument at face value, the evidence does warrant the claim that posting private information on social networking sites is dangerous.

In our experience, we've found that some public speakers take the warrant for granted—assuming that the audience will automatically draw the connection between the evidence and the claim. Although that might be a relatively safe assumption with the example provided here, it could become risky as your arguments become more complex and when large segments of the audience are hostile to your advocacy. In such cases, it might be necessary to state the warrants explicitly.

We've also found that some students fail to critically reflect on their warrants, which results in a serious disconnect between the evidence offered and the claim advanced. Consider the following example:

> Power lines are dangerous to human health because my sister lives near power lines and all of her cats have developed cancer.

Source Citations:
[5] Reynolds, R. A., & Reynolds, J. L. (2002). Evidence. In J. P. Dillard & M. Pfau (Eds.), *The persuasion handbook: Developments in theory and practice* (pp. 429–430). Thousand Oaks, CA: Sage.

[6] Morley, D. D., & Walker, K. B. (1987). The role of importance, novelty, and plausibility in producing belief change. *Communication Monographs, 54*, 436–442.

See also

Reinard, J. C. (1998). The persuasive effects of testimonial assertion evidence. In M. Allen, & R. W. Preiss (Eds.), *Persuasion: Advances through meta-analysis* (pp. 69–86). Cresskill, NJ: Hampton Press.

Reinard, J. C. (1988). The empirical study of the persuasive effects of evidence: The status after fifty years of research. *Human Communication Research, 15*, 3–59.

We admit that this is an exaggerated example; however, it closely parallels an actual argument we've heard in the classroom. For the moment, let's overlook the glaring problems with the evidence offered here. Our concern is with the relationship between the evidence (my sister's pets all developed cancer) and the claim (power lines are dangerous to human health). Does the fact that her cats developed cancer warrant the claim that power lines are dangerous to human health? Clearly, the physiology of cats and humans differs substantially, making this warrant untenable. Constructing arguments using Toulmin's model makes it easy to identify potential problems with the relationships between the claims you are advancing and the evidence you are using to support those claims.

Qualifiers

As a persuasive speaker, you should avoid using terms such as *always* or *never*. **Qualifiers** admit exceptions and demonstrate that argumentation is not an exact science. After all, issues can rarely be discussed in absolute terms. According to Toulmin,[7] your credibility with the audience will suffer if you use such terms—especially if they are aware of exceptions to the claim. Also, acknowledging your degree of certainty safeguards you against the appearance that you are taking an unreasonable position on the topic.

Source Citation:
[7] Toulmin, S. E. (2003). *The uses of argument.* New York: Cambridge University Press.

Let's consider more carefully our claim about the dangers of posting personal information on social networking sites. Can you think of any instances where posting such information might actually be advantageous? Even some university administrators have acknowledged that social networking sites can help students transition from high school to college by providing a vehicle for students to form networks and connect with others before they set foot on campus.[8] Therefore, a speaker advancing the case against posting certain types of private information on the Internet would be well advised to qualify her or his remarks by noting instances where doing so might be appropriate. In fact, a speaker making this case could even provide specific tips for safely posting information.

Source Citations:
[8] Lombardi, K. S. (2007, March 21). *Make new friends online and you won't start college friendless.* Retrieved September 6, 2008 from the New York Times website: http://www.nytimes.com/2007/03/21/education/21friends.html

Rebuttals

Given the nature of persuasive communication, you are likely to have at least some audience members who do not agree with your position. So, in what circumstances should you address audience objections to your advocacy? This is a question that all persuasive communicators must deal with whenever they speak to an audience. First, let's distinguish between one- and multi-sided messages. Simply put, **one-sided messages** give arguments in favor of the speaker's position on the issue and **multi-sided messages** present the multiple perspectives of the controversial issue. A **rebuttal** not only states the other sides or **counterarguments** to your position but also attacks them head on. According to Toulmin, speakers must address objections to their position directly if they are to successfully persuade the audience.[9]

Why is it so important that you acknowledge the counterarguments to your position? Research indicates that by addressing the objections of the audience, the speaker demonstrates that she or he is aware of the (opposing)

[9] Toulmin, S. E. (2003). *The uses of argument.* New York: Cambridge University Press.

Source Citation:
[10] Allen, M. (1998). Comparing the persuasive effectiveness of one- and two-sided message. In M. Allen & R. W. Preiss (Eds.), *Persuasion: Advances through meta-analysis* (pp. 87–98). Cresskill, NJ: Hampton Press.

[11] Hale, J., Mongeau, P. A., & Thomas, R. M. (1991). Cognitive processing of one- and two-sided persuasive messages. *Western Journal of Speech Communication, 55,* 380–389.

information, has taken it into account, and still finds that the weight of the evidence favors her or his position.[10] However, research also shows that speakers must go beyond merely mentioning opposing positions on a given topic, because it is essential to strongly refute those counterarguments.[11] Consider the following example of a rebuttal:

> Many people believe that social networking sites are entirely safe. In fact, when I conducted my audience analysis for this speech, one audience member specifically indicated that she didn't think that posting personal information is a problem because, as she said, "nobody but college students will ever look at my Facebook site." However, a recent study reported in Campus Safety Magazine indicates that Internet predators are enrolling in single classes, then dropping, but still maintaining their university e-mail address so that they can have access to sites such as Facebook. Again, the U.S. Department of Justice has warned that posting personal information on social networking sites is a major cause of stalking in America.

It should be apparent that formulating an effective argument requires you to do a good job of researching the multiple perspectives on your topic. In addition, you must carefully analyze where your audience stands on the topic and rebut any counterarguments they may hold to your position. Constructing an effective argument also depends on your use of logos, ethos, and pathos.

Preparing to Participate 15.1
Defining Argument

Knowledge
Define the term *argument*.
What are the six elements of the argument model?

Application
What's the difference between an argument and a disagreement?
What are the consequences of neglecting one of the six elements in a persuasive speech?

Persuading Through Logos

Source Citation:
[12] Aristotle. (1960). *The rhetoric of Aristotle* (L. Cooper, Trans.). New York: Appleton-Century-Crofts. (Original translation published 1932.)

Communication scholars have devoted a significant amount of time and energy to better understanding the strategies speakers can utilize to influence others. Indeed, as far back as Ancient Greece, Aristotle was theorizing about three modes of persuasion he called *logos, ethos,* and *pathos*.[12] According to Aristotle, the term ***logos*** refers to the rational proofs you use to support the arguments you make in a persuasive speech. **Rational proofs** are made up of a series of **premises**, or declarative statements, that lead to a conclusion. There are several types of rational proofs, including those based on inductive, deductive, causal, and analogical reasoning.

Inductive Reasoning

When reasoning inductively, you begin with specific instances and formulate a reasonable generalization or conclusion from them. In short, **inductive reasoning** moves from the particular to the general. Consider the following example from a persuasive speech about unethical business practices in America:

> Enron engaged in unethical business practices.
> Tyco International engaged in unethical business practices.
> Adelphia Communications engaged in unethical business practices.
> Conclusion: Unethical business practices are common in America.

Has the speaker provided enough examples to warrant the conclusion that unethical business practices are common in America? If you use inductive reasoning in your persuasive speech, it is important that you avoid jumping to conclusions based on a small number of examples. Consider the following argument:

> My cousin has no interest in politics.
> My sister has no interest in politics.
> None of my friends have any interest in politics.
> Conclusion: Young people have no interest in politics.

Persuasive Proofs. Though he died over 2300 years ago, much of what Aristotle wrote and taught about persuasion still has relevance today.

Although these examples are a bit exaggerated, they clearly illustrate a **hasty generalization**—a fallacy of reasoning that occurs when the conclusion offered is based on insufficient evidence. Beyond gathering more examples to support the conclusion, what else might the speaker do to strengthen the argument? Following the argument model proposed in this chapter, one strategy might be to qualify the conclusion—perhaps the speaker could discuss the percentage of young people that have no interest in politics rather than stating that all young people lack interest. You can further enhance the persuasiveness of your argument by adding credible statistics from reliable sources. In addition, when you construct inductive arguments, you should apply the tests for supporting material discussed in Chapter 7 to make sure they are sound. The instances or cases that you advance in support of your conclusion must be typical, representative, and timely.

Deductive Reasoning

Unlike inductive reasoning, **deductive reasoning** begins with a generalization and moves logically to an application in a specific case:

> Killing people is always wrong.
> Capital punishment involves killing people.
> Therefore, capital punishment is always wrong.

This example follows the classic form of deduction by beginning with a major premise ("Killing people is always wrong"), moving to a minor premise

("Capital punishment involves killing people"), and ending with a specific conclusion ("Capital punishment is always wrong"). Aristotle deemed this full version of a deductive argument a **syllogism**. As you might guess, speakers frequently rely on syllogisms in persuasive speeches. When the *premises* are true and the conclusions can logically be derived from the premises, the syllogism is highly persuasive. Consider the following example:

> People who drive drunk are more likely to have accidents than those who drive sober.
> Jimmy regularly drives drunk.
> Therefore, Jimmy is more likely to have an accident than are persons who drive sober.

Utilizing the same form of deduction, let's consider the following example based upon a faulty major premise:

> People who drive sober are more likely to have accidents than are those who drive drunk.
> Jill drives only while she is sober.
> Therefore, Jill is more likely to have an accident than are those who drive drunk.

In this example, we can assume that the minor premise is true ("Jill drives only while she is sober") and we can see that the conclusion clearly flows logically from the premises; however, the argument must be rejected because it is based on a flawed major premise. This example vividly demonstrates how erroneous conclusions can be reached if you begin with an unfounded major premise. As a result, you must carefully scrutinize the premises and conclusions you advance in your persuasive speech.

Persuaders often do not provide the entire syllogism in their arguments. For example you might say, *"Capital punishment? That means the state kills people!"* and allow your audience to discern the necessary connections. Relying on such truncated arguments may work well when you and your audience share similar knowledge, values, and experiences related to the topic under discussion; however, such a strategy may not work at all if you don't share this common ground with your audience.

Causal Reasoning

Causal reasoning asserts that one condition or event (cause) brings about another condition or event (effect). In order to be a cause, one condition or event must obviously precede the other. Although this is a necessary condition to meet when using causal reasoning, it is not by itself sufficient. As a result, the speaker must also demonstrate that the preceding event caused the effect. The key to effective causal reasoning is to produce enough reasons to warrant the link between the cause and the effect. In the following example, the author develops an effective causal argument by describing the effects on marine life of low-frequency noises caused by oceangoing merchant shipping:

> The second aspect is the high level of low-frequency sounds produced by vessels while cruising in the sea. These sounds can travel long distances and

may change local acoustic environments, impacting marine mammals that use sound in reproductive interactions and interfere with predator/prey detection. In extreme cases, noise pollution may cause habitat avoidance in these animals.[13]

Source Citation:
[13] Sharma, D. (2006). Ports in a storm. *Environmental Health Perspectives, 114*(4), A223–A231. (p. A226)

Persuasive speakers using causal reasoning should avoid offering a single cause or effect when others are known to exist. The reality is that most events have multiple causes. For example, what factors cause tropical deforestation? Population pressure? Clear cutting for cattle pasture and other agricultural needs? Economic debt? Commercial logging and mining? All of these factors—and others—contribute to the problem of deforestation. In addition, there are many effects of deforestation, including climate change, loss of biological diversity, and displacement of forest-based societies. When multiple causes or effects exist, be sure to note them.

It is equally important that you avoid the **false cause fallacy** when using causal reasoning. The Latin name for this fallacy of reasoning is *post hoc, ergo propter hoc,* which translates to "after this, therefore because of this." Consider the following argument:

> The town council erred in permitting the adult bookstore to open, for shortly afterward two women were assaulted.

The simple fact that one event (i.e., the council allowed the bookstore to open) preceded the other (i.e., two women were assaulted) does not mean that one caused the other.

Analogical Reasoning

You can use **analogical reasoning** to help clarify complex situations by comparing them with situations more familiar to the audience. As we noted in Chapter 7, *literal analogies* compare the similarities in things that are alike. Literal analogies may be especially useful in building a case for the adoption of policies. Consider the following example:

> Smoking bans have been successfully employed without harming businesses in large cities like New York and Washington, DC. As a result, a smoking ban should be adopted in Chicago.

Figurative analogies draw upon metaphors to identify the similarities in two things that are not alike, but that share some identifiable characteristics. Dr. Martin Luther King, Jr. used an elaborate figurative analogy in his famous 1963 "I Have a Dream" speech to compare racial discrimination to a bad check:

> And so we've come here today to dramatize a shameful condition. In a sense we've come to our nation's Capitol to cash a check. When the architects of our republic wrote the magnificent words of the Constitution and the Declaration of Independence, they were signing a promissory note to which every American was to fall heir. This note was a promise that all men—yes, black men as well as white men—would be guaranteed the inalienable rights of life, liberty, and the pursuit of happiness. It is obvious today that America has defaulted on this promissory note insofar as her citizens of color are concerned. Instead of honoring this sacred obligation, America

Making Analogies. Dr. Martin Luther King, Jr. delivered the "I have a dream" speech on Aug. 28, 1963. The quality of his arguments has made this one of the most famous speeches of all time.

Source Citation:
[14] King, M. L., Jr. (1963, August 28). *I have a dream.* Speech given at the March on Washington. Washington, DC. From "I Have a Dream" by Martin Luther King, Jr. Copyright 1963 by Dr. Martin Luther King Jr.; copyright renewed 1991 Coretta Scott King. Reprinted by arrangement with The Heirs to the Estate of Martin Luther King Jr., c/o Writers House as agent for the proprietor New York, NY.

has given the Negro people a bad check—a check which has come back marked "insufficient funds."[14]

As we noted in Chapter 7, the analogies you use to support your ideas should compare cases that share similar characteristics. The argument that a smoking ban could be adopted in Chicago because it has worked in other large cities rests on the assumption that the cities are essentially alike. An **invalid analogy** occurs when the items being compared are not sufficiently similar.

Persuading Through Ethos

The term **ethos** refers to credibility. Think of a speaker you've heard recently whom you perceived to be highly credible. Is that credibility something that the speaker possesses, or is it something that exists in your head, as the receiver of the message? Most researchers argue that credibility is a perception in the mind of the receiver or listener. Therefore, speakers are only as credible as their listeners perceive them to be. This receiver-oriented focus has led persuasion scholars to define speaker credibility, or *ethos*, in terms of the perceptions listeners hold about the following factors of speaker **credibility**: competence, character, and goodwill.

Factors of Speaker Credibility

Competence refers to the audience's perception of the speaker's intelligence, expertise, and overall knowledge on the topic. **Character** refers to the audience's perception of the speaker's trustworthiness and sincerity. Finally, **goodwill** reflects the extent to which an audience perceives that the speaker is concerned about them.

In general, research suggests that we are more likely to accept the message recommendations of sources we perceive to be highly credible, and we tend to discount the recommendations of those we perceive to be less credible.[15] This does not mean that we base our decisions on our perceptions of the source alone, but these perceptions do figure into the decision-making process. It is important to recognize that, beyond establishing your own credibility as a source on your topic, you must also establish the credibility of the information sources you are using to support your ideas. As noted in Chapter 7, if the audience evaluates your sources positively, they are more likely to accept your arguments. It is also important that you be aware that the audience's perception of your credibility is likely to fluctuate throughout your speech.

Source Citation:
[15] Cialdini, R. B. (2001). *Influence: Science and practice* (4th ed.). Boston: Allyn and Bacon.

Types of Speaker Credibility

Initial credibility refers to your credibility before you give the speech. It may well be the case that your audience will know very little about your experiences and knowledge of your persuasive speech topic before you actually deliver the speech. As you learned in Chapter 10, you can build your credibility in the introduction of the speech by revealing your training, credentials, experiences, and research on the topic.

Derived credibility is the credibility a speaker develops during the speech. As your persuasive speech progresses, you can continue to enhance your credibility by citing sources, developing quality arguments, and sharing your own personal experiences on the topic. In addition, you can work to establish common ground with your audience by highlighting similarities you share with them. Analyze your audience carefully to determine where shared attitudes, values, beliefs, and experiences can be utilized to establish common ground. So, why is establishing common ground so important in the persuasive speech? In short, we like people whom we perceive to be similar to us. In addition, researchers have found that we are often motivated to comply with the wishes of others based simply on the fact that we like them.[16] Establishing rapport with your audience and demonstrating that you care about them will go a long way toward enhancing your credibility.

Source Citation:
[16] Cialdini, R. B. (2001). *Influence: Science and practice* (4th ed.). Boston: Allyn and Bacon.

We've already noted that delivery is related to audience assessments of speaker credibility. (See Chapter 13 for a more extensive discussion of delivery.) Clearly, the more prepared, energetic, and comfortable you are, the more credible your audience will perceive you to be. By employing the strategies discussed in this chapter, you will also enhance your **terminal credibility**—the credibility given to a speaker at the end of the speech.

Persuading Through Pathos

The term **pathos** refers to appeals to *emotion*. Persuasive speakers can target a number of emotions in their audience including fear, anger, pity, envy, love, and pride. Research substantiates that emotional appeals can operate

Source Citation:
[17] Wood, W. (2000). Attitude change: Persuasion and social influence. *Annual Review of Psychology, 51*, 539–570.

as powerful persuasive tools.[17] For example, a speaker might attempt to arouse the audience's anger in order to motivate them to evaluate a particular policy negatively. Alternatively, a speaker interested in motivating action (e.g., to donate money to a charitable cause) might appeal to the audience's pity.

Developing Emotional Appeals

One excellent example of the power of pathos can be found in Dr. Martin Luther King, Jr.'s "Letter from the Birmingham Jail." Written in 1963, this letter was a response to other civil rights leaders who suggested that rather than engaging in acts of civil disobedience to prompt societal reform, members of the movement should simply wait for life to get better. King responded by arguing that:

> I guess it is easy for those who have never felt the stinging darts of segregation to say, "Wait." But when you have seen vicious mobs lynch your mothers and fathers at will and drown your sisters and brothers at whim; when you have seen hate filled policemen curse, kick, brutalize and even kill your black brothers and sisters with impunity; when you see the vast majority of your twenty million Negro brothers smothering in an airtight cage of poverty in the midst of an affluent society; when you suddenly find your tongue twisted and your speech stammering as you seek to explain to your six-year-old daughter why she can't go to the public amusement park that has just been advertised on television, and see tears welling up in her eyes when she is told that Funtown is closed to colored children, and see the depressing clouds of inferiority begin to form in her little mental sky, and see her begin to distort her little personality by unconsciously developing a bitterness toward white people; when you have to concoct an answer for a five-year-old son asking in agonizing pathos: "Daddy, why do white people treat colored people so mean?"; when you take a cross-country drive and find it necessary to sleep night after night in the uncomfortable corners of your automobile because no motel will accept you; when you are humiliated day in and day out by nagging signs reading "white" and "colored"; when your first name becomes "nigger," your middle name becomes "boy" (however old you are) and your last name becomes "John," and your wife and mother are never given the respected title "Mrs."; when you are harried by day and haunted by night by the fact that you are a Negro, living constantly at tip-toe stance never quite knowing what to expect next, and plagued with inner fears and outer resentments; when you are forever fighting a degenerating sense of "nobodiness"; then you will understand why we find it difficult to wait.[18]

Source Citation:
[18] King, M. L., Jr. (1964). Letter from the Birmingham jail. In M. L. King Jr. (Ed.), *Why we can't wait* (pp. 77–100). New York: Penguin. From "Letter from Birmingham Jail" by Martin Luther King, Jr. Copyright 1963 by Dr. Martin Luther King Jr.; copyright renewed 1991 Coretta Scott King. Reprinted by arrangement with The Heirs to the Estate of Martin Luther King Jr., c/o Writers House as agent for the proprietor New York, NY.

For emotional appeals to be effective, the speaker must recreate the event that would provoke an emotional response from the audience in "real life." In other words, one of your goals in using pathos is to stimulate the audience to relate to your speech on a personal level. King does this very effectively by using his own lived experiences to help his audience understand how it feels to be so pervasively oppressed by racism and segregation.

King also does an excellent job developing vivid examples that bring the content home for receivers in very personal terms. As you develop your speech, consider using rich examples that personalize the content of the speech for your audience. Perhaps one of the most compelling components of this text is King's sincerity and conviction about the cause. Your sincerity and conviction will be evident to the audience in all of your verbal (e.g., the words you say) and nonverbal (e.g., tone of voice, rate, gestures, etc.) actions.

Applying Ethics to Emotional Appeals

It is important to recognize that some scholars have suggested that an over-reliance on emotion neglects the role of logical reasoning in argumentation. We agree that you have a responsibility to construct an ethical persuasive speech and that you should carefully scrutinize the appeals you are exposed to, whether they are based upon emotion or not. However, we strongly believe that, as seen in the example provided by Martin Luther King, Jr., it is entirely possible to effectively and ethically combine emotional and logical appeals. After all, who would rightly argue that Americans should not have been angered by the racist oppression King described? Ultimately, we encourage you to develop an optimal mix of logos, ethos, and pathos as you construct a persuasive speech.

Preparing to Participate 15.2
Persuasive Appeals

Knowledge
What are the three persuasive appeals?

Application
Which of these appeals do you think is most effective for classroom speeches?
How might you use all three appeals in your next persuasive speech?

Critically Evaluating Arguments for Fallacies

A **fallacy** occurs when an argument is based on unsound reasoning or evidence. As a producer of messages, you should be careful to avoid fallacies in your speeches. As a consumer of messages, you should be able to detect fallacious arguments. In short, you should draw upon your *critical thinking* as well as information and media literacy skills as you produce and consume persuasive messages. Throughout this chapter we have already highlighted a number of fallacies, including hasty generalization, false cause, and invalid analogy. Although logicians have identified well over 100 fallacies,[19] we'll focus next on a few most relevant to public speaking.

Source Citation:
[19] Van Eemeren, F. H., & Gootendorst, R. (1992). *Argumentation, communication, and fallacies: A pragma-dialectical perspective.* Hillsdale, NJ: Lawrence Erlbaum.

Ad Hominem

Translated from Latin to English, **ad hominem** means *against the person*. This fallacy occurs when a speaker attacks the character of the person making an argument rather than the argument itself:

> Bill's arguments against capital punishment don't matter because he was arrested for driving while intoxicated.

In this case, the speaker attempts to divert attention away from the argument and toward Bill's character. On its face, this character attack has no bearing to Bill's arguments regarding capital punishment. Given the amount of time we've devoted to source credibility in this text, you might be asking yourself if there are circumstances where it would be reasonable to question the character of the source. Yes, but only if the person's character has direct bearing on the truth or falsity of the claim being made (see the examples of tests of evidence in Chapter 7).

Bandwagon

The **bandwagon** fallacy suggests that something is correct, good, or true because many other people agree with it or are doing it. You are surrounded by bandwagon appeals—politicians, advertisers, and even your friends use these types of arguments frequently. Consider the following claim:

> Recent polls suggest that the vast majority of Americans oppose the war in Iraq. Obviously we must bring the troops home and end the war.

This type of appeal is particularly effective given our tendency to base our actions on what others are doing.[20] Although this tendency can serve us well in some circumstances (e.g., everyone avoids drinking water contaminated with mercury, so I will too), it can also result in poor decisions (e.g., all of my friends drink and drive, so I will too). When you experience a bandwagon appeal, take the time to critically evaluate the evidence and reasoning offered for the proposed action. Also, regardless of who else thinks it's a good idea, ask yourself if accepting the idea serves your interests.

Source Citation:
[20] Cialdini, R. B. (2001). *Influence: Science and practice* (4th ed.). Boston: Allyn and Bacon.

Slippery Slope

The **slippery slope** fallacy occurs when a speaker asserts that some event must inevitably follow from another down a steep slope toward disaster. In many cases, there are a series of steps between events that lead toward an ultimate conclusion. Consider the following examples:

> We have to stop the tuition increase. The next thing you know, they'll be charging $100,000 a semester!

> If we restrict the publication of magazines such as the *National Enquirer*, then the First Amendment will be weakened and the whole country will be controlled by the government.

Speakers advancing such arguments face the burden of substantiating each of the links in the chain of reasoning. As a consumer of these types of arguments, you should carefully analyze the proof offered and reflect on whether the proposed chain of events is really leading inevitably toward disaster.

False Dilemma

The **false dilemma** fallacy (also known as the *either-or* fallacy) asserts that a complicated question has only two answers, when more actually exist. One easy way to identify this fallacy is to listen for the words *either* and *or*:

> Look, you're going to have to make up your mind. Either you decide that you can afford this MP3 player, or you decide you're going to do without music for a while.

This example presents a false dilemma—you can certainly identify other ways to access music that do not require you to purchase an MP3 player. Such arguments are problematic because they are designed to prevent the receiver from considering other, perhaps better, alternatives.

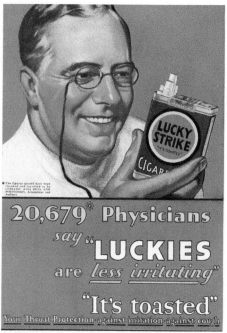

Appeal to Authority

An **appeal to authority** rests on the assumption that because an authority figure says something, it must be true. We have provided a number of examples of how to use appeals to authority (e.g., evidence credibility statements) throughout this text. As a result, we want to be very clear about the fact that the mere presence of an appeal to authority does not constitute fallacious reasoning. Instead, such arguments go "bad" when the appeal is based on a statement made by a person who is actually not an authority or when the person is situated in some circumstance that undermines her or his credibility. Think back to our example of source bias in Chapter 7. Would it be reasonable for a speaker seeking support for an argument for relaxing restrictions on carbon dioxide production to appeal to an authority figure who was paid to develop this type of research by coal companies? For the critical consumer of information, the obvious presence of bias in this case should overwhelm any persuasive effects of the source's authority. Indeed, you can easily detect fallacious appeals to authority by applying the tests of evidence and other information literacy skills discussed in Chapter 7.

Appeal to Authority. Many years ago cigarette advertisements routinely featured statements from doctors to give credibility to the claim that tobacco products were safe to use.

Critical Interaction 15.1
Thinking Critically about Advertisements

Please choose and analyze an advertisement.

Description of Advertisement (provide if possible):

1. After a quick glance, what are your first impressions of the advertisement?
2. Whom do you believe is the target audience for the advertisement? Why?
3. What emotional appeals (pathos) were advertisers using in this ad? Explain.
4. What logical appeals (logos) were advertisers using in this the ad? Explain.
5. How did the advertisers use credibility (ethos)?
6. What is the slogan, if any?
7. Are there any fallacies used in the ad? If so, which ones? Explain.
8. What is your overall impression of the advertisement based on what you have discovered in the earlier questions? Are you persuaded to buy the product?

Red Herring

The term **red herring** has its roots in English fox hunting traditions. Prior to a hunt, farmers often dragged a herring (a stinky fish) around the fields to mask the scent of the fox and throw the dogs off its trail. Speakers commit the red herring fallacy when they introduce irrelevant information into an argument in an attempt to mask the real issue under discussion. The following example illustrates this fallacy:

> Senator Johnson has argued that I completely support President Obama's strategy for stimulating the economy. His most recent ads have attacked me as a tax and spend liberal. In fact, Senator Johnson, like many Senate Republicans, has accepted money from the very financial institutions that created our current economic problems. Clearly, it's time for a new start.

In this example, the speaker fails to address the key issue—current strategies for stimulating the economy. Instead, the speaker introduces an entirely new issue designed to divert attention away from the central point.

As you produce and consume persuasive messages, use the critical thinking skills discussed throughout this text to detect fallacious arguments. As a consumer of persuasive messages, identifying fallacies will help insulate you from the kinds of bad decisions that fallacies promote. As a producer of persuasive messages, eliminating fallacies from your speech will bolster your credibility and enhance your persuasiveness.

Media
Interaction 15.1

Skeptic's Dictionary: Fallacies

For this media interaction, please visit the Skeptic's Dictionary website (http://www.skepdic.com/refuge/ctlessons/lesson5.html).

1. Try to find at least three examples of fallacies mentioned in the chapter on this website.
2. Bring your examples to class to share.

Preparing to Participate 15.3
Fallacies of Reasoning

Knowledge
What are the common fallacies of reasoning?

Application
What are the consequences of using fallacies in your speech?
What are your perceptions of speakers who use fallacies?

SUMMARY

The systematic study of the methods of argumentation and persuasion dates back to the days of the Ancient Greeks. As we noted in this chapter, an argument consists of several elements: claims, evidence, evidence credibility statements, warrants, qualifiers, and rebuttals. Understanding the relationships among each of these elements is critical to effective persuasive speaking and *competent* communication.

This chapter also introduced you to logos, ethos, and pathos as major modes of persuasion. Logical appeals make use of inductive, deductive, causal, and analogical reasoning. Appeals to credibility are rooted in the audience's perception of the speaker's competence, character, and goodwill. Appeals to emotion tap into the audience's feelings and are especially effective when used in combination with logical and credibility appeals.

Finally, fallacies are errors in logic that result from unsound reasoning or evidence. Fallacies are unethical, obscure the central argument, and can represent a threat to decision making. As a producer of persuasive messages, you should avoid the use of fallacies in your speeches. In addition, as a consumer of messages, you should be able to detect and defend yourself from fallacious argument. Understanding the principles in this chapter will not only improve your *ethical communication* but your *critical thinking* skills as well.

KEY TERMS

argument (232)

argument model (232)

claim (232)

evidence (233)

evidence credibility
    statement (233)

warrant (234)

qualifier (235)

one-sided/ multi-sided message (235)

rebuttal (235)

counterargument (235)

logos (236)

rational proof (236)

premise (236)

inductive reasoning (237)

hasty generalization (237)

deductive reasoning (237)

syllogism (238)

causal reasoning (238)

false cause (239)

analogical reasoning (239)

figurative analogy (239)

invalid analogy (240)

ethos (240)

credibility (240)

competence (240)

character (240)

goodwill (241)

initial credibility (241)

derived credibility (241)

terminal credibility (241)

pathos (241)

fallacy (243)

ad hominem (244)

bandwagon (244)

slippery slope (244)

false dilemma (245)

appeal to authority (245)

red herring (246)

ADDITIONAL ENGAGEMENT OPPORTUNITIES

Now that you have finished reading the chapter, it is also important to make connections between the course content and your own experiences. These activities will help you understand, apply, analyze, evaluate, or synthesize course concepts. You can use these activities to provide evidence of your preparation for participation in class as well as to plan additional contributions to class discussion. The Civic Engagement Opportunities (CEOs) are designed to help you become more engaged in campus and community life and apply course concepts to important social issues.

1. Write an evidence credibility statement for one of your sources in your persuasive speech.
   - Identify the claim to be supported by evidence.
   - What type of evidence will you use to support the claim (example, statistics, testimony)? Is this the most appropriate means of supporting this claim?
   - Is this evidence appropriate for this audience?
   - Identify the author(s) of the evidence and develop a brief statement of credibility. Is the person(s) an expert on the subject? Is the person(s) reasonably objective? List the credentials of the author(s).
   - Identify the date of publication. Is this evidence timely? Does it account for what is currently happening with your topic?
   - Where was the information published? Is this a credible source? Can you identify source bias?

- Write a paragraph description that includes the claim and evidence as well as the information you would use to create an oral citation (author, credibility of author, date of publication, source information). This paragraph is what you will actually say in your speech.

2. 🗨 Visit the Annenberg Political Fact Check website (http://www.factcheck.org/) and view a recent political advertisement. Did the advertisement present an effective argument (including claim, data, warrant, evidence credibility statement, etc.)? Did the advertisement rely on a particular form of proof (i.e., logos, ethos, pathos) or offer a mix of persuasive strategies? Were you able to identify any fallacies in the advertisement?

Using Communication in the 21st Century

As long as there are human rights to be defended; as long as there are great interests to be guarded; as long as the welfare of nations is a matter for discussion, so long will public speaking have its place.
—William Jennings Bryan

CHAPTER OBJECTIVES

After reading this chapter, you should be able to:

- Understand how to use communication skills in a democracy.
- Understand how to use communication skills for the common good.
- Understand how to critically consume messages.

A few hundred years ago, if you obtained a university education, you pretty much learned everything that was known in the Western world. As you no doubt realize, when you graduate with a degree in the 21st century, you don't know everything. With increased literacy and education, the world has produced a glut of information, requiring much greater specialization among its citizens.

You have probably declared a major course of study or will be expected to do so very soon. The farther you advance in your education, the more specialized your knowledge will become. There's nothing wrong with that, of course, but we still have to communicate with others who may not share our educational or experiential backgrounds. Hopefully, you have come to understand the importance of **audience analysis** as a result of taking this course, so that you can adjust your message and delivery based on the knowledge and experience levels of the people with whom you are speaking. Recall in Chapter 4 on listening that we discussed the importance of critical thinking for effective public speaking. The speaking, listening, and thinking skills listed in Figure 4.2 are useful in a variety of contexts, not just giving speeches in a classroom. Our wish is that you will take what you have learned and practiced in this course and will be able to apply it in your own personal and professional lives. The public speaking and thinking skills you have honed will allow you to participate as an active member of your community by enabling you to share your unique talents and perspectives. By becoming better public speakers, we become better communicators. By becoming better communicators, we become better citizens.

Communicating in a Democracy

Competent and **ethical communication** is central to the tenets of democratic self-governance. The founders of our nation were products of the Enlightenment, and as such, had an unshakable belief in the power of reason. In fact, our democracy depends on people acting in good faith using the best possible information to reach some sort of consensus about how best to create a free and just society. That's why the first amendment protects freedom of speech and freedom of the press. Thomas Jefferson, third president and author of the Declaration of Independence, went so far as to state:

> The basis of our governments being the opinion of the people, the very first object should be to keep that right; and were it left to me to decide whether we should have a government without newspapers or newspapers without the government, I should not hesitate a moment to prefer the latter. But I should mean that every man should receive those papers, and be capable of reading them.[1]

When Jefferson wrote those words, there was no such thing as photography, radio, television, or the Internet. That's why being able to read and write and having the freedom to share one's thoughts (both orally and in writing) was so important to him. In other words, democracies function as a result of citizens communicating with one another. It is important for us, too, which is why we have written a book to help you with your *oral communication competencies*. However, new literacies are required in today's world. Recall our

Source Citation:
[1] As cited in Commission of Freedom of the Press (1947). *A free and responsible press; a general report on mass communication: Newspapers, radio, motion pictures, magazines, and books.* Chicago: University of Chicago Press.

discussion in Chapter 7 (Integrating Supporting Material) about **information literacy**. Because it is not possible for us to know everything, despite being highly educated, it is crucially important that we be able to locate and evaluate information from those experts whose specialties we don't share. Likewise, recall Chapter 12 (Designing Presentation Aids) and the idea of **visual literacy**. Humans have a long history of determining the truth or falsity of spoken and written propositions, but judging visual messages requires a different sensibility.[2] Many of the fallacies discussed in Chapter 15 (Building Arguments) have been known since the time of the ancient Greeks and were developed specifically for examining spoken and written arguments. What is new, however, is the meaning and persuasive appeal inherent in the images we see in books and magazines and on television and the Internet.

Hopefully, since you have now had the chance to produce visual materials for your own speeches, you will be more alert and critical when encountering them in your everyday life. Information and visual literacy are vitally important, but we would like to add one more category to the list: media literacy. That is, it is important to consider the channel or medium a message is delivered in, and to be aware of political, organizational, and ideological biases that affect the content of mediated communication. Throughout this book we have pointed you to **media interactions** that we hope have honed your **critical thinking skills** regarding the mass media. Now, where do you go from here?

How would you go about finding information about a political candidate? Well, it is certainly possible (probably unavoidable) to view each candidate's 30-second television spot during the campaign season. How much and what kind of information do those messages contain? Do those TV spots tell you about the candidate's position on the important topics of the day? Is 30 seconds sufficient time for a candidate to expound on plans to accomplish campaign goals? During presidential campaigns we have the opportunity to witness debates between the candidates—this is a great way to put your critical thinking and listening skills to the test. Can you spot faulty reasoning? Logical fallacies? Importantly, can you recognize when the candidate you favor makes a mistake in his or her reasoning?

Neil Postman reports that in 1854 in Peoria, Illinois, Abraham Lincoln and Stephen Douglas engaged in seven hours of debate (with a break for dinner).[3] This wasn't unusual and the audience thought nothing of it! I wonder how well that would play in Peoria today? Today's citizens are not likely to listen to seven hours of debate, but if short debates and television spots don't answer your questions, where would you seek more information about political candidates? Once you locate more in-depth information, how can you tell if that source is factual or overly biased? These are difficult questions, but if we want to govern ourselves, they have to be answered. **Democracy** requires informed citizens. Citizenship implies responsibility. Responsibility means acting in mutually beneficial ways with others. We owe it to one another to be media literate, but what if we don't share a "range of common experiences"?

It is now possible for each of us to receive only the information that we seek. Through the use of computers and the Internet, each of us can consume only those media messages or news items that we deem important or useful.[4] In effect, we can create and live in our own informational worlds, cut off from those around us. As we mentioned earlier, to create and sustain a public realm

Source Citation:
[2] Postman, N. (1985). *Amusing ourselves to death: Public discourse in the age of show business.* New York: Penguin Books.

Source Citations:
[3] Postman, N. (1985). *Amusing ourselves to Death: Public discourse in the age of show business.* New York: Penguin Books.

[4] Sunstein, C. (2001, March 16). Exposure to other viewpoints is vital to Democracy. *The Chronicle of Higher Education,* p. B10.

Informed Decision-Making.
Abraham Lincoln's Peoria speech on Oct. 16, 1854 lasted over three hours and was later transcribed by Mr. Lincoln himself *from memory!*

worthy of a democracy, we have to share common goals and experiences. Although specialized expertise is needed in today's professional world, we also need to maintain broad civic interests. And although our ability to locate and organize information on any topic is practically limitless, we need to resist hemming ourselves into informational backwaters where only other specialists can understand what we say.

Preparing to Participate 16.1
Citizenship

Knowledge
What does it mean to be a citizen in a democracy?

Application
What have you learned in this class that will enable you to become a citizen in democracy?

Calvin and Hobbes

CALVIN AND HOBBES ©1993 Watterson. Dist. By UNIVERSAL PRESS SYNDICATE. All rights reserved.

1. How does understanding communication help us to deal with the demands of the 21st century?

2. How have channels changed? How will they continue to change?

3. How has the context changed? How will it continue to change?

Use Communication for the Common Good

Our economic system is based on the belief that the best ideas, goods, and services will flourish when people behave in mutually beneficial ways. That is, when we enter into consensual economic transactions in an informed manner, everyone should get what they want. Now, it should come as no surprise to you that we do not always live up to our ideals. Why is that? Are our experiences so different that we can't hope to achieve the ideals set forth in our constitution? Landon Beyer and Daniel Liston point out that **common**, **community**, and **communication** all share the same linguistic root, and that without these, it would be impossible to "establish a widely held social good."[5]

Back in Chapter 1, we discussed the **personal**, **professional**, and **social benefits** of studying communication and we stated that our goals were that you would become *competent, confident,* and *ethical communicators.* Through classroom discussions and group activities, you practiced interpersonal communication and hopefully gained new insight into how to make those interactions more pleasant and effective. With your public speeches you learned and practiced many new skills on your way to becoming more competent and confident presenters. We have tried to stress the idea that all of us are both producers and consumers of messages. That is, we are all communicators. But, as you no doubt realize, there are many other **channels** and **contexts** (remember the communication process model?) in which you will be expected to function in your life other than the ones practiced in this course.

Fortunately, the skills and techniques you used to interact successfully with your classmates and instructor can be put to use in other social situations. In addition, the **research**, **argumentation**, and speaking skills that you practiced when preparing and delivering your presentations can be extended into job interviews and business meetings or used to write reports or compose emails.

The channels and contexts in which we now consume and produce messages are numerous and will only expand over time. Do you surf the web? e-mail? blog? chat room? IM? Perhaps you have your own website? If not, maybe you have a profile on MySpace, Facebook, or LinkedIn. Have you ever contributed to a threaded discussion list? Did you receive a new

Source Citation:
[5] Beyer, L. E., & Liston, D. P. (1996). *Curriculum in conflict: Social visions, educational agendas, and progressive school reform.* New York: Teachers College Press. (p. 88).

Don't Take My Word for It. Dr. Michael Shermer, the founding publisher of *Skeptic* magazine, encourages critical skeptism.

Source Citations:

6 Shermer, M. (1997). *Why people believe weird things: Pseudo-science, superstition, and bogus notions of our time.* New York: MJF Books.

7 Sagan, C. (1996). *The demon-haunted world: Science as a candle in the dark.* New York: Ballantine Books.

digital camcorder for your birthday? Perhaps a video could get your point across. A video conference or podcast over the web may extend your influence farther than your parents or grandparents could ever imagine.

Perhaps you prefer communicating with old-fashioned tools. How about a letter to the editor? Have you ever spoken at a school board meeting or zoning commission? Maybe you are an officer in a club and often have to conduct meetings. Perhaps you have a part-time job as a telemarketer. Are you confident that what you have learned about the communication process can serve you and others well in these areas?

Recall that being an *ethical communicator* requires you to be truthful, accurate, honest, and reasonable. While conducting research for your speeches, you probably came across conflicting information. How did you resolve those conflicts, and how will you resolve them in the future? How can you judge the quality of the information you encounter? If you are going to persuade co-workers, family members, or voters to adopt your viewpoint to enhance the common good, you should have good evidence for what you say.

Recall the strategies we discussed in Chapter 7 about how to locate supporting material. Specifically, we encouraged you to develop your *information literacy* by developing research questions to guide yourself and to keep your audience in mind as to what information was likely to persuade them. As you are well aware, there is no shortage of information in today's world. The trick is locating relevant information and then determining its quality. Generally speaking, information that has been through some sort of review process is more reliable than the casual thoughts of some individual ranting on a web page. For example, journalists usually have to go through a series of editors before they get their stories on the air or in print. Scientists must submit their studies to a peer-review process meant to weed out faulty thinking and results. In short, this information tends to be more useful and accurate because many eyes have had a chance to catch errors or sloppy reasoning.

Of course, you should approach all information with a critical eye. Michael Shermer, publisher of *Skeptic* magazine, once was asked by a journalist, "why should we believe anything you say?" And he replied, "You shouldn't."[6]

In your own life, ask questions, consult multiple sources, and suspend judgment until you have enough high-quality information before making decisions that affect you personally, professionally, and socially. Astronomer Carl Sagan offered this sage advice: "Have an open mind but not so open your brains fall out!"[7] Do you remember the material in Chapter 15 about logical fallacies? Once you have located high-quality information, can you reach a logically justified conclusion? Once you have perfected your argument, how do you present it to others? Should you address them face-to-face? If this is not possible, how about a website? If this is too impersonal, how about an e-mail message?

As you can see, as a producer and consumer of messages, you are faced with a great array of choices. Does that give you option anxiety, or does it thrill you that you are limited only by your imagination? Much of our

Being Open-Minded. Dr. Carl Sagan, who was an astronomer at Cornell University, encouraged keeping an open but critical mind. He hosted the 13-part *Cosmos* series on PBS which has been seen by half a billion people worldwide.

communication is **goal-directed**. That is, we create messages to accomplish personal, professional, or social goals. To reach a goal, you must have a strategy. Luckily, you now know something about the communication process and can use that knowledge to devise a strategy for producing and consuming messages. Communication always takes place in a context, and it requires a receiver or an audience. That audience may be one person or many. Who are they, and what do they know, want, or believe? What will be the setting and why are they there? What is the message that you want to convey? Do you have the necessary information to back your claims? What channel makes the most sense for your message, context, and audience? What types of interference may hinder your efforts? Can you foresee any "noise," and are you able to take steps to eliminate or minimize it?

Consider a slightly different question: How might you utilize your freshly honed communication skills to participate in our democratic system for the common good? 🖥 To begin with, you are certainly now better equipped to make informed choices at the ballot box. However, you are also now in a position to employ these skills more proactively for political engagement. Take a moment to look over the skills for **political engagement** provided in Figure 16.1.[8]

How many of these skills rest on the foundation of the *communication, critical thinking,* and *information, visual,* and *media literacy skills* covered in this text? All of them! This realization should reinforce a central theme of this chapter (and text): As

Political Engagement

Visit the New York Times Political Engagement website (http://www.nytimes.com/college/collegespecial10/) and peruse the pilot profiles of the eight participating institutions.

1. What is the objective of the national Political Engagement Project?
2. Are there activities on other campuses that you would like to see at your school? If so, what specific activities might work best?
3. The *New York Times* has made a commitment to publish meritorious student PEP-related work. What projects have you completed this semester that could be submitted to this site?

Source Citation:
8 Colby, A., Ehrlich, T., Beaumont, E., & Stephens, J. (2003) *Educating citizens: Preparing America's undergraduates for lives of moral and civic responsibility.* San Francisco, CA: Jossey Bass. (p. 276).

Critical Interaction 16.1
Promoting Political Engagement through Public Speaking/Communication

Based on the Political Engagement skills presented in Figure 16.1 and the information you find in Media Interaction 16.1, create a plan that will convince others at your institution to participate in these activities.

- What is your central message?
- Who is your intended audience?
- What channel(s) will you use to communicate?

Source Citation:
9 Hillygus, D. S. (2005). The missing link: Exploring the relationship between higher education and political engagement. *Political Behavior, 27*, 25–47.

you become a more *competent communicator*, you become better prepared to participate in our *democracy*. For example, in order to engage in political persuasion, you must have the verbal and argumentation skills to communicate a position. To further substantiate this point, research regarding the effects of higher education on political involvement demonstrates that the best predictor of students' future political engagement is training in communication skills.[9]

Skills for Political Engagement

Work together with someone or some group to solve a problem in the community where you live.

Contact or visit a public official—at any level of government—to ask for assistance or to express your opinion.

Contact a newspaper or magazine to express your opinion on an issue or issue a press release detailing your issue.

Call in to a radio or television talk show to express your opinion on an issue.

Attend a speech, informal seminar, or teach about politics.

Take part in a protest, march, or demonstration.

Sign a written or e-mail petition about a political or social issue.

Work with a political group or for a campaign or political official.

Boycott something because of conditions under which the product is made, or because you dislike the conduct of the company that produces it.

Buy a certain product or service because you like the social or political values of the company that produces it.

Work as canvasser going door to door for a political candidate or cause.

FIGURE 16.1

Skills for Political Engagement

We have clearly made the point that studying communication will benefit you personally and professionally, and all of us join together in wishing you the best of luck in your future endeavors. However, we agree with researchers Anne Colby, Thomas Ehrlich, Elizabeth Beaumont, and Jason Stephens, all prominent civic education advocates, that whatever else you do the rest of your life, we hope you will also be "active citizens and positive forces in the world."[10]

You are likely aware that many prominent scholars have argued over the last several years that political disengagement among the youth of this country is a significant problem.[11] This is a problem worth addressing because the withdrawal of a cohort of citizens from our political system places democracy at risk. If our country ever needed a new generation of savvy critical thinkers that know how to access, use, and evaluate information, as well as how to use their communication skills for the common good, we need them now. In the end, you can be the vehicle for positively affecting the attitudes and lives of others in your community.

Source Citations:
[10] Beaumont, E., Colby, A., Ehrlich, T., & Torney-Purta, J. (2006). Promoting political competence and engagement in college students: An empirical study. *Journal of Political Science Education, 2*, 249–270.

[11] Galston, W. A. (2003). Civic education and political participation. *Phi Delta Kappan, 85.*1, 29–33.

Preparing to Participate 16.2
Common Good

Knowledge
What does it mean to use communication for the common good?

Application
How will you use the skills learned in this class for the common good?

Consuming Messages

Many times, you may not be in the position to inform or persuade anyone, but you may need to be informed or persuaded yourself. That is, you may only be interested in consuming information. No doubt, you are inundated by messages every single day. Your voice mail is full of messages from friends

Critical Interaction 16.2
Common, Community, and Communication

Based on what you have learned in this class, write one sentence using the terms *common*, *community*, and *communication*.

Comic 16.2

1. Have the media put our democracy at risk? If so, how?

2. What are the consequences of an unengaged democracy?

CALVIN AND HOBBES ©1993 Watterson. Dist. By UNIVERSAL PRESS SYNDICATE. All rights reserved.

[12] Shenk, D. (1997). Data smog: Surviving the info glut. *MIT's Technology Review, 100*, 18–26.

and family vying for your attention. Your e-mail box is full of spam trying to sell you things you don't really need, your car radio seems only to play commercials rather than music, and billboards block out the beautiful neighborhoods that lie beyond them. Why in the world would anyone seek more information in a world that spews so much of it? The sad fact is that in our world there is a glut of information, which makes it difficult to locate and analyze the best possible messages to help us make decisions about our personal, professional, and social lives.[12]

Have you ever wanted to lose weight? Why? Is it for health-related reasons, or is it because you're trying to match the "ideal" body image we see on television or in fashion magazines? How many different diet books or pills do you think there are on the market? Are they all the same? Is one more effective, healthier, or cheaper than another? Whom do you believe? Why? Is it because the source is attractive, eloquent, and seemingly knowledgeable? Or do you believe based on the quality of evidence and force of logic? Where would you look for diet/health information? Are you in a position to evaluate it once you find it? Are you aware that the Federal Trade Commission (FTC) and the Food and Drug Administration (FDA) routinely examine health claims made by various businesses and individuals? For example, for a prescription drug to make it to the market, the manufacturers must submit scientific evidence to support their claims. The FDA is then faced with the possibility of making two kinds of errors: accepting a bad drug or rejecting a good drug.[13] Statisticians call them *type 1* and *type 2* errors. The FDA makes its judgments based on the quality and amount of evidence offered about the safety and effectiveness of the drug in question. If accepted, the drug can then be put on the market. But even this precaution is not foolproof. For example, in the late 1990s, the diet drug Phen-fen was pulled from the market—not because the drug didn't help people lose weight, but because some people using the prescription drug had died. Those are serious consequences that even the FDA did not foresee when it approved Phen-fen's use.

Two important considerations when you are trying to make a decision are to ask yourself: *What is the likelihood of being right?* and *What are the consequences of being wrong?* For example, there are thousands of diet products that are marketed as supplements and not as drugs, so the FDA has little or no control over them. The claims made about the effectiveness of these products range greatly, but those claims are not often reviewed by the FDA.

Source Citation:
[13] Paulos, J. A. (1988). *Innumeracy: Mathematical illiteracy and its consequences.* New York: Hill and Wang.

See also

DeMars, C. E., Cameron, L., & Erwin, T. D. (2003). Information literacy as foundational: Determining competence. *Journal of General Education, 52*, 253–265.

Perhaps you have noticed the label on a supplement bottle or the fine print on a television commercial that says something to the effect that the FDA has not reviewed these claims. That is because the product is categorized as a supplement and not as a drug.

So, as you can see, being able to consume media messages critically and draw conclusions based on that information can have serious consequences for you. It is not always easy to make decisions because of the glut of contradictory messages that we encounter, but it is our responsibility to weigh the information carefully and act accordingly. Again, consider the consequences of making a decision.

This form of reasoning is important for personal decision making such as choosing a new diet, and it is common in many professional settings as well. Most businesses engage in cost/benefit analyses before launching new products and services. It is likely that you will have to perform these types of analyses during your career. Basically, it involves the weighing of advantages and disadvantages before making a decision. In an organizational setting, your findings and recommendations will need to be reported to others in a persuasive manner in order to effect **policy changes**.

Finally, as we're sure you have already concluded, these skills are essential to the functioning of our democracy. Aren't you glad you've studied public speaking and persuasion?

Preparing to Participate 16.3
Consuming Messages

Knowledge
What does it mean to be a consumer of messages?

Application
How has taking this class made you a better consumer of messages?

SUMMARY

New skills and sensibilities are required for citizens wishing to participate in a 21st century democracy. Speaking and listening are still crucially important, but they now require literacies that have only recently been understood and taught. *Information, visual,* and *media literacies* allow today's citizens to locate and evaluate information, view and design images, and critically engage media messages. Democratic self-governance requires engaged, *informed citizens* who know how to operate in today's informational world.

Creating a widely held social good is difficult in a society where citizens have highly specialized knowledge and seldom communicate with those who are different from themselves. The modern *competent* and *ethical communicator* seeks out a broad range of information and media messages so that they can be civically and *politically engaged* with their communities.

Likewise, when faced with personal and professional choices, these communicators exercise their *critical thinking skills* and consider a broad range of options and information before making crucial decisions. In the end, *competent, confident,* and *ethical communicators* become successful in their *personal, professional,* and *social lives.* That's our hope for you.

KEY TERMS

audience analysis (252)

competent
communication (252)

ethical communication (252)

information literacy (253)

visual literacy (253)

media interactions (253)

critical thinking skills (253)

democracy (253)

common, community,
communication (255)

personal, professional, and
social benefits (255)

channels (255)

context (255)

research (255)

argumentation (255)

goal-directed (257)

political engagement (257)

policy change (261)

ADDITIONAL ENGAGEMENT OPPORTUNITIES

Now that you have finished reading the chapter, it is also important to make connections between the course content and your own experiences. These activities will help you understand, apply, analyze, evaluate, or synthesize course concepts. You can use these activities to provide evidence of your preparation for participation in class as well as to plan additional contributions to class discussion. The Civic Engagement Opportunities (CEOs) are designed to help you become more engaged in campus and community life and apply course concepts to important social issues.

1. Find a company that you like because of the social or political values they embody. Write a short letter to the company to show your appreciation and endorsement of their products.

2. If someone asked you to describe in one minute what you have learned from this class, what would you say?

3. For this CEO go to http://www.gopetition.com/ to find a petition you deem worthy of signing. You can complete a quick keyword search to find a topic that interests you (perhaps from one of the class persuasive speeches) or you can select a currently featured topic. Be prepared to share with the rest of the class which petitions you selected and why they were worthy of their consideration.

Appendix

OUTLINE FOR INFORMATIVE SPEECH

Tornadoes

Purpose: To inform the audience about tornadoes.

Thesis: In order to better understand tornadoes, it is important to explore what causes tornadoes to develop, how researchers classify types of tornadoes, and odd occurrences that may be associated with tornadoes.

Organizational Pattern: Topical

I. **Introduction**
   A. **Attention Getter:** What can hurtle automobiles through the air, rip ordinary homes to shreds, defeather chickens, and travel at speeds over 60 mph?
   B. **Relevance:** Illinois rests on the boundary of what tornado researchers call *Tornado Alley*. This is the area of the country that receives the most tornadoes every year. According to a 1995 brochure distributed by the *National Oceanic and Atmospheric Administration* (NOAA), Illinois averages 27 tornadoes a year. Also, nearly five people die every year in Illinois as a result of tornadoes **[VISUAL AID]**. In fact, according to *Tornado Project Online!*, a website hosted by a company that gathers tornado information for tornado researchers that I accessed earlier this month, the deadliest tornado in U.S. recorded history occurred in Murphysboro, Illinois. In 1925, a violent tornado killed 234 people in this Southern Illinois town.
   C. **Credibility:** I grew up in the heart of Tornado Alley and have been interested in this weather phenomenon for a very long time. Also, I am a trained weather spotter for the Bloomington/Normal civil defense agency.
   D. **Thesis:** In order to better understand tornadoes, it is important to explore what causes tornadoes to develop, how researchers classify types of tornadoes, and odd occurrences that may be associated with tornadoes.
   E. **Preview:** So, let us crash through the causes of tornadoes, twist around the types of tornadoes, and blow through some of the oddities associated with tornadoes.

Transition: Initially, I will crash through the causes of tornadoes.

II. Body

  A. There are several causes of tornadoes.

    1. According to the *USA Today Tornado Information* website, which was last updated on June 20, 2000, a tornado is a "violently rotating column of air in contact with the ground and pendant from a thunderstorm." Therefore, thunderstorms are the first step in the creation of a tornado.

    2. The *USA Today Tornado Information* site also indicates that there are three key conditions for thunderstorms to form.

      a. First, moisture in the lower to mid levels of the atmosphere.

      b. Second, unstable air. This is air that will continue rising once it begins rising from near the ground.

      c. The final condition for the formation of tornado-producing thunderstorms is a lifting force. A lifting force is a mechanism that causes the air to begin rising. The most common lifting force is heating of the air (which is why we experience so many thunderstorms in the spring as the air begins to warm).

    3. The same source indicates that the strongest thunderstorms typically form in warm, humid air that's east or south of advancing cold air.

    4. I mentioned in the introduction that Illinois sees its fair share of tornadoes. The following graph, adapted from the *USA Today Tornado Information* website, illustrates areas in the U.S. that receive the greatest number of tornadoes (Tornado Alley). Thunderstorm-producing tornadoes are likely to form in this area as cold air from the west and north clashes violently with warm air from the Gulf of Mexico **[VISUAL AID]**.

Transition: Now that we have crashed through the causes of tornadoes, let's twist around the types of tornadoes.

  B. There are several types of tornadoes.

    1. According to renowned weather historian Dr. David Ludlum, author of the 1997 edition of the National Audubon Society's *Field Guide to North American Weather*, tornado researchers use a scale, known as the Fujita-Pearson Tornado Intensity Scale (named after its creators) to rate the intensity of tornadoes **[VISUAL AID]**.

    2. Tornado statistics from *NOAA* (cited above) **[VISUAL AID]**

      a. Weak tornadoes

        (1) Account for 69% of all tornadoes.

        (2) Winds are less than 110 mph.

      b. Strong tornadoes

        (1) Account for 29% of all tornadoes.

        (2) Winds range from 110 to 205 mph.

      c. Violent tornadoes

        (1) Represent only 2% of all tornadoes.

        (2) Winds exceed 205 mph.

    3. According to *Tornado Project Online!*, although violent tornadoes account for only 2% of all tornadoes, they are responsible for 67% of all deaths in tornadoes **[VISUAL AID]**.

    4. In addition, astrogeophysicist Dr. Robert Davies-Jones notes in a 1995 edition of *Scientific American* that most tornadoes have damage paths 150 feet wide,

move at about 30 miles per hour and last only a few minutes. However, extremely violent tornadoes, like the one that ripped through Murphysboro, Illinois, may be over a mile wide, travel at 60 miles per hour and may stay on the ground for more than one hour.

Transition: Now that we have a better understanding of the causes and types of tornadoes, I will blow through some of the oddities associated with tornadoes.

  C. There have been many oddities associated with tornadoes.

    1. Stories of strange events are typical in the wake of the damage caused by tornadoes. Indeed, much of what makes stories of tornadoes unusual is irony. Consider the following story from the *1996 Weather Guide Calendar*. In a 1984 Kansas tornado, a man, apparently thinking that his mobile home would be destroyed, ran to shelter in another building, only to have that building destroyed (killing the man), while his trailer survived just fine.

    2. As noted by *Tornado Project Online!*, the Great Bend, Kansas tornado of November 1915 is a tornado which seems to have the greatest number of oddities associated with it.

      a. At Grant Jones' store, the south wall was blown down and scattered, but shelves and canned goods that stood against the wall were not moved.

      b. The Riverside Steam Laundry, build of stone and cement block, was completely destroyed, yet two nearby wooden shacks were untouched.

      c. A canceled check from Great Bend was found in a corn field, one mile outside of Palmyra, Nebraska . . . . 305 miles to the northeast. This is the longest known distance that debris has ever been carried.

    3. *Tornado Project Online!* also reports that the "plucked chicken" remains today as perhaps the most talked about tornado oddity **[VISUAL AID]**. Indeed, this oddity has been associated with many Illinois tornadoes.

      a. Within the damage descriptions of rural tornadoes, there are often stories of a chicken "stripped clean of every feather."

      b. It has long been thought that the feathers explode off the bird in the tornado's low pressure.

      c. The most likely explanation for the defeathering of a chicken is the protective response called "flight molt." As noted by *Tornado Project Online!*, "chickens are not stripped clean, but in actuality they lose a large percentage of their feathers under stress in this flight molt process." In short, when the chickens become scared their feathers become loose and are simply blown off.

Transition: Summary

III. Conclusion

  A. Thesis/Summary: In this speech I have explored the key factors that cause tornadoes to develop, how researchers classify types of tornadoes, and odd occurrences that may be associated with tornadoes.

  B. Memorable Close: So, the next time you see a Ferrari flying through the air, your college dorm being dismantled floor by floor, or a chicken without wings, take cover because tornado season is here.

References

Davies-Jones, R. (1995). Tornadoes: The storms that spawn twisters are now largely understood, but mysteries still remain about how these violent vortices form. *Scientific American, 273*(2), 48–58.

Grazulis, T. (1995). Chasing tornado oddities. In L. Sessions (Ed.), *1996 Weather guide calendar with phenomenal weather events*. Denver, CO: Accord Publishing.

Ludlum, D. M. (1997). *National Audubon Society field guide to North American weather*. New York: Chanticleer Press.

National Oceanic and Atmospheric Administration. (1995). *Tornadoes: Nature's most violent storms* [Brochure]. Washington, DC: National Weather Service.

Tornado Project Online. (2000, June 19). *The top ten U.S. killer tornadoes*. Retrieved August 5, 2000, from http://www.tornadoproject.com/

USA Today Tornado Information. (2000, June 20). *Understanding tornadoes*. [On-Line]. Retrieved August 7, 2000, from http://www.usatoday.com/weather/tornado/wtwisto.htm

OUTLINE FOR INFORMATIVE SPEECH

Roman Coliseum

Specific Purpose: To inform the audience about the Roman Coliseum.

Thesis/Central Idea: To truly understand the historical impact the Coliseum has had on civilization, it is important to learn of the architectural wonders of the Coliseum, the terror of the Roman Games, and the present plans for its restoration.

Organizational Pattern: Topical

I. **Introduction**
   A. **Attention Getter:** Imagine yourself being ushered up a dark hallway and into a huge, outdoor theatre. Here you are greeted by 50,000 screaming spectators and one man—crazy for your death, hungry for the thought of ripping you apart limb from limb. You and Blood Thirsty are the only ones inside an arena encompassed by a 15-foot wall, and the 50,000 people are waiting for you to die.
   B. **Relevance:** From professional football and basketball games to the sporting events at ISU's Redbird Arena, much of our culture is influenced by the success of one great sports arena built nearly 2000 years ago. The author Alan Baker, in his book, *The Gladiator*, published in 2001, makes the connection between the ancient Roman games and our culture today. Our own athletes, he states, ". . . are merely the pale echoes of the ancient fighters . . . [they] display their skill and aggression before thousands of screaming spectators, with millions more watching on television. This is exactly what happened in the ancient world."
   C. **Credibility:** As a history major focused on Roman studies, I have always been enamored with the stories surrounding the Coliseum. Further, a tour of Ancient Rome this past summer intensified my horror and fascination with this great monument.
   D. **Thesis:** To truly understand the historical impact the Coliseum has had on civilization, it is important to learn of the architectural wonders of the Coliseum, the terror of the Roman Games, and the present plans for its restoration.
   E. **Preview:** Therefore, [show transparency] we will first lay the foundation by describing its design and construction, next, live through a day at the games, and finally, learn of the present plans to restore and renovate this ancient monument to its original glory.

Transition: To begin, we will lay the foundation by describing its design and construction.

II. **Body**
   A. First, the Coliseum's construction will be discussed.
      1. According to John Pearson, author of *Arena: The Story of the Coliseum*, published in 1973, the Emperor Vespasian, to curry the favor of the Roman people, commissioned the construction of the Coliseum.
      2. Considering the games were held 1900 years ago, the construction was considered pure genius.

a. The outdoor theatre boasted 80 entrances, with a design so incredibly pragmatic that each was equipped with a numbered staircase, ensuring the simultaneous exit of about 50,000 individuals in three minutes flat. Our sports stadiums today cannot even accomplish this feat.

b. Just as we look down from gymnasium bleachers, spectators would look down upon the wooden arena floor. However, the Coliseum's floor was covered with sand, which served to soak up large quantities of blood. The floor also concealed a labyrinth of tunnels, trapdoors, and a complicated system of chains and pulleys, similar to our modern-day elevators.

Transition: Now that we have laid the foundation of the Coliseum's construction, let us live through a day at the Roman Games.

B. A Day at the Games can be compared to a day watching football at the Redbird Arena.

1. As ISU students, part of our tuition pays for Redbird Arena. However, at the Coliseum's inception, it was a Roman citizen's right to attend the games free of charge. And just as we are treated to semesters of games, it was not uncommon for emperors to treat their subjects to many months of games.

2. The mornings began with fights between wild animals. One battle involved a bull and a panther, each at the end of a chain. They could barely reach other, and they were forced to tear each other apart piece by piece. Lions would be matched against tigers and bears pitted against bulls.

3. Lunchtime executions followed. The scholar Baker, as cited earlier, states that the infliction of pain was an essential part of punishment in ancient Rome. Therefore, common methods included crucifixions, being burned alive, and being thrown to wild beasts. In fact, Emperor Constantine would order molten lead to be poured down the condemned's throats.

4. The best attraction was saved for the afternoon: gladiatorial combat. The following videoclip is taken from the 2000 epic film, *Gladiator*, in which Russell Crowe stars. As stated earlier, notice the concealed trapdoors in the arena floor. [Show videoclip.]

Transition: Now that we have lived through the terror of the Roman Games, let us learn of the present plans to restore and renovate this ancient monument to its original glory.

C. The present life of the Coliseum is undergoing change.

1. After 300 years of this publicly accepted entertainment a monk named Telemachus ran into the arena, screaming for them to stop. However, the mob was not to be cheated of their entertainment, and he was torn to pieces.

a. Although gladiatorial combat was subsequently banned, the battles and executions involving wild beasts took another 100 years to end.

b. Stones were taken from the Coliseum to construct other buildings during the Middle Ages, and the inner arena, as shown here [show transparency] became overgrown with weeds and vegetation.

2. Recently, [show transparency] the National Geographic website reported in July of 2001 that a restoration project is underway to reinstate the Coliseum, which is located near the center of modern Rome.

   a. It will take eight years and cost 18 million dollars.
   b. It will also allow international tourists to attend Greek plays
       and gladiatorial exhibitions.

Transition: Once restored, it will encompass, as historian Dr. Alison Futrell states
in her 1997 book, *Blood in the Arena*, "all the glory and doom of the Roman Empire."

III. Conclusion

   A. **Thesis/Summary:** In many ways, the Coliseum has influenced the development
       of civilization and will likely do so for years to come. The Coliseum's construc-
       tion was truly genius, bearing witness to the wealth of the Roman Empire. The
       games, unlike those at Redbird Arena, served bloodshed and agony, in the form
       of wild beasts, executions, and gladiators. Hopefully, the restoration of the
       Coliseum will see much less bloodshed.
   B. **Memorable Close:** To quote the 7th century historian and monk, the Venerable
       Bede, in his famous *Ecclesiastical History of the English People*, "While the
       Coliseum stands, Rome shall stand; when the Coliseum falls, Rome shall fall;
       when Rome falls, the world shall fall."

References

Auguet, R. (1998). *Cruelty and civilization: The Roman games*. New York: Barnes & Noble.

Baker, A. (2001). *The gladiator: The secret history of Rome's warrior slaves*. New York:
   St. Martin's Press.

Bede, V. (1849). *The Venerable Bede's ecclesiastical history of England*. London: H. G. Bohn.

The Coliseum on Eliki. (n.d.) *The Coliseum*. Retrieved July 20, 2002, from http://www.
   eliki.com/coliseum/

Core Tour Europe 2003. (2002). *Coliseum*. Sponsored by Saint Joseph's College.
   Retrieved July 22, 2002, from http://www.saintjoe.edu/~mjoakes/europe/images/
   photos_01/coliseum.jpg

Futrell, A. (1997). *Blood in the arena: The spectacle of Roman power*. Austin: University
   of Texas Press.

National Geographic News. (2001, June 29). *Rome Coliseum being restored for wider
   public viewing*. Retrieved July 22, 2002, from http://news.nationalgeographic.com/
   news/2001/06/0625_wirecoliseum.html

Pearson, J. (1973). *Arena: The story of the Coliseum*. London: Thames & Hudson.

Wick, D. (Producer), & Scott, R. (Director). (2000). *Gladiator* [Motion picture].
   United States: Dreamworks Pictures and Universal Pictures.

OUTLINE FOR INFORMATIVE SPEECH

Delta Blues: Where the Soul of Man Never Dies

Purpose: To inform the audience about Delta Blues.

Thesis: To really understand the roots of popular American music, it's necessary to journey back to the early 20th century and examine the music of three men who epitomize Mississippi Delta Blues.

Organization Pattern: Chronological

I. **Introduction**
   A. **Attention Getter:** "This is where the soul of man never dies." So says Sun Records founder Sam Phillips . . . the man who discovered and first recorded Elvis Presley, Jerry Lee Lewis, and Johnny Cash. However, Sam wasn't referring to the King, the Killer, or the Man in Black. He wasn't even referring to Rock and Roll. He was referring to the Blues . . . . the real reason he opened Sun Studios in Memphis way back in the early 1950's.
   B. **Relevance:** I know many of you are from the Chicago-land area. Through the many books and magazine articles I've read, I've discovered that the world famous "Chicago Blues" sound owes its origins to Mississippi Delta Blues—since many of those players migrated to Chicago in the 40's and 50's. In fact, the blues classic "Sweet Home Chicago" was written by a Delta musician. According to Nicholas Leman in his book *The Promised Land: The Great Black Migration and How It Changed America*, the black migration from the rural south to Chicago represented one of the largest and most rapid mass internal movements of people in history. And, most of those who relocated were from the Mississippi Delta.
   C. **Credibility:** I have been a blues fan for several years now. I was first introduced to the music by reading interviews with famous rock musicians like the Rolling Stones, Eric Clapton, and Bad Company. These English guys kept mentioning people with funny names . . . Blind Lemon Jefferson, Muddy Waters, Howlin' Wolf. They said these musicians were the first ones to inspire them to play. I started reading books and listening to the music, and just generally finding out about the blues and its players. . . . Especially Pre-War Country Blues . . . the music created in the 20's and 30's in the Delta region of Mississippi. I've even traveled to the area to attend music festivals and visit historic blues sites.
   D. **Thesis:** To really understand the roots of popular American music, it's necessary to journey back to the early 20th century and examine the music of three men who epitomize Mississippi Delta Blues.
   E. **Preview:** First, we'll examine Charley Patton, one of the earliest Delta musicians; next Son House, his friend and protégé; and finally Robert Johnson, a man shrouded in myth and legend.

Transition: William Barlow, in his 1989 book *Looking Up at Down: The Emergence of Blues Culture*, called Charley Patton the heart and soul of the early Delta Blues tradition.

II. Body

   A. Charley Patton was a flamboyant and charismatic performer.

      1. He was not the first blues musician in the Delta. . . . he just happened to be the first one to record—therefore, he's the first one to emerge from the anonymous oral tradition.

      2. Patton lived and played around the Dockery Plantation near Ruleville, Mississippi . . . leading some people to call Dockery's the birthplace of the blues.

      3. Whether he was playing for change on a street corner or for corn liquor at a juke joint, Charley was the consummate showman.

         a. Barlow reports that Patton played the guitar behind his back and between his legs, and would sometimes toss it high into the air—all to work the crowd into a frenzy.

         b. The young Howlin' Wolf was watching and listening and later incorporated some of those moves into his own performance style. And, Jimi Hendrix took some of his cues from Wolf—so Patton may very well be the prototype for rock stage performance.

      4. Though he died in 1934, Patton still inspires many musicians. On a recent recording, Bob Dylan dedicated his song "High Water" to Charley Patton.

Transition: Though Patton never lived to see the worldwide acceptance of the blues, one of his disciples did.

   B. Eddie "Son" House was born in Riverton, Mississippi in 1902.

      1. In the article "Trail of the Hellhound" on the National Park Service's website last modified on April 30, 2001, we find that Son first tried his hand at preaching but the seductive pull of women and music was just too great to keep him in the church.

      2. He played at many of the same juke joints and parties as Charley Patton and the two even made a trip together in 1930 to Grafton, Wisconsin to record.

      3. House played slide guitar in a rudimentary fashion, but very few bluesmen could match his vocal intensity. The band Lynyrd Skynyrd put it this way in their song "Swamp Music": *When that hound dog starts barking, sounds like old Son House singing the blues!*

      4. Like most bluesmen, Son knew trouble first hand. He spent some time in Parchman Penitentiary for murdering a man, but was subsequently released.

      5. In the 40's he moved to Rochester, New York and was out of the music business until 1964 when he was "rediscovered" during the folk music boom. Throughout the rest of the 60's he played the "real folk blues" at several festivals.

      6. By the 1970's he had fallen into ill health and had to retire from music.

      7. He died of throat cancer in 1988.

Transition: When Son House used to play juke joints, he would sometimes notice a skinny little kid hanging around. When Son would stop playing to take a break, the would-be musician would pick up his guitar and start to play. The kid wasn't very good and Son would say "Little Robert, put that thing down, you're going to drive everybody away."

   C. Robert Johnson was that kid.

      1. Well, Robert Johnson took the hint and went away by himself for about a year.

      2. When he came back, he played so well that Son House remarked that "he

must have made a deal with the devil," as reported in a 1966 magazine article in *Down Beat Music* by Pete Welding. So begins one of the most famous and oft told stories in blues lore. Years later Muddy Waters would recall that he saw Robert playing in front of this drugstore in Friars Point, MS, but fled the scene frightened because of the devil stories.

3. These stories, some recent documentaries, the movie *Crossroads* with *Karate Kid* Ralph Macchio . . . they all play into the "Robert Johnson sold his soul to the devil at the crossroads" myth. That's too bad, because the myth overshadows what is probably the pinnacle of the Delta Blues form in terms of musicianship and performance. Keith Richards of the Rolling Stones said that when he was a young man trying to learn the music from Johnson's records, that he was flabbergasted to find out that it was just one person playing.

4. Robert Johnson left the world 29 songs from two recording sessions—one in San Antonio and one in Dallas.

5. Robert Johnson died a mysterious death in August of 1938.
   a. According to Peter Guralnick in his 1989 book *Searching for Robert Johnson*, he was playing a gig at Three Forks Store just outside of Greenwood, Mississippi on a Saturday night.
   b. Many blues researchers believe he drank poisoned whiskey given to him by a jealous husband (Robert was a notorious womanizer). But no one really knows for sure.
   c. He died three days later.
   d. However, no one knows for sure where he was buried either.

6. This monument at Mt. Zion Church was erected by Sony music in 1990 after the reissue of the complete Robert Johnson catalog.

7. A few miles down the road at Payne chapel, you'll find this headstone. Notice that blues pilgrims leave spare change, guitar picks, and flowers.

8. Truth is, he's probably not buried in either location.
   a. *Rolling Stone* magazine reported in October of 2000 that Rosie Eskridge knows where Robert is buried. She said her deceased husband was the man that buried him.
   b. I'm sure we'll never know for sure.
   c. Blues researcher Gayle Dean Wardlow recently placed this monument where Rosie says he is buried.

Transition: Charley Patton, Son House, Robert Johnson—three men who lived and played their music in the harshest of places, in the worst of times.

III. Conclusion
   A. **Thesis/Summary:** These men didn't have multimillion dollar recording contracts . . . they played to survive and to avoid the back breaking labor of the cotton fields. Nevertheless, their impact is still being felt today. They directly influenced some of the greatest blues musicians from the heyday of Chicago blues like Howlin Wolf and Muddy Waters, who in turn influenced a whole generation of rock and rollers.
   B. **Memorable Close:** If you keep your eyes and ears open you may hear one your musical heroes cover a Delta Blues song or list these musicians as an inspiration. The roots of modern American music run deep. Muddy Waters once sang. "The blues had a baby and they named it rock and roll." Charley, Son, and Robert may no longer be with us, but they left us a great musical legacy—where the soul of man never dies.

References

Barlow, W. (1989). *Looking up at down: The emergence of blues culture.* Philadelphia: Temple University Press.

Guralnick, P. (1989). *Searching for Robert Johnson.* New York: Penguin Group.

The National Park Service. (n.d.). *Trail of the Hellhound: Delta Blues in the lower Mississippi Valley.* Retrieved May 19, 2003 from http://www.cr.nps.gov/delta/blues/people/son_house.htm

Robert Johnson's Grave Found. (2000, Oct. 12). *Rolling Stone,* 29, 33.

Welding, P. (1965). Hellhound on his trail: Robert Johnson. *Down Beat Music '66:* 73–76, 103.

Glossary

abstract language   General and vague language choice.

accuracy   Language that is grammatically and structurally correct.

acronyms   First letter abbreviations for longer terms.

action model   Views communication as a linear process.

action statement   Statement that indicates what you want your audience to believe or do.

active voice   The subject performs the action.

ad hominem   Fallacy occurs when a speaker attacks the character of the person making an argument rather than the argument itself.

advocate   To support a position, policy, or way of viewing the world.

agent of action   Entity who is responsible for taking action in a policy claim.

alignment   Creating lines and edges on the tops, bottoms, and sides of a visual element.

alliteration   Repetition of sounds that are near each other.

analogical reasoning   Comparison of a situation to a situation that is more familiar to audience; using analogies helps clarify complex situations for audience members.

analogy   Comparison using defining characteristics of one concept to another.

antithesis   Strategy used to explain what something *is* by describing what it *isn't;* the contrast of ideas creates a memorable effect.

appeal to authority   Fallacy that rests on the assumption that because an authority figure says something, it must be true.

appreciative listening   Listening for personal enjoyment.

appropriate language   Word choices that are appropriate to the topic, occasion, and audience.

arbitrary   Words have no meaning in and of themselves. They get their meaning from the people who use them.

argument   Process of advancing claims supported by evidence and reasoning.

argument model   Developed for understanding the critical components of effective arguments; these elements include claims, evidence, evidence credibility statements, warrants, qualifiers, and rebuttals.

articulation   Clear formation of words.

attention getter   A strong opening statement that uses some kind of creative device to capture your audience's attention and motivate them to listen.

attitude   Describes how your audience feels about your topic. Also, a relatively enduring set of beliefs around a person, group, idea, or event that predisposes an individual to respond in a particular way.

audience analysis   Process by which we gather and analyze information about our listeners and adapt our message to their knowledge, interests, attitudes, and beliefs.

audience demographics   General characteristics about each person, such as age, sex, gender, sexual orientation, cultural background, income, occupation, education, religion, group membership, political affiliation, and place of residence. Knowing this general information about your audience will help you choose and develop topics with your audience in mind.

audience-based apprehension Feeling anxious to interact with a specific person(s).

bandwagon   Fallacy suggests that something is correct, good, or true because many other people agree with it or are doing it.

belief   Acceptance that something is true even if we can't prove that it is true.

bias   Source that provides an opinion that is so slanted to one perspective that it is not objective or fair. Also, a source that has something to gain or lose in people accepting a point of view.

body   Portion of the speech containing the main points.

brainstorming   Techniques used to generate topic ideas.

brief example   Specific case used to support a claim.

bulleted list   Presentation aid that shows items that are related, but are in no particular order.

burdens of proof   Obligation a persuasive speaker faces to provide sufficient reasons for changing what already exists and is accepted in the status quo.

captive audience   Group of individuals who are required to attend a presentation and who may not have an inherent reason for listening to a speech.

causal pattern   Organizational strategy that highlights the cause-effect relationships that exist among the main points.

causal reasoning   Assertion that one condition or event (cause) brings about another condition or event (effect).

channel   The medium through which we communicate.

character   Listeners perceive a speaker to possess good character if he or she is honest and trustworthy, and has the listener's best interests in mind.

childhood reinforcement   Apprehension that is learned through modeling or past experience.

chronological pattern   Organizational strategy that arranges ideas by a time sequence.

citizen in a democracy   One who uses critical thinking skills to advance local, state, national, or international causes.

claim   Assertion or point that a speaker advocates.

claim of fact   A position considering what is or is not true, what does or does not exist, or what did or did not happen.

claim of policy   A position considering what should be done, what law should be changed, or what policy should be followed.

claim of value   A position considering right or wrong, moral or immoral, just or unjust, or good or bad.

clarity   Using words that are specific and familiar to your audience.

classroom code of conduct   List of rules that will govern speakers and listeners in your class during discussions and speech presentations.

closed question   Gives the interviewee a choice between options such as yes or no.

cognitive restructuring   Strategy used to manage psychological effects of communication apprehension; restructures thoughts from irrational to rational.

commemorative speech   A speech presented as part of celebrations of anniversaries, national holidays, or important dates and are accompanied by tributes to the person or persons involved.

communication apprehension   An individual's fear or anxiety associated with real or anticipated communication with others (McCroskey, 1977).

communication process   Six elements that are necessary for any communication event; these include people (speaker and listener), the message, channel, interference, feedback, and context.

comparative advantage order   Organizational pattern for a persuasive speech that organizes the main points around the advantages and disadvantages of at least two competing solutions.

competence   Listeners perceive a speaker to be competent if he or she is prepared, organized, and knowledgeable.

competent communicator   One who has the knowledge, skill, motivation, and judgment necessary for a communication encounter.

comprehensive listening   Listening occurs when understanding a message for a particular reason, to gain knowledge or complete a task.

concept mapping   A brainstorming technique that creates a visual organizer of the narrowing down of ideas to create a manageable topic.

conclusion   The end of the speech, which summarizes the key points of the presentation as well as provide a memorable close.

concrete language   Specific, detailed, and tangible language choice.

confident communicator   One who has decreased apprehension in public, personal, and professional contexts.

connotative meaning   Emotional response to a word.

constructive comment   Feedback for the speaker that acknowledges the need for improvement in the speech and provides specific direction or detail on how to improve.

context   The time of day, location, or social situation surrounding the communication encounter.

context-based apprehension   Feeling anxious in certain settings, such as one-on-one, groups, meetings, or public speaking.

contrast   Design principle that suggests varying the size of the visual elements used.

coordination   Arrangement of points of the speech into successive levels, with the points on the same level having the same importance and grammatical structure.

counterargument   Other side to your position.

credibility   Audience's perceptions about the speaker's competence, character, and goodwill.

credibility statement   Statement made to the audience that explains why the speaker is interested in, has personal experience or connection with, or shows expertise about the topic.

credo   Code of ethics to guide our communication behaviors.

criterion   Standard by which the value judgment is to be made.

critical listening   Listening to make judgments about the messages we receive.

critical thinking   Ability to make reasonable decisions about what to believe or do based on careful evaluation of available evidence and arguments.

data graphic   Pictures of numbers that make complex information much easier to understand.

data map   Data graphic that compares space elements.

deductive reasoning   To begin with a generalization and move logically to an application in a specific case.

delivery notes   Reminders written into a speaking outline regarding delivery elements, such as when to adjust your rate, tone, or movement.

denotative meaning   Literal dictionary meaning of a word.

derived credibility   Credibility a speaker develops during the speech.

design principles   Presentation aid guidelines that include contrast, repetition, alignment, and proximity.

diagram   Visual representation that shows relationships between abstract ideas.

dialogical perspective An ethical standard used to promote the development of self, personality, and knowledge.

discriminative listening Listening occurs when we distinguish between verbal and nonverbal messages.

display technology Technologies that can display your information on screen or on paper.

empathetic listening Listening to support or help another person, to understand and feel for the other person.

empathy The ability to feel for another person.

entertainment speech A speech that is designed to make an important point or have a serious message presented in a creative or humorous way.

ethical communication Application of our ethical standards to the messages we produce and consume.

ethical communicator One who is honest, clear, accurate, open-minded, and willing to listen to others in communication situations.

ethical norms Rules of behavior.

ethical standards Guidelines that help us make responsible decisions. These standards can be based on political, dialogical, human, or situational perspectives.

ethics Set of standards that offer guidance about the choices we make and why we behave as we do.

ethos Credibility.

evidence Used to substantiate a speaker's claim and may take several forms including statistics, analogies, facts, examples, and testimony.

evidence credibility statement Brief statements that establish the quality of the information you are using to support your ideas.

example Specific instances developed at varying lengths and used by speakers to make an abstract idea concrete.

extemporaneous speech Speech delivered with a prepared outline or speaking notes; allows a speaker to gauge the audience's reactions (feedback) and adapt his/her message accordingly.

extended analogy Explain metaphors in detail; speaker recalls the previous example and extends it.

extended example Substantially more developed example compared to brief examples; also referred to as *narratives, stories*, or *anecdotes*.

external effect Behavioral issues such as avoidance or disfluency that can stem from communication apprehension.

external interference Static or noise that distracts the speaker or listener from the message such as loud music, traffic, people laughing or talking, or a bad connection on your telephone or email server.

eye contact Purposefully looking at your audience to both communicate with them and receive feedback from them.

facial expressions Using your face to communicate consistency between a verbal and nonverbal message.

fact Statement that is verifiable as true.

factual distraction Internal source of interference that occurs when we concentrate so hard on a speaker's message that we miss the main point.

fallacy Argument based on unsound reasoning or evidence.

false cause fallacy Assumes that because one event precedes another, it caused the other event.

false dilemma Fallacy that asserts that a complicated question has only two answers, when more actually exist.

feedback The responses to either the speaker's or the listener's verbal or nonverbal message.

figurative analogy Comparison that draws upon metaphors to identify the similarities in two things that are not alike.

frame of reference A person's experiences, goals, values, attitudes, beliefs, culture, age, gender, and knowledge that he/she brings to the communication encounter.

general-purpose statement   Overall intent of the message; typically, to inform, persuade, entertain, or commemorate.

gestures   Use of your body in some way to reinforce an idea.

global plagiarism   Intentionally taking entire passages or speeches from someone else's work.

goodwill   Audience's perception of how much the speaker is concerned about them.

hasty generalization   A fallacy of reasoning that occurs when the conclusion offered is based on insufficient evidence.

hereditary   A cause of communication apprehension resulting from an enduring personality trait.

human perspective   An ethical standard that guides our responsibility to ourselves and to others to be open, gentle, compassionate, and critically reflective in our choices.

HURIER model   The steps in the listening process including hearing, understanding, remembering, interpreting, evaluating, and responding (Brownell, 2006).

hypothetical example   Imaginary situation that could conceivably take place in the way it is described.

immediate action   Audience members are motivated to engage in a specific behavior or take a specific action as a result of the speech.

impromptu speech   Speaking engagement where speaker has little to no time to prepare remarks.

inclusive language   Language choices that avoid excluding anyone for any reason; language choice that considers and respects all types of people.

inductive reasoning   To begin with specific instances and formulate a reasonable generalization or conclusion from them.

inflection   Varying pitch.

information literacy   Ability to find appropriate sources, analyze the material, evaluate the credibility of the sources, and to use and cite those sources ethically and legally.

informative speech   A speech that presents information that contributes something of significance to the body of knowledge of your audience; most typically about a(n) *object, person, event, process,* or *concept* that they would not know otherwise.

inherent barrier   Obstacle preventing the status quo from acting to solve the problem.

initial credibility   Credibility before a speaker gives a speech.

intentional plagiarism   Knowingly stealing someone else's ideas or words and passing them off as your own.

interaction model   Views feedback as part of the communication process.

interference   Anything that gets in the way of shared meaning between the speaker and listener.

internal effects   Psychological issues that may become physical due to communication apprehension.

internal interference   Causes speaker or listener to lack concentration; includes personal concerns, physical ailments, stress, or conflict.

internal preview   Brief statement of what the speaker will discuss next.

internal summary   Brief review of what has just been discussed before moving on to the next point.

interview   Method of collecting information about audience members; done by asking members about their knowledge, interests, and attitudes on a topic.

introduction   Beginning of a speech that prepares the audience to listen to the speech; it includes attention getter, relevance statement, credibility statement, thesis statement, and preview statement.

invalid analogy   Fallacy that occurs when the items being compared are not sufficiently similar.

jargon   Language that is specific to a particular group.

line graph   Data graphic that plots one or more variables against a time interval; also called *time-series plots*.

listening   A complex process that involves the steps in the HURIER Model.

literal analogy   Analogy that is based on a comparison of actual events.

logos   Refers to the rational proofs used to support arguments made in persuasive speech.

manuscript speech   Speech read word for word.

media literacy   Ability to critically evaluate what is heard and seen in the mass media.

membership   Items communicated in a bulleted list that are related, but are in no particular order.

memorable close   The last statement made in a speech that indicates in a powerful way that the presentation is complete and should be remembered.

memorized speech   Speech committed to memory.

mental distraction   Internal sources of interference that occur when our own mind gets in the way of our ability to concentrate and listen.

metaphor   Figure of speech that uses *implied* comparisons between two unlike things.

monotone   Not varying pitch.

Monroe's motivated sequence
Organizational pattern for persuasive speech; the objective of this pattern is to gain immediate action by identifying the problem and solution as well as the consequences of implementing your plan. The five steps of this sequence are attention, need, satisfaction, visualization, and action.

movement   Speakers should plan meaningful times to move during a presentation.

multi-sided message   To present multiple perspectives of the controversial issue.

natural nervousness   Extra adrenaline that provides a speaker with added energy before a presentation.

negative comment   Feedback for the speaker that criticizes the speech without providing suggestions for improvement.

nonverbal delivery   Delivery through the eyes, face, body (posture and gesture), and movement (use of space).

nonverbal message   Actions or behaviors; how you say your words and use gestures.

numbered list   Presentation aid that can display rankings or other ordered content, making it easy for the audience to grasp important relationships.

one-sided message   To give arguments in favor of the speaker's position on the issue.

onomatopoeia   Strategy uses sounds that mimic the meaning of words such as "tick tock" or "snap."

open question   Allows the interviewee to respond in-depth.

oral citation   Information that the speaker says aloud to the audience during a speech; consists of information about who authored the material, a statement about the credibility of the author, the date the information was published (or the date the interview was conducted), and relevant information about the source (e.g., title of the journal, magazine, or website).

oral organizational strategies
Plans that will allow you to devise an effective structure for your speech and enable your audience to better follow and comprehend your message.

oral style   Writing for the listener (not reader).

partial plagiarism   Intentionally taking key words and phrases from someone else's work and using them within your own speech.

passive agreement   The audience is motivated to adopt a new attitude without the speaker asking them to engage in a specific behavior.

passive voice   Subject is acted upon.

past fact   Claim that something did or did not happen.

pathos Appeals to emotion.

pause A well-timed moment of silence; can be used to emphasize a point, collect the speaker's thoughts, or transition to a new point.

people Speaker and listener involved in the communication encounter.

personal inventory A brainstorming technique that organizes thoughts by creating different categories and listing topics under each category.

personification Speaker gives human qualities to inanimate objects, ideas, or animals.

persuasive communication Any message that is intended to shape, reinforce, or change the responses of another, or others.

persuasive speech A speech that is controversial in some way and attempts to influence the audience's attitudes, beliefs, or actions with regard to the issue; typically about current events, social issues, local issues, or beliefs.

physical distraction External sources of interference that distract us from focusing on the speaker and the message; these could include time of day, temperature in the room, and noises both inside and outside of the room.

pie graph Data graphic constructed from small data sets with the values reported as percentages; also called a *pie chart.*

pitch Highness or lowness of voice.

plagiarism Presenting someone else's words or ideas as if they were your own.

political perspective An ethical standard used to understand ethical practices based on a value system.

positive descriptive comment Feedback for the speaker that says the speaker did a good job, and specifically describes or details what was liked about how the speaker accomplished his/her task.

positive nondescriptive comment Feedback for the speaker that says that the speaker did a good job, but does not describe or detail how the task was accomplished.

posture Distribute weight evenly on both legs; with legs shoulder width apart.

premise Declarative statement in an argument.

preparation outline Detailed outline that helps a speaker prepare his/her speech; it includes the title, general and specific purpose, organizational pattern, introduction, main points and subpoints, transitions, and references used in the speech.

present fact Claim that something is true or not true.

preview statement A statement that provides more detail about each of the main claims before speaking about them.

primary/recency effect Theory that suggests people pay more attention to and remember information that is presented first and last.

priority List of most important factors; communicated in a numbered list.

problem To show harm exists.

problem-cause-solution order Organizational pattern for a persuasive speech that devotes the first main point to establishing the problem, second main point to explaining why there is a problem, and the third main point to solving the problem.

problem-solution order Organizational pattern for a persuasive speech that devotes the first main point to establishing the problem and the second main point to solving the problem.

projection fact Claim that something will be true or not true in the future.

pronunciation How a word is said and stressed.

proximity Design principle that suggests if two or more visual items are related, they should be grouped closely.

public speaking anxiety Person's anxiety specifically associated with giving presentations.

qualifier To admit exceptions and demonstrate that argumentation is not an exact science.

questionnaire Method of gathering information about audience members in which the audience provides written answers to questions.

rate Speed with which you speak.

rational proof A series of premises that lead to a conclusion.

rebuttal To state the other sides or counterarguments to your position, and attack them directly.

red herring Fallacy that introduces irrelevant information into an argument in an attempt to mask the real issue under discussion.

relevance statement Statement made to the audience that explains how the speech will specifically relate to the audience.

repetition Repeating a phrase or word.

representative sample Critical measure of the reliability and validity of statistics.

research questions Questions that guide the research process; probes the researcher's as well as the audience's knowledge on the topic.

rhetorical question Question that is posed aloud to an audience with the purpose of having them think about, not state, the answer.

scaled/continuum questions Type of question that allows you to gauge attitudes on a continuum.

semantic distraction Internal source of interference that occurs when we have an emotional response to particular words or concepts the speaker is presenting.

sequence Proper order of steps in a process; communicated in a numbered list.

significant topic Topic that allows you to contribute information that your audience would not have known had you not given the presentation.

signpost Words that signal the next point to be made.

simile Direct comparison of unlike things using the words *like* or *as*.

situational perspective An ethical standard using context to guide a decision.

situation-based apprehension Feeling anxious temporarily due to a particular event at a particular time.

skills deficit Apprehension caused by lack of knowledge of the skills involved in public speaking.

skills training Communication apprehension strategy that involves learning about the steps necessary to plan and present a public speech as well as gaining practice in doing so.

slippery slope Fallacy that occurs when a speaker asserts that some event must inevitably follow from another down a steep slope toward disaster.

spatial pattern Organizational strategy that arranges ideas according to place or position.

speaking outline Brief outline that helps you remember key points as you are speaking.

speaking situation Situation composed of the size and type of audience, the setting and audience's interests, knowledge, and attitudes toward the topic.

specific purpose statement Statement indicating the direction or focus the speaker will take with his/her topic.

statistics Numerical method for summarizing data; statistics can take such forms as means, medians, ratios, and percentages.

status quo All of the laws, regulations, and attitudes that currently exist.

status quo bias People are generally predisposed to favor what they currently believe as well as what currently exists.

subordination Ranking of ideas from the most to least important.

summary Review of main points that prepares your audience for the end of the message.

syllogism Three part argument containing a major premise, minor premise, and conclusion.

symbolic Words stand for or symbolize things.

systematic desensitization Relaxation technique used to manage physical symptoms of communication apprehension.

table Presentation aid that includes numbers as well as words.

target audience The portion of the whole audience that you most want to influence.

terminal credibility Credibility given to a speaker at the end of the speech.

testimony Quotes or paraphrases from an authoritative source.

thesis statement A clear and concise sentence that provides an overview of the entire presentation.

timely Speakers should incorporate recent information that accounts for the laws, regulations, and attitudes that currently exist.

topical order pattern Organizational strategy that arranges each main point by subtopic of a larger topic.

trait-like communication apprehension A genetic predisposition for feeling anxious in most situations.

transaction model Views communication as the simultaneous sending and receiving of messages that occur in context.

transitional devices Transitions, internal previews, internal summaries, and signposts that provide links to claims throughout the speech, provide a sense of organization, and ultimately make it easier for the audience to follow and remember the ideas presented.

transitions Words or phrases that demonstrate key relationships among ideas and also indicate a speaker is leaving one point and moving on to another.

triangle of meaning Figure that helps us to understand the symbolic and arbitrary nature of words; triangle of meaning consists of the symbol, thought, and referent.

typicality Test that assesses the extent to which your example is normal.

unintentional plagiarism Neglecting to cite your source appropriately, because of careless note-taking or documenting during the research process.

value Deeply held, stable conviction about what is good or bad, right or wrong with respect to human existence including such concepts as fairness, justice, freedom, love, security, and honesty.

verbal delivery Use of pauses, clear articulation and pronunciation, and varied volume, rate, pitch, and inflection.

verbal message Words spoken in a communication encounter.

vertical bar graph Data graphic that plots one or more variables against a time interval; much like a line graph, but the data set is not as large as one used for a line graph. Good for quick comparisons between groups. Also called a *column graph*.

visual literacy "The learned ability to interpret visual messages accurately and to create such messages" (Heinich, R., Molenda, M., Russell, J. (1982).

visualization A technique for managing apprehension in which the speaker imagines giving a successful presentation.

vivid Language used to evoke a certain emotion or image from an audience; language that appeals to the audience's senses.

vocal variety Verbally varying volume, rate, pauses, and pitch.

vocalized pauses Words or phrases used to fill gaps of time that can decrease a speaker's credibility, such as *like, you know, um.*

volume Loudness or softness of voice.

voluntary audience Group of individuals attending a presentation with a particular interest in doing so.

warrant To provide the justification and reasoning to connect the evidence with your claim.

written language Presentation aid that can take the form of bulleted lists, numbered lists, or tables that you can easily incorporate into a PowerPoint presentation.

Index